Indigenous Confluences

Charlotte Cotè, Matthew Sakiestewa Gilbert, and Coll Thrush, *Series Editors*

CALIFORNIA THROUGH NATIVE EYES

Reclaiming History

WILLIAM J. BAUER, JR.

UNIVERSITY OF WASHINGTON PRESS

Seattle

© 2016 by the University of Washington Press
Printed and bound in the United States of America
Composed in Charter, a typeface designed by Matthew Carter
20 19 18   5 4 3 2

All rights reserved. No part of this publication may be reproduced or transmitted in any form or by any means, electronic or mechanical, including photocopy, recording, or any information storage or retrieval system, without permission in writing from the publisher.

UNIVERSITY OF WASHINGTON PRESS
www.washington.edu/uwpress

LIBRARY OF CONGRESS CATALOGING-IN-PUBLICATION DATA
Names: Bauer, William J., Jr., author.
Title: California through Native eyes : reclaiming history / William J. Bauer Jr.
Description: [1st edition] | Seattle : University of Washington Press, [2016] | Series: Indigenous confluences | Includes bibliographical references and index.
Identifiers: LCCN 2016005513 | ISBN 9780295998343 (hardcover : alk. paper) | ISBN 9780295998350 (pbk. : alk. paper)
Subjects: LCSH: Indians of North America—California—History. | Indians of North America—California—Folklore. | Konkow Indians—Folklore. | Pomo Indians—Folklore. | Paiute Indians—Folklore. | Indian mythology—California. | Indians of North America—California—Wars. | Indians, Treatment of—California.
Classification: LCC E78.C15 B3225 2016 | DDC 979.4004/97—dc23
LC record available at https://lccn.loc.gov/2016005513

The paper used in this publication is acid-free and meets the minimum requirements of American National Standard for Information Sciences—Permanence of Paper for Printed Library Materials, ANSI Z39.48–1984. ∞

CONTENTS

Preface vii
Acknowledgments xi
Maps xiv

INTRODUCTION 3

CHAPTER 1 Creating 10

CHAPTER 2 Naming 28

CHAPTER 3 Discovering 49

CHAPTER 4 Fighting 73

CHAPTER 5 Cleansing 88

CHAPTER 6 Persisting 105

CONCLUSION 120

Notes 125
Bibliography 147
Index 161

Illustrations follow page 62

PREFACE

I was slogging my way through a roll of microfilm at the University of California's Bancroft Library when my great-grandfather's name, Charles Wright, woke me from my trancelike state. I was using a collection of ethnographic field notes and had high hopes for the next pages of black and white notebook paper projected on the small screen. Perhaps my great-grandfather provided oral histories of work in northern California, like other Concows in this particular collection. I had found a packet of letters about him in the National Archives, and the oral histories might augment the written record. Born in the late 1840s (he claimed 1849 on the 1928 California census) at a Concow town called Koyoom K'awi, near modern-day Oroville, California, Wright's early life belied his rather tranquil elderly years. In 1862 U.S. troops marched 460 Concows from their homeland in present-day Butte County to the Round Valley Reservation; only 270 survived the horrible trek. Wright's parents died sometime after his birth, perhaps during this ethnic cleansing, and his grandmother raised him.[1] In 1935, when the oral traditions were collected, Wright lived a quiet life on northern California's Round Valley Reservation, herding cattle, performing odd jobs, and taking care of his four children. Still, government officials worried about the elderly Wright and his young children (my grandmother was born in 1923) and considered him an ideal candidate for a New Deal public works project sponsored by anthropologist Alfred Kroeber that recorded ethnographic information with some of California's indigenous people.[2] Rather than providing an oral history of Native-newcomer encounters, ethnic cleansing, or federal Indian policy, though, Wright told a creation story about a figure named Jesus. Deep in time three people lived on earth: a husband, his wife, and their daughter. One day the daughter went to pick clover, and on her return home she found several arrows on the ground. The daughter picked up the arrows. After she grabbed the third one, God appeared before her and declared that he owned the arrows. The girl left and soon gave birth to twins. One day one of the twins, named Jesus, looked outside and saw geese flying south. The young woman gave Jesus a slingshot, and he hunted the geese. With one shot Jesus killed one thousand geese. After gathering his geese Jesus encountered Fishworm, who demanded the slain animals. Jesus asked his grandfather, God, who appeared in different forms, such as a stump and a rock, for guidance. God told Jesus to wait for Fishworm to stick his head out of his hole and then shoot him. Jesus did as instructed and killed Fishworm. After this, Jesus killed all of the mean people, animals, and birds and took their hearts.

Jesus and God went north. They came to a swift and deep stream. Jesus asked Crane how they could cross, and Crane extended his leg and allowed the duo to cross. As God reached the middle of Crane's leg, Crane bent his leg and let God fall in the stream. God nearly drowned. When Jesus attempted to cross, Crane also tried to drown him. However, Jesus walked on water and killed Crane. In the North, Jesus and God found a sweathouse in which many animals sat on a floor of ice. In order to avoid slipping, Jesus put down a bed of straw. Then Jesus gambled with the animals. Jesus bet all of his beads and lost. He bet his grandfather's eyes and lost. Jesus bet his grandfather's life and lost. He bet his eyes and lost. Jesus bet his life and won. He continued to gamble until he won back all that he had lost and his opponents' lives. Jesus asked God what he should do next. God instructed Jesus to dry up all the water and give it to him. After the water dried up and the animals died, Snake Hawk carried Jesus to present-day Chico, California. Jesus took his slain enemies' hearts and threw them into a lake. The next day people were laughing and talking at the lake. Jesus named the different tribes and sent them away from the lake with their respective languages. After the people left, Jesus and Coyote negotiated how the people would live. Jesus wanted the people to die at night and be reborn the next day; to harvest seeds, nuts, berries and fruit from one large tree; to bring down game by only looking at it; and to catch salmon as they moved up the falls. Coyote wanted the people to die permanently; for women to gather seeds on the ground and men to climb trees to knock off acorns; men to hunt with bows and arrows and encounter difficulties while fishing. Coyote eventually got his way. After setting up the world, Jesus invited the people into a sweathouse and told them he was leaving: "If people get mean as they were before, I'll come back. But if you're all good people I'll not have to come back. So treat everyone kind."[3]

At the time, I did not know what to do with this oral tradition and the others I read that day. Providing ethnographic information to an anthropologist certainly constituted work and labor. Yet what did these oral traditions mean to Wright and other California Indians during the Great Depression? The book that follows provides one answer to that question.

A couple of years later I flew from Las Vegas to Sacramento right before the spring semester began. I planned to visit Table Mountain, outside of Oroville, drive through Chico, and visit West Mountain, now known as Lassen Peak.

PREFACE ix

Before their ethnic cleansing, Concows came to Table Mountain to collect flint and the place had a role in Concow oral tradition. Concow Annie Feliz told a story about the time Mole turned into a rock and remained at Table Mountain. It was a cool California winter day when I pulled my car into the gravel parking lot at Table Mountain. Cows now graze on this plateau, which is not as flat as its name suggests. I spent a couple of hours dodging cow manure, scrambling out of ravines, and admiring the patches of volcanic rock. Eventually I paused. To my left, partially shrouded by the Delta fog, sat Middle Mountain, or Sutter's Buttes, the mountain on which the Concow dead climb a rope of feathers to the sky. I could faintly (I hoped I could) see West Mountain, or Lassen Peak, the place where Mouse stole fire from Eagle, which Coyote then stole and dropped, starting a fire in the Sacramento Valley and causing Mole to lament and turn into stone. I could see, at least partly, how Concows linked these important places in the Sierra Nevada foothills to their history. At any rate, thinking about the oral traditions I realized I stood in a very different California, one known to Wright and other Concows. I stood near the center of the Concow world, to which they continued to connect during the Great Depression.

I could not keep these stories to myself. After the semester ended, my oldest daughter and I boarded a plane for Sacramento. I spent the better part of a week bailing hay for my dad. After reminding myself why being a professor was slightly better than being covered in grease and hay dust, I drove with my daughter from the Round Valley Reservation to West Mountain, Table Mountain, and Koyoom K'awi. Table Mountain was different than it had been in January; the grass had dried considerably, and grasshoppers buzzed in front of us as we walked. Rather than a cool Delta fog, a heavy haze of the central valley partially obscured Middle Mountain. On this trip I told my daughter, again, the story of how Mouse stole fire from Eagle at West Mountain and Mole was frozen at this place. In an oral tradition, telling stories retains and perpetuates knowledge. Charles Wright shared his stories with his daughter Eva Wright; other California Indians told these stories to friends, relatives, or younger Indians. I could not completely replicate the experience of being in an oral tradition, but telling my great-grandfather's stories in the place where they were created helped to enunciate some aspects of how Concows understood their world and history.

These two trips helped me to rethink what it means to tell California history from an Indigenous perspective. For one, the history that follows is place-centered. Rather than dwell on when events took place, California Indians such as my great-grandfather emphasized where their oral traditions and history took place. Second, the stories in this book are bound by a host of relationships—between interviewer and interviewee, between person and place, between people and animals—that structured how California Indians understood their past. Third, the history told in this book is grounded in the particular moment of the Great Depression. Charles Wright and other Californians used their oral traditions to gain control over the changing historical circumstances around them and provide a path for their descendants to follow. This book attempts to follow that path.

ACKNOWLEDGMENTS

I could not have completed this book without the support of several individuals and institutions. The American Indian Studies Program at the University of California, Los Angeles (UCLA) provided me with a semester-long fellowship to begin writing this book. I thank Angela Riley for making this appointment possible. I also had the opportunity to teach a California Indian history class at UCLA; it was a rare treat, and I was honored to work with exceptional undergraduate students at UCLA in addition to graduate students Caitlin Keliiaa (Washoe) and Lawrence Mojado (Cahuilla). I will never forget teaching that course. The Research Institute of Comparative Studies in Race and Ethnicity at Stanford University offered a second semester-long fellowship to continue work on this book. Thanks to Heidi Lopez, Elizabeth Wahl, and everyone at RICSRE for making Stanford a welcoming space. I appreciate Bridget Ford, Ramón Saldívar, and other participants in the monthly workshops for their feedback on the initial phases of this project.

In addition to UCLA and Stanford, several institutions provided financial support for the research and publication of this book: at the University of Nevada–Las Vegas the Research and Economic Development Program awarded me a Faculty Opportunity Award; Dean Chris Hudgins and the College of Liberal Arts provided generous funding for research and subvention of images included in this book; and the Department of History, led by, first, David Wrobel and, second, David Tanenhaus, offered financial support for the purchase of microfilm and travel to other archives.

Several colleagues have invited me to present aspects of this book to public and academic audiences. Laurie Arnold (Colville) invited me to speak at my alma matter, the University of Notre Dame. Thanks to Brian Collier for attending the lecture and accompanying us to dinner. Richard Burrill brought me to Oroville to spend the weekend attending the annual Ishi gathering and seminar. Annette Reed (Tolowa) invited me to provide a keynote lecture at the annual California Indian Conference in Sacramento. Denni Diane Woodward (Mescalero Apache) asked me to give the Pam Hantichak Lecture for the Native American Cultural Center at Stanford University. Cal Winslow and the California Institute brought me to Caspar for a weekend conference on the beautiful northern California coast. I appreciate the comments I received on this work from my panelists at academic conferences: Damon Akins, Cathleen Cahill, Duane Champagne, Tai Edwards, Paul Kelton, and Julie Stidolph.

Since 2009 I have called UNLV home. I thank my colleagues who welcomed me to UNLV and commented on aspects of this book: Raquel Casas, Kevin Dawson, Marcie Gallo, Greg Hise, Andy Kirk, Colin Loader (my partner in the early morning), Cian McMahon, Miriam Melton-Villaneuava, Mark Padoongpatt, Todd Robinson, Jeff Schauer, Paul Werth, and A. B. Wilkinson. Andy Fry chaired the search committee that brought me to Las Vegas; I appreciate his willingness to read this manuscript in its roughest form, serving as a mentor for the Faculty Opportunity Award, and entertaining my comments on college basketball. David Wrobel captained the History Department when I arrived at UNLV. David Tanenhaus assumed the role of department chair after Wrobel left for "sooner" pastures. David supported UNLV's membership in the Newberry Consortium in American Indian Studies and always had his door open for me, even if it was to talk about rotisserie baseball. I am honored to call him my friend. I must also thank David's son, Isaac, for playing with my daughter, Scout; without their easy friendship it would have been difficult to get any work done over the summer. Last but certainly not least, a special thanks goes to Annette Amdal, Kathy Adkins, Matt Fledderjohann, Therese Chevas, Heather Nepa (who, oddly, listens to the same sports radio I do), and Lynette Webber, who kept the History Department running.

As I have advanced in my academic career, I have been blessed to work with a fantastic cohort of graduate students. I assigned a draft of this book to my graduate colloquium. I extend my sincere gratitude to Bridget Baumgarte (Alaska Native), Bridger Bishop, Stephen Bohigian, John Crandall, Anthony Graham, Leslie Lewis, and Benjamin Roine for their comments. It has been a joy to watch David Christensen, Brandi Hilton-Hagemann, Margaret Huettl, and Julie Stidolph grow as scholars. I look forward to working with all of you in the future.

I am also blessed to have an extended network of colleagues and friends whose eyes did not glaze over when I discussed this book with them. Thanks to Damon Akins, Stephen Amerman, Cathleen Cahill, Brenda Child (Ojibwe), Steven Crum (Western Shoshone), Jeani O'Brien (Ojibwe), Josh Reid (Makah), Khal Schneider (Pomo), and Louis Warren. David Chang accompanied me on a trip to the Concow Valley several years ago; I appreciate his bravery for driving with me through northern California's winding roads.

At the University of Washington Press, Ranjit Arab expressed interest in this project from its earliest stages. Thanks for sticking with me and this project. I know I was tardy on hitting deadlines, but it has been a pleasure to work with you. Ranjit identified Cathleen Cahill and Donald Fixico to review this manuscript. I appreciate their comments and criticisms; this book is a better product for their insights.

Finally I must recognize my family for all their support. For a long time Albert Hurtado has been a mentor, adviser, and friend. I look forward to our encounters at conferences, and I thank him for everything that he has done for me. My aunt Betty Matthews has been an unflappable supporter. She has never failed to miss an opportunity to attend one of my public presentations in northern California. My grandmother Anita Rome, whose father sparked my interest in writing this book, passed away as I completed this project. My own parents, William and Deborah, have never failed to support me in all endeavors. I can never repay their love, kindness, and support. My partner, Kendra Gage, puts up with too much. Her patience and support is otherworldly. I love you. I dedicate this book to my children, Temerity and Scout. Watching television and movies, attending basketball games, dance recitals, and *Star Trek* conventions, and listening to the story of their day have been welcome escapes from writing this book and teaching classes. Writing this book and passing along the stories that our ancestors told to them is part of what I consider to be the importance of this book.

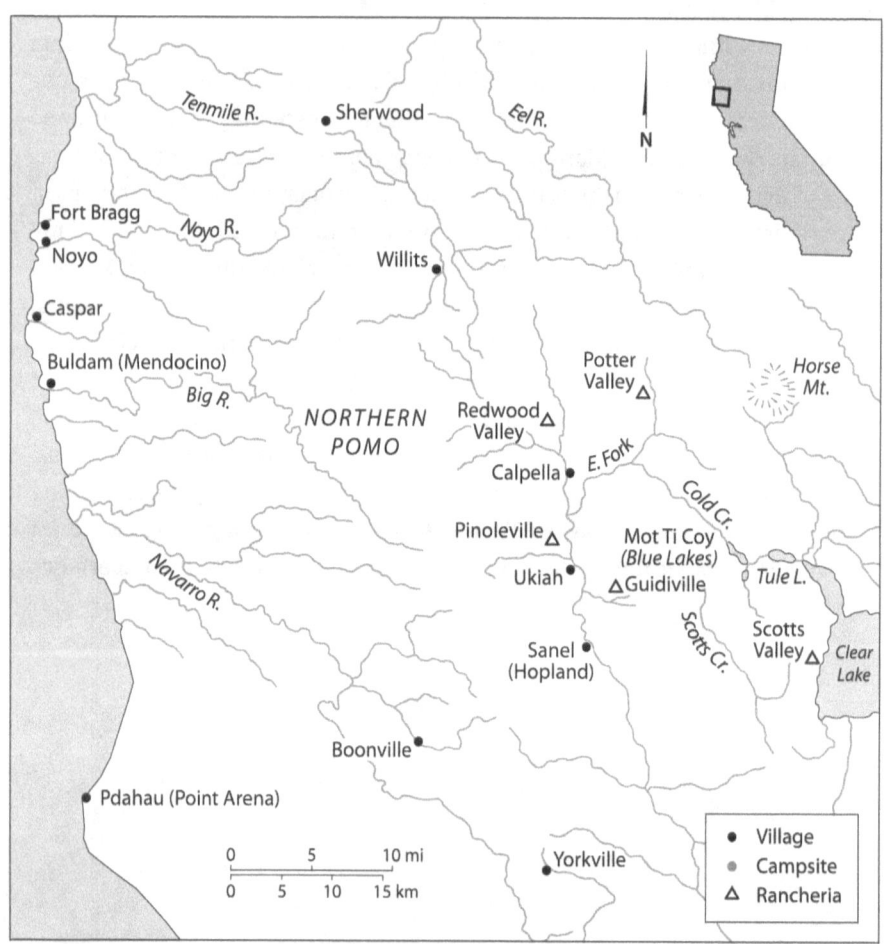

MAP 1. Pomo territory. Adapted from Sally McLendon and Robert J. Oswalt, "Pomo: Introduction," in Robert Heizer, ed., *Handbook of North American Indians*, vol. 8: *California* (Washington, DC: Smithsonian Institution Press, 1978), 283. Map by Bill Nelson.

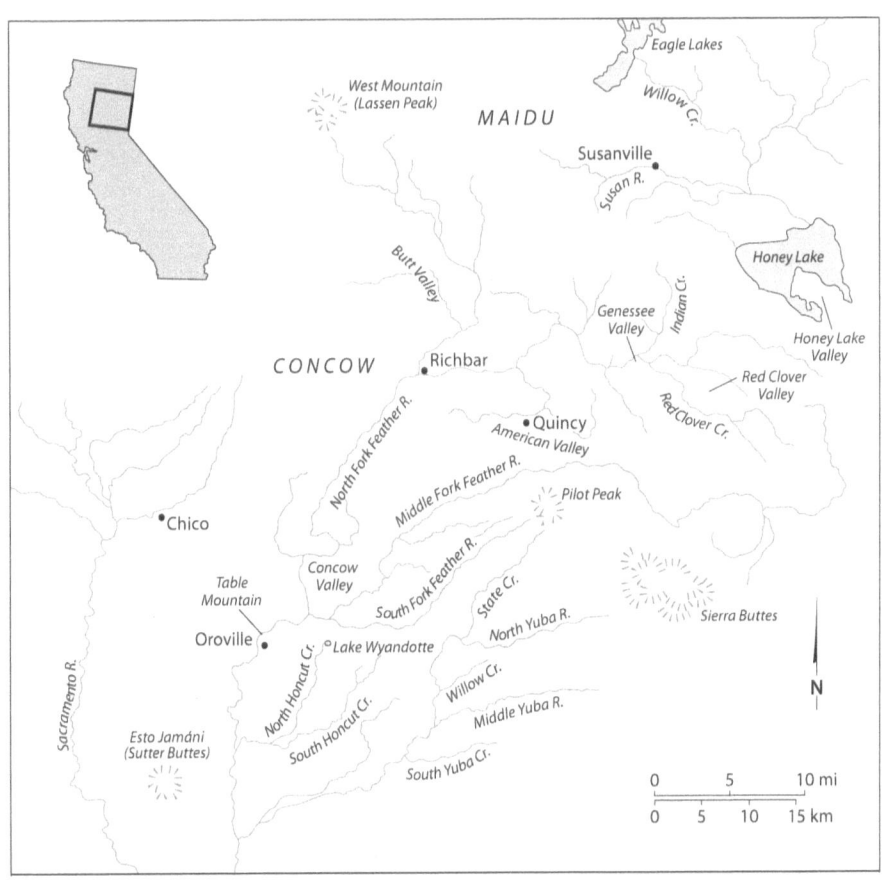

MAP 2. Concow and Maidu territory. Adapted from Francis A. Riddell, "Maidu and Konkow," in Robert Heizer, ed., *Handbook of North American Indians*, vol. 8: *California* (Washington, DC: Smithsonian Institution Press, 1978), 371. Map by Bill Nelson.

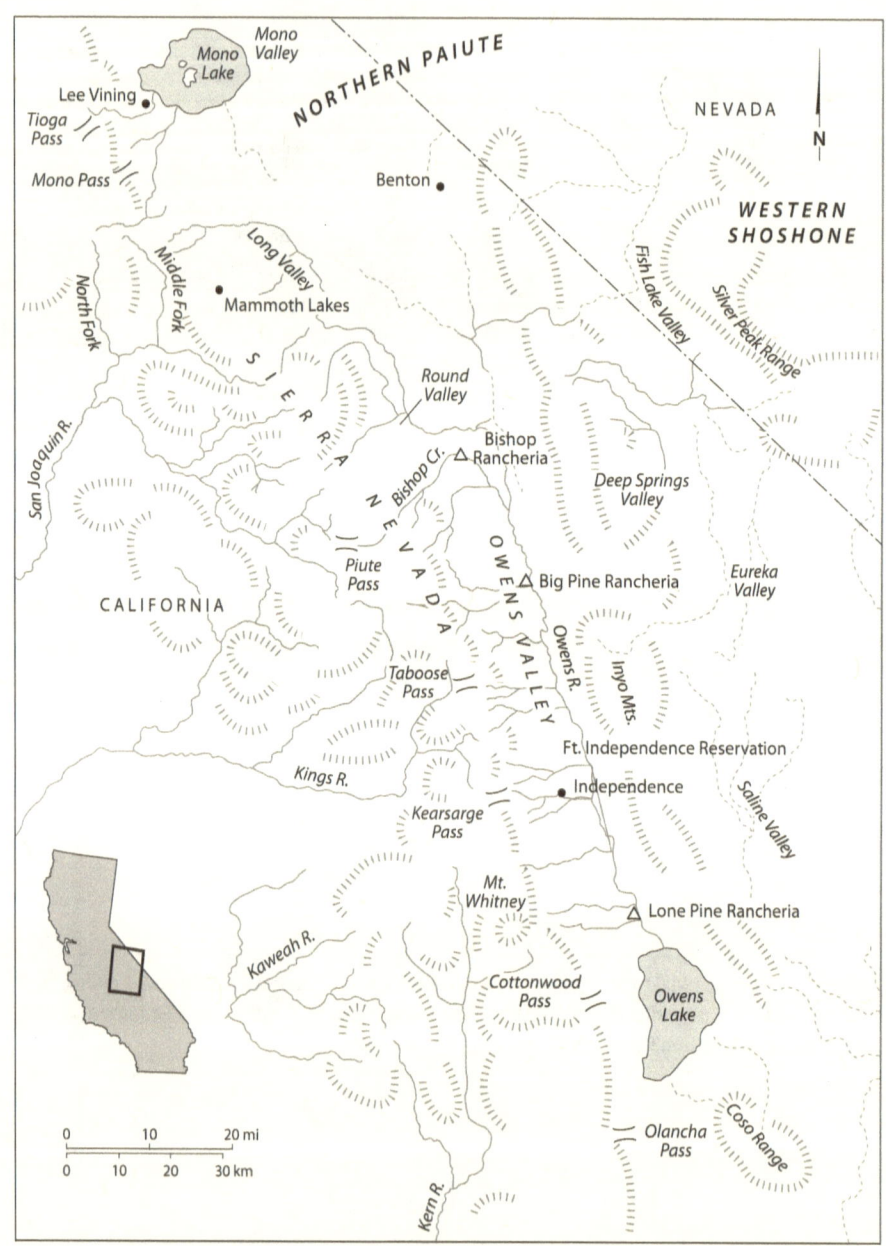

MAP 3. Owens Valley Paiute territory. Adapted from Sven Liljeblad and Catherine S. Fowler, "Owens Valley Paiute," in Warren L. d'Azevedo, ed., *Handbook of North American Indians*, vol. 11: *Great Basin* (Washington, DC: Smithsonian Institution Press, 1986), 283. Map by Bill Nelson.

CALIFORNIA THROUGH NATIVE EYES

Introduction

LASSIK LUCY YOUNG, ALSO KNOWN AS T'TCETSA, LIVED ON THE ROUND Valley Indian Reservation with her husband, Sam Young, who was from Hayfork, California. She was a contemporary of my great-grandfather Charles Wright, but I do not know if they ever met. Born in the late 1840s, Young, like Wright, experienced the traumas of the U.S. colonization of California. In 1861 and 1862 U.S. troops and volunteers wiped out Young's male relatives and marched her female relatives to Fort Seward, located along the Eel River northeast of modern-day Garberville. After arriving at the fort, settlers abducted her and sold her into indentured servitude. She eventually married one of her employers, although it is likely this was a nonconsensual relationship. During the Great Depression Young worked with non-Indians in Round Valley, providing information on indigenous plants. In 1935 she and Sam, her third husband, worked on the same public works project as Charles Wright. Young recalled, "[The Wailackis and Lassiks] were very healthy till after the white People came in among them." She explained that, between guns and diseases, nearly all of northwestern California's Native People died: "After about two years they began to die off by the hundred[s]." Wailacki and Lassik healers attempted to combat the illnesses, but to no avail: "There were sickness all the time and it has been so ever since." Young's oral history provided a Native view of a common ethnohistorical topic: the encounter between Indigenous and Settler societies.[1] She highlighted the devastating impact of disease and the new technologies that arrived with Settlers. Young also understood her story's value as a historical source: "If you could only know the truth of [how] the Indian has been treated since the first white man came into his part of the country, it would make an ordinary man shake and shudder. I would like to tell you the whole story from 1846 up to the present date. I am afraid it would not be allowed to be put in print."[2]

During the Great Depression, California Indians in Mendocino County and Owens Valley told oral histories that challenged contemporary understandings of California history. Taken together, California Indians told an alternative, Indigenous version of California history that began at creation, assessed the impact of cultural encounters in the mid-nineteenth century, and concluded with pressing issues in California Indian communities in the 1930s. The goal of this book is to put into print Lucy Young's history and that of other California Indians from the Great Depression.

Anthropologists recorded Wright's and Young's oral histories as part of a New Deal work relief project, similar to the better known WPA slave narratives.[3] In 1935 anthropologist Alfred Kroeber secured a grant from the State Emergency Relief Administration (SERA) to conduct ethnographic research among California Indians. Kroeber proposed projects in four areas—northwestern California (Shasta, Siskiyou, Trinity counties), northeastern (Mendocino, Sonoma, Lake counties), Humboldt County, and Inyo County—but completed only two. He dispatched two graduate students, Frederick Hulse and Frank Essene, to Mendocino and Inyo counties, where they hired elderly California Indians, like Young and Wright, to serve as ethnographic informants and younger California Indians, such as Eva Wright, Charles's daughter, as interpreters. After Eva and others interviewed their elders, they gave the notebooks to the anthropologists, who edited and transcribed some of the interviews. For this book I relied on the handwritten notebooks rather than the printed transcripts, which revealed substantial editing on the part of the anthropologists. Although the project failed to cover as much territory as Kroeber hoped, it surveyed a wide range of Native People who lived in different parts of the state and possessed distinct historical experiences.[4]

Unlike the WPA slave narratives, in which white fieldworkers interviewed elderly African Americans, California Indians interviewed other California Indians in the SERA project. From the beginning Kroeber envisioned this division of labor in order to spread work relief money throughout California Indian communities.[5] The relationship between interviewer and interviewee enabled California Indians to determine the interview's structure and content. Jeff Joaquin, an eighty-nine-year-old Pomo man from Hopland, began his interview, "As a ghost story is fresh in my memory this morning I will start with it."[6] Joaquin controlled the production of knowledge by deciding which stories to tell and in what order. California Indian storytellers insisted on their own methods to determine historical authenticity. Lucy Young understood that knowledge was historically valid within her lived experience and that written sources excluded Indigenous understandings of the past. She restored Lassik understandings of the state's history over which Settler historians, such as Hubert Howe Bancroft, had glossed.[7] Although we cannot ignore the colonial relationships that shaped these sources, we should also be aware that California Indians found ways for their ways of knowing to intervene in the history of California.

In the Great Depression, California Indians restored Indigenous ways of history to understanding California's past.[8] For one, California Indians used oral traditions to narrate California's history. According to Dakota historian Waziyatwain, oral tradition "refers to the way in which information has been passed on rather than to the length of time something has been told."[9] Oral histories and so-called mythic tales are included in oral tradition. Wright, Young, and other California Indian storytellers communicated their narratives through what Native Hawaiian scholar Noenoe Silva calls a "genealogical world view."[10] Wright, for instance, told the story of Jesus and several others to his daughter Eva, who translated them from Concow to English and transcribed them into a notebook. Wright and Young anchored their narratives in specific, known places on their landscapes, creating what anthropologist Keith Basso calls a "place world."[11] Jesus created the People at a lake near Chico, the Concow world's geographic center. Young centered her stories in the Eel River watershed of northeastern California. Both narratives revealed a particular California history that they uniquely experienced. Wright and Young were part of a generation of California Indians who experienced the horrors and trauma of mid-nineteenth-century California. Wright's story explained the origin of the Concow People, language, and culture—indeed the creation of a part of the state—whereas Young described the harrowing experiences of Indigenous People in mid-nineteenth-century California.[12] Both narratives subverted orthodox historiographies. Young concluded her story by criticizing how Settler historians ignored the manner in which Settlers treated Indigenous People. Although Wright did not overtly reveal his politics, as Young had done, his oral narrative challenged historical and ongoing colonial structures.[13]

California Indian oral histories operated on three levels: past, present, and future. In looking to the past California Indians narrated a history of California's long nineteenth century. By the time of the Great Depression, Settler historians had created what writer Tony Platt calls the "California Story," a historical narrative of nineteenth-century California that depicted California Indians as "racially inferior, predestined to doom and salvageable only by an authoritarian regime."[14] The "California Story" rationalized Settler colonialism, exculpated white Americans for nineteenth- and twentieth-century violence, and erased Indigenous People from the historical and contemporary scene.[15] California Indians reframed and reinterpreted this history. They recited histories about the creation and (re)naming of the state, Indigenous Peoples' discovery of Americans, the violence of warfare and ethnic cleansing, and the consequences of state and federal policies in ways that clashed with the prevailing "California Story."[16]

When considering the present, California Indians "revisioned" their traditional stories to address events occurring in the Great Depression.[17] They argued that California Indian People and knowledge systems endured settler colonialism. California Indians and their stories attempted to stall and reverse settler colonialism, claim and reclaim lands, and define identities during the Great Depression. California Indians engaged in two separate events in 1930s California. In 1928 the state of California brought a lawsuit against the United States on behalf of California Indians for failure to ratify treaties.[18] At the same time, Owens Valley Paiutes struggled to secure land and water rights after Los Angeles purchased those rights in the early twentieth century.[19] Both events came to a head during the Great Depression and weighed heavily on the storytellers in his book.

In looking to the future, California Indians delineated a path for their descendants to follow. California Indians used their traditional stories as teaching tools, providing lessons to future generations as they defined and maintained their sovereignty. These stories insisted that Indigenous People would persevere and possessed the power and resources to reclaim land and broaden their sovereignty in the future.[20]

Wright and Young shared their stories at the same historical moment, the summer of 1935, when the world was in the throes of a depression and California Indians' relationship with the nation-state was changing.[21] The SERA project and the contemporaneous Indian New Deal was part of a folk, multicultural, decolonial, but, ultimately, limited historical moment.[22] The Indian New Deal promoted and preserved American Indian arts and crafts.[23] WPA guidebooks used American Indians as historical foils, often placing them in the timeless mists of American history.[24] However, during the Great Depression, California Indians wedged their cultural and political expressions into American life.[25] Although the folk, multicultural, and anticolonial ethos of the Great Depression provided an opportunity for California Indians to indigenize the state's history, the social, political, and economic context of the times stunted California Indians' decolonization project.

This book is purposefully synchronic. These oral histories provide a snapshot of California Indian views on history in the mid-1930s. In chapters 1 and 2 California Indians tell and interpret what historian Donald Fixico calls the *longue durée* of American Indian history.[26] In chapter 1 I discuss how California

Indian creation stories challenged the California stories that historians Charles Lummis and Hubert Howe Bancroft situated in the Spanish missions and the California Gold Rush, respectively. Settler creation myths praised the pioneering virtues of Franciscan priests and the 49ers, while denigrating California Indians as racially inferior in order to justify the taking of Indian land. California Indian oral histories described the creation of California's land, People, and culture. California did not begin at Mission San Diego or when John Marshall discovered gold at Coloma; California began when Earth Maker transformed the ocean into land and placed the People there. Moreover California Indians used creation stories to articulate Indigenous land claims. In 1928 the state of California sued the federal government on behalf of the "Indians of California" for failing to compensate them for lands taken in 1850 and 1851. Although lawyers and the anthropologists who testified on behalf of and against California Indians ignored California Indian oral traditions, California Indian creation stories, grounded in place, People, and culture, claimed California's land.[27]

Chapter 2 examines how California Indians named the state's geographic features. Place-names articulated a deep history for Indigenous People on the land, an intimate knowledge of California places, and a network of relationships that made life function. Upon arrival in the state Settlers *renamed* those landmarks and invested their own historical meaning in California places. Settler place-naming practices are part of the doctrine of discovery, which, in part, asserted that Indigenous lands were *terra nullis* (land belonging to no one). Naming California had different meanings for California Indians. Pomos used oral traditions and place-names to challenge western and California historiography by claiming that Native People were, in their words, the true "pioneers" and lived on the "frontier." Paiutes, who still lived in their homelands but were marginalized by white Settlers, used place-names in their indigenous language to claim the places they saw everyday but could not use. Concow place-names reclaimed the place from which they had been ethnically cleansed.

In chapters 3, 4, and 5 I explain how California Indians told and interpreted the violence of mid-nineteenth-century California. Chapter 3 considers how prophecy narratives—oral narratives that foretold the coming of Settlers—explained how California Indians discovered and encountered Settlers. California Indian prophets criticized contact and lamented the arrival of Settlers and their domesticated livestock, tools, and diseases. These oral histories questioned progressive narratives of western and California history and empowered California Indians, giving foreknowledge of the contact experience.

Chapter 4 uses oral narratives to assess how California Indians defended their homelands. Histories of the "Indian Wars" are common in western and

U.S. history. Scholars have argued that the Indian Wars reconciled the United States after the Civil War and portended the "last days" of Indian Nations. Histories of the California Indian Wars portrayed Natives as docile and racially inferior to Anglo Americans. Pomo war stories featured battles between different Pomo People; in the process Pomos defied the racialization of California Indians as inherently docile, reclaimed land, and discussed how California Indians survived the violent conquest of the state. Owens Valley Paiutes narrated a history of the Owens Valley War. They argued that their *puha*, or power, emboldened them in their conflict with the United States and Settler society.

If there is one word that applies to nineteenth-century American Indian history, it may be *removal*. In the early nineteenth century white Americans advocated the removal, or ethnic cleansing, of American Indians from the Ohio Valley and Southeast at the same time that white frontier Settlers "removed" themselves to lands on which Native People previously lived. In the 1850s California Settlers advocated removing California Indians to Baja California or Nevada. Pro-removal groups argued that ethnic cleansing was necessary for American democracy and the market economy to grow and to protect Indians from aggressive Settlers. Chapter 5 considers how Concows and Paiutes told histories of their respective ethnic cleansings from their homelands. Rather than describing these removals as being in their best interests, California Indians interpreted removal as a violent and traumatic event, one that they survived only with the strength of their kinship networks.

In chapter 6 I relate how California Indians discussed political events that occurred in their communities. In the early twentieth century two crises gripped Indian Country. Reservations were the sites of epidemic rates of trachoma and tuberculosis. In response the Office of Indian Affairs attempted to standardize and professionalize the Indian health service. These new health professionals often blamed Native People for the poor health conditions that prevailed on reservations (ignoring government policies that forced Indians to live in crowded circumstances) and attempted to eradicate long-standing Indian folk-healing methods. California Indians used their oral narratives to insert themselves into this debate about public health in Indian country. Healing, or doctoring, stories emphasize how California Indian healing methods often worked better than Settler medicine and highlighted the importance of Native knowledge when federal officials attempted to eradicate these practices. In eastern California, Indigenous People faced disputes of their water rights. Perhaps the most famous of these water rights battles occurred in the Owens Valley, with the City of Los Angeles siphoning the area's water. Long ignored in histories of the Owens Valley Water Wars, Paiute oral histories articulated the meaning of water in Paiute life and history and offered a positive path to the future in which Paiutes reclaimed the water Los Angeles had taken from them. California Indian stories offer insight into the way California Indian ways of knowing persisted into the Great Depression.

This Indigenous version of California's history questions the origins of ethnohistory and new western history. California Indians asked scholars to tell more complicated histories of cultural encounters between Indigenous People and Europeans. They insisted that scholars consider the legacies of conquest in the state's history. Yet few scholars were prepared to heed the historiographical arguments that Lucy Young and Charles Wright articulated. This book argues that it is time for us to listen.

CHAPTER 1

Creating

ALL PEOPLE HAVE A CREATION STORY, A NARRATIVE THAT EXPLAINS their origins, sense of place, and uniqueness. California Indian creation stories begin on the water. Austin McLaine, an eighty-one-year-old Concow man living on the Round Valley Reservation, said that long ago water covered the entire world. Light existed, but the sun and human beings did not. A man, sometimes identified as Earth Maker, floated in a boat on a vast sea.[1] A Paiute narrative—told by Hank Hunter, a one-hundred-year-old man from Independence—starts with two brothers, the brown dragonfly Esha and the white dragonfly Oonoop, flying over a large body of water.[2] Yuki creation, as told by sixty-eight-year-old Lizzie Tillotson from the Round Valley Reservation, opens with water covering the whole world. The water's foam resembled a feather, from which arose the image of man, whom the Yuki know as Taikomol', "he who walks alone."[3] McLaine, Hunter, and Tillotson proceeded to describe how creators formed California's land, People, and culture on this blank slate of water. Creators used a tremendous amount of work and a proper division of labor to form the Earth for a specific and special People. After resting, creators prepared that world for human beings. Creators centered the storyteller's People at the heart of the known world and established boundaries between the storyteller's People and their neighbors. California Indians used colors, physical appearance, and language to define who belonged with the storyteller's People and who did not. Then, through intense negotiations, creators and Coyote developed the social, political, economic, and cultural practices that structured human life, such as kinship, birth, death, and work.

Creation narratives were not inert historical sources and interpretations. Rather they are living understandings of what happened in the past. During the Great Depression, creation stories challenged the prevailing "California Story," which Settlers used to justify colonialism in the state. Simultaneously oral histories confronted prevailing ideas about California Indian land and identity. California Indians used their creation stories to articulate Indigenous identity, sovereignty and land.

The image of water covering the entire world is an appropriate place to begin California Indian creation stories. For terrestrial People like the Concows, Paiutes, and Yukis, water is a formless but powerful landscape.[4] The vast body of water over which the Dragonfly brothers flew or on which sat Earth Maker or Taikomoĺ evokes the image of an amorphous landscape. Sometime in the People's deep history, the land sat outside their realm of experiences.[5] Before creation Concows and Yukis had not listened to the wind rustle the leaves of oak trees. Paiutes had not diverted mountain streams to irrigate crops of indigenous plants. The People had not tracked deer through the foothills and valleys. The land did not exist—it was a blank ocean—until the People arrived, created identities, and experienced a life there.

Creating the land required a tremendous amount of work. Tillotson explained that after appearing on the ocean foam, Taikomoĺ stood up on a feather, stretched his arms out, and asked, "What am I going to do?" The water carried him north, and from there he moved south, creating the Earth. This job took several days and exhausted Taikomoĺ. On *me căus cō*, the seventh day, Taikomoĺ rested. After taking the day off he returned to work. Tillotson did not know how long it took Taikomoĺ to complete the Earth. When he finished, Taikomoĺ looked in each direction—north, south, east, west—and said, "My beautiful Earth." Next he formed mountains, on which he engraved river valleys and springs.[6]

For Concows the stupendous amount of work necessary to create the world required the effort of more than one individual. McLaine explained that Turtle swam from the north and met Earth Maker on the boat. Earth Maker asked, "How are you on diving?" Turtle replied, "I am good at that. Why do you ask me these questions?" Earth Maker responded, "Because we do not want to live on the water all our lives, we want to live on the ground." Turtle asked, "How are we going to do that?" Earth Maker replied, "I'll make a rope and tie it around you and you can dive to the bottom and get all the dirt you can." Earth Maker tied a rope around Turtle, who dove down into the water. When Turtle reached the bottom of the water, he filled his ears, fingernails, and mouth full of dirt. Turtle tugged on the rope and Earth Maker pulled him up. When Turtle resurfaced, he had only a small amount of dirt left in his mouth. Earth Maker asked Turtle to dive again. When Turtle gathered all the dirt he could carry, he yanked again on the rope, and Earth Maker pulled him up. Turtle had just as much dirt as he had before. Earth Maker flattened the dirt and put the disc on the boat's south stern. Earth Maker instructed Turtle, "We shall lie down and rest." When Earth Maker awoke, the water had receded, land appeared, and Turtle had left, following the water.[7]

Paiute creators, like Concow creators, cooperated in order to create the world. Esha, the brown dragonfly, asked his brother, Oonoop, the white dragonfly, to make land. After flying for several days Oonoop finally said, "Esha, I have figured a way to make land, but you must help me as best as you can." Oonoop asked Esha to sing as they flew. After singing for a few days, a dab of dirt appeared in Oonoop's hand. He threw the dirt into the water, and it floated. Oonoop and Esha sang again, and another bit of dirt appeared in Oonoop's hand. He threw the dirt into the water, and it spread out to make a small island.[8]

Concows, Yukis, and Paiutes understood creation as the product of everyday actions and relationships, buried deep in their respective histories. The first Yukis, Concows, and Paiutes who arrived in their homelands expended considerable energy to transform the unknown landscape into a known place. They identified the best places to fish for steelhead or salmon. They hiked the Sierra Nevadas or North Coast Range's hillsides to find the most productive acorn or pine nut groves. This work was as exhausting as creation. As with Taikomol' and Turtle, who slept after creating the world, the People must have rested after they prepared the land.[9] Work, like creation, required a suitable division of labor. At creation Earth Maker and Turtle divided the tasks of creation according to their abilities. Turtle possessed a prodigious ability to swim and hold his breath. Alternatively Earth Maker had the ability to manipulate the land into form. Family labor strategies reflected the way Earth Maker and Turtle divided their labor. Native Peoples organized their work activities according to kinship and gender. Kin had obligations to pool their work power to harvest acorns, hunt game, fish for salmon, or construct irrigation networks. By the 1930s Native families continued to organize their work by gender in California's agricultural and pastoral economies.[10] These labor systems produced food and resources for the People and re-created creation on a seasonal basis. By cooperating to hunt deer or rabbit, fish, harvest acorns and pine nuts, build irrigation networks, or pick hops, Indigenous People reenacted the work and labor that brought their worlds into being.

Owens Valley Paiutes used singing, not labor, to describe the significance of kinship in creation. Paiutes sang in various contexts. They sang during gambling matches to produce good luck and confuse opponents. Healers learned healing songs to cure illnesses. During a healing an assistant accompanied the healer and translated parts of the song to the audience. When hearing the Paiute creation story, listeners might provide a song or join in the singing, much as the audience did when the healer and his assistant sang to heal a person. In addition to gambling and healing singers, communities hired singers for Round, or Circle, Dances (a social dance). Held in the fall, these dances united Paiutes after they had dispersed for the summer. A town headman invited Paiutes from neighboring communities for the dance. Women tapped prospective dance partners on the shoulder, and they proceeded to hold hands. All dancers then formed a circle and hopped or side-shuffled in a clockwise direction. Singing remained a vital aspect of Paiute life during the Great Depression. Paiutes sang deer songs during fandangos, celebrations that occurred when seasonal agricultural work ended. Singing united Paiute People and activated the creative power needed to heal the sick, tell sacred histories, and celebrate a new season.[11]

Human-animal relationships, in addition to human-human, created parts of California. Nonhumans, such as the Dragonfly brothers and Turtle, had to work with humans to find dirt underneath the water and sing the world into existence. California Indians owed respect and reciprocity to the animals they hunted, the steelhead they fished, and the plants they harvested. Furthermore animals taught the People important traits. Twentieth-century Paiutes, Concows, and Yukis still had much to learn from Turtle's industriousness and sacrifice and the Dragonfly brothers' ability to work together and their singing power.[12]

Gradually creators made the land suitable for People. After creating the land, Esha asked Oonoop to enlarge the island. Oonoop sang into being another bit of dirt and used it to increase the size of the island. He said, "Brother Esha, see if the island is big enough for you and I. Run along the edge of the island and circle the island." At this point Esha transformed into Coyote, the famous shape-shifting trickster in American Indian oral tradition, and started out. He returned in a few minutes. "Brother Oonoop," Esha said, "I am afraid the island is too small for you and I to live on." Oonoop sang again and the island grew. Esha ran around the island, and it took him a little longer to return. Still Esha considered the island too small. Oonoop once again expanded the island. This time it took Esha a couple of days to return to his brother. Panting, Esha said, "Brother Oonoop could you put just one more handful on the island?" Oonoop replied, "Esha, you must be satisfied. I am going to put a little more than a handful." Esha set out again and, several days later, flopped down at Oonoop's feet. "Brother Oonoop," gasped a hungry and tired Esha, "I am perfectly satisfied. The land is big enough for you and I to roam on." Oonoop created a bounded island specifically for himself, Esha, and their Paiute descendants.[13]

Once the various creators made the land, they placed plants and animals there. Little Toby, a seventy-five-year-old Yuki man from the Round Valley

Reservation, said that Taikomoĺ planted foods for all the Yuki to gather: acorns, clover, nuts, and seeds. Then Taikomoĺ put animals, such as bear, deer, elk, grouse, rabbits, squirrels, and fish, on the earth for Yukis to eat.[14] Mary Saulque and Emma Washington, Paiute women from Benton, said that Kama (Rabbit) appeared after the creator made the Paiute world. Esha (Coyote) hunted, killed, and ate Kama.[15] Creators made the land suitable for the People by providing them with plants and animals.

Creators made the land, animals, and plants for a specific and distinct People. Polly Anderson, a seventy-seven-year-old Concow woman from the Round Valley Reservation, observed, "The Indians said that over on the Feather River, there were big flat rocks where they could stand right out in the river and catch their fish. They believed that Jesus left these rocks there mainly for them."[16] The creator made these rocks for Concows, and no one else, to use in fishing. Taikomoĺ, the Yuki creator, called his creation a "beautiful Earth." Only the Yuki, Lizzie Tillotson suggested, appreciated the mountains climbing out of the valley floor and encircling the People like a well-made basket.[17] Only the Yuki thought that the life sustaining oak groves that dotted the valley were beautiful. That land was ideally suited for the specific People who Taikomoĺ eventually created there.

California Indians argued that if the Creator made the land specifically for the People, then the Creator made a People expressly for that land. Paiutes Mattie Bulpitt, Jim Tom Jones, and George Robinson shared slightly different versions of this story. Their histories about the creation of People begin with a solitary male figure living in a rock house or a cave, located in Inyo County's Round Valley.[18] Although the three stories varied, Bulpitt, Jones, and Robinson knew exactly where Coyote lived: a stone house in Round Valley. The trio did not attempt to invalidate each other's story; instead they added their narratives to the rich corpus of Paiute knowledge and strengthened Paiutes' connection to places in their homeland. Coyote's home was a powerful place. Paiutes believe that a force called *puha* permeates all living things. Rocks, rock homes, and rock art, like those mentioned in the stories, are sites for obtaining or communicating with *puha*.[19] Round Valley was the origin of Paiute People, knowledge, and religious beliefs.

After precisely locating Coyote's house in Round Valley, Jones, a ninety-five-year-old from Bishop, explained that Coyote was making a blanket out of rabbit skin when a beautiful woman passed by. She looked into his house and then went on her way. Mesmerized, Coyote followed the woman as she traveled west, out of Round Valley, through Pine Creek Canyon. Coyote caught up with this beautiful woman at Pine Lake. The bashful couple only smiled at one another and did not speak a word. After spending two days together near the lake, the duo descended the mountains and set up camp at Pine Creek Canyon's mouth. "This camp," Jones explained, "was the camp of where Mother and Father of all Indian races lived. Here the Mother of all Indians had a lot of children."[20] In the version of the story told by Robinson, a seventy-five-year-old man from Independence, after catching up with the woman, Coyote killed some ducks to prove that he was a good hunter. He took the ducks to the woman, who lived with her mother. Coyote spent the night at the house, where he attempted to sleep with the beautiful woman. However, she had teeth in her vagina. Coyote used a stick to take out the teeth and impregnated the woman. She then lived with Coyote and became the mother of all Indians.[21]

Robinson's and Jones's creation stories reminded listeners of the process by which Paiute ancestors enlarged their homeland. In the 1930s Settler historians believed that California Indians lived remote and isolated lives before the arrival of Americans.[22] Yet Paiutes understood their history as one in which they continually expanded the space in which they lived. Recall that in Hank Hunter's creation story, Esha and Oonoop created a small island, which Oonoop increased to accommodate his brother's request. Like Esha's laps around the island, Coyote's pursuit of First Woman enlarged the world they inhabited. The listener follows Coyote as he drops his work and trots west, through Pine Creek Canyon and up to Pine Lake. Coyote and First Woman stretched the Paiute world to include Round Valley, Pine Creek, and Pine Lake.

The Paiutes' understanding of their history was not of ancient knowledge. In the 1930s Paiutes constructed a "place-world," in which they knew the exact places of their creation.[23] They could follow Coyote's footsteps and re-create the story of Coyote and First Woman conceiving the People. Paiutes and their ancestors followed this path in the summer when they left the blisteringly hot Owens Valley for Pine Lake's cool sanctuary. As they made this trip, Paiutes could travel comfortably, knowing that their ancestors and cultural heroes had already made this trip.[24] Storytellers placed their People at the heart of the world by mentioning the exact places of creation.

California Indians understood that, in fundamental ways, the People differed from one another. Creation stories accounted for and explained the dissimilarities between California's ethnic groups. Wailackis used colors to distinguish between the People. Wailacki Nancy Dobey, an eighty-year-old woman from the Round Valley Indian Reservation, told a version of Wailacki creation that begins with two men and women already on the land—one white pair and one dark pair. The white pair left and the dark pair remained. Then plants and animals emerged into the Wailacki world. Colors figured prominently in this story. Dark and light are complementary pairs and possess positive and negative attributes. Wailackis perceived darkness was a germinal force and maternal symbol. The dark pair gave birth to the People. The white or light pair were linked to death or an "other" since they left the site of creation. From a Wailacki perspective, the dark pair of humans remained in the homeland and prepared the land for their offspring. These ideas of dark and light clashed with those held by Americans. Dating to the sixteenth century, western European cultures identified positive traits, such as purity, with light or white, and negative traits, such as sin and death, with dark or black. Wailackis reversed this chromatic understanding of the world, thereby centering their ways of knowing when interpreting ethnic differences.[25]

Paiutes meanwhile attributed human differences to the antics of the mischievous Coyote. Paiute Susie Butcher, a seventy-five-year-old Paiute women from Big Pine, informed Evelyn Butcher that an old woman asked her son-in-law, Coyote, to carry a basket to their home. She warned Coyote not to open the basket until he reached home. To no one's surprise, Coyote's curiosity overwhelmed him and he looked inside the basket. As he did, human beings jumped out and stood around him. Coyote did not know what to do with all the People, so he sent them off in different directions to start their own families. The ugliest People went east; the People that owned plenty of ornaments and buckskins traveled north; the common People went south; and the prettiest went west. Butcher's story placed Paiutes in a web of social, political, and economic relationships. The four groups complemented each other. Note the way the cardinal directions frame Butcher's account, with physical appearance existing on the east-west axis and wealth on the north-south. The People living in the North may have been just as important as those who lived in the West, with their valuable trade items.[26]

Although Wailackis and Paiutes used color and location as ways to determine ethnicity, Concows and other Paiutes reckoned differences by language. After the creation of People, Concow Austin McLaine explained, the Creator told everyone, "If you wish and are tired of living in one place, you have the privilege to go wherever you may wish. There will be supplies enough for you, you will have a place to fish, to hunt, or gather acorns or any kind of food to eat. But there is one thing I want to tell you: when you leave this place you will be a tribe of your own and will speak a different language." Some left and spoke another language.[27] Paiute Jim Tom Jones told Billy Williams that the Father of all Indians told his children, "Now go where you like, have language to suit yourself."[28] Language, as these stories convey, set groups apart from one another and the land. The People who left the site of creation speak other languages, while those who remain speak the language of the land. Historically language served as a principal means to differentiate one California Indian polity from the other. In 1835 Luiseño Pablo Tac wrote a history of Luiseno contact with the Spanish and Mission San Luis Rey. Tac argued that before the Spanish arrived, "always there was war, always strife day and night with those who spoke in another language."[29]

The Creator provided for those who remained at the place of creation, whether a "dark pair," a "pretty People," or those who spoke the language of the land. Paiutes Mary Saulque and Emma Washington said that after humans had left the homeland, Esha addressed those who stayed behind: "My children, what few of you that are left here, you may have wars with the others, but you shall be peaceful. But if you have to fight, you shall never be defeated." Saulque and Washington continued, "It has been said that the Indians in this valley years ago had many wars with the other Indians but has never been defeated."[30] Jones's version of creation also referred to the Paiutes' martial prowess. The Creator told the Paiutes, "Now you, the ones that are left will be the best warriors." That is why, Jones explained, the Paiutes are not good-looking but strong.[31] Paiute George Robinson told Arthur Richards that one day Coyote went to find water, and when he returned, he found People going in all directions. Only a small group of People stayed. Coyote observed, "These People were not as fine looking as the People that had left." Coyote then said "the People who were with him would be superior to others that had left in anything they might take up or do."[32] The Paiutes were a chosen People, wise enough to remain in the homeland and selected by the Creator for greatness for they possessed the appropriate cultural traits. Paiute history verified this knowledge.

After creating the land and People, creators formed the respective cultures of California Indians. If creator figures placed the chosen People in specific and known places, it follows that those places were the wellspring of California Indian lifeways.[33] Narratives of cultural development featured two characters—Wolf and Coyote for the Paiutes, and Earth Maker and Coyote for the Concows—who negotiated how the People would survive at the center of the world. In their consultations creator figures and Coyote established idealized patterns of interethnic and intraethnic behavior.

California Indians established the kinship relationships between the two creators of their culture. "To begin with," Paiute Mose Weyland said, "Wolf and Coyote were brothers." After Earth Maker made the Concow world, Coyote trotted over to him and addressed him as "cousin."[34] Kinship established a set of protocols and relationships that regulated how People acted within a community.

California Indians transmitted knowledge through the kinship relationships established at creation. According to Wailacki Nancy Dobey, First Man and his grandson traveled north to find other People with whom to play grass game. It took the pair so long to travel to the North and back that when First Man returned to the site of creation he was "pretty gray." When the duo had left, only four People lived at the site of creation. First Man and his grandson returned to find many People. These fecund People "were Indians," Dobey explained, "like we are today." In addition to humans, animals and birds had increased in number. The People split into smaller groups and lived apart from one another. Grandfather taught his grandson how to live in the place of creation. Wailacki ancestors built housing appropriate for their seasonal locations. In the summer they escaped the heat by retreating to the mountains, where they erected houses "wherever it was suitable." In the winter Wailackis descended the mountains and lived along the more temperate Eel River, where they constructed permanent pine bark and grass houses. The process of transporting the materials and building the houses was quite laborious. Wailackis brought the bark from as far away as two miles from the campsites. In a similar fashion older kin taught younger relatives methods of living on the land. Elderly men shared hunting methods and songs with younger relatives. Older women taught younger women how to make baskets. The People's way of life proceeded from these kinship relations.[35]

After the various Peoples left the site of creation and began talking different languages, they developed ways to maintain connections with each other. According to Paiute Mose Weyland, Wolf told other men, "We are going visiting. We are going to visit girls in yonder places. So let us tan our hides as soon as we can and tan them so soft that [they] will be a fine present for the fair ones." Wolf took out his *woina*, a flute made from elderberry and used for doctoring and singing, inserted it into the ground, and blew. This action opened a hole in the ground and into the women's house. The men arrived in a vacant house. An old woman and the men of the village were hunting. The younger women, however, sat outside the house. One of the women sensed that strangers were around and sent her younger sister to investigate. She looked into her house's smoke hole and saw Wolf, Coyote, and other men lounging around. Wolf asked the woman to bring his party some water. The woman, no doubt a bit incensed by the men lying about her home and demanding water of her, brought back stale water. Wolf saw immediately that the water was unfit to drink, so he again asked the woman to bring him some water. This time the woman brought a small container of potable water. Wolf told her to give the water to the other men first. Although the container that held the water was small, Wolf's generosity ensured that everyone had a drink. The young woman then brought a bit of food. Once again Wolf instructed her to give the food to the other men first. Although the woman brought a small amount of food, there was enough to go around. The exchange of food and water softened relations between the woman and Wolf's group. That evening the men and women "gossiped and told stories; all had a good time."[36]

Visiting another community, as Wolf and his followers did, provided an opportunity to create interethnic ties in Indigenous California. After the exchange of gifts, the men and women socialized by telling stories and gossiping. No doubt the courting couples had a good laugh at Coyote's expense, for an old woman had fallen in love with him, but he "treat[ed] her rough." The old woman declared, "You are not treating me very good. So I am going out." When the old woman left the house, she instantly turned into a beautiful young woman. Coyote quickly realized his mistake and ran after the woman, but he never found her. Perhaps this was Coyote's punishment for attempting to cheat on his spouse or acting outside proper social decorum.[37] Exogamous marriages, often created when different groups camped together, permitted Indigenous People to establish friendships, trade, hunt, or go to war.[38]

Weyland also explained what Paiute spouses looked for in a potential mate. Women shared food and water with the visiting men, which demonstrated their ability as providers. Women gathered seeds, cooked, and tended to the home and used the fruits of their labor to assert a political role in their communities. They hosted visitors and served as conduits by which outsiders discussed important matters with the local headman. Paiute men had to prove they possessed complementary abilities, such as hunting and providing essential items that the family desired. Wolf, after all, exhorted his men to acquire and prepare soft hides.[39] By sharing food and water with his followers, Wolf proved that he was a good provider and a wise and generous leader.

After the courting process had concluded, the creator figure and Coyote developed proper childbirth procedures. Paiute Mose Weyland said Wolf proposed that after a couple married, they would just find their children. Coyote disagreed: "No, it cannot be. When they marry, the women must suffer to bear their children." Here storyteller Weyland interjected, "Like it is now."[40] Women, historically and in the 1930s, experienced difficulties in childbirth because Coyote acted against the good of humans. When a Paiute woman was ready to give birth, she entered the *cutü'vida*, an enclosed depression that the *tuduamudukudu* (midwife, "bring baby's birth") had heated for six to eight hours by a fire and lined with fresh, cool dirt. After the tuduamudukudu placed a blanket over the expectant mother, attendants steamed the woman by placing hot rocks in an *apa*, a basket filled with water. The midwife sat behind the kneeling mother and kneaded the baby down the mother's belly.[41] Wolf's recommendation for childbirth would have made for a much easier process.

Death arrived in a manner similar to childbirth: an argument between Creator and Coyote. According to Concow Austin McLaine, Earth Maker made a pool of water and proposed that when Concows grew old or sick, relatives would throw them into the water, and the elderly or ill would become healthy or young again. Coyote demurred, "We don't want such a thing as that. We have to have it so that if anyone gets sick, let him die so we have given a good time, crying and burning him."[42] In a Paiute story told by Weyland, Wolf suggested, "We will die for one year and after that we will live again." Coyote responded, "It cannot be. When we die we must die once and that be the end."[43]

California Indians understood that death, like birth, offered a moment for extended kinship networks to come together. Coyote insisted that death was important because Concows needed a time for "crying and burning." Unfortunately for Coyote, the world's first cry came at his expense. Coyote approached the Concow captain (likely Earth Maker under a new title) and said, "Cousin, it is about time we should have a big time." The captain asked, "What kind of big time do you want?" Coyote stated, "We want to have footraces and dances, all kinds of excitement." The captain replied, "All right, go and call all the People up to gather in the sweathouse, and we will have a meeting and talk about it, but do not have a big time without first doing so." Coyote then called People to the sweathouse and began to tell them what to do without consulting anyone. He ordered the women to gather seeds for pinole and acorns for soup. He told the men to hunt for deer and other animals for meat. With the feast prepared, the People readied for a footrace. All the young men in the community, including Coyote's son, lined up for the race. When the race started, the captain took a piece of joint grass and threw it in a hole near Coyote's son, likely because Coyote disobeyed the captain and held the big time without first consulting him. The grass turned into Rattlesnake. When Coyote's son, in the lead, neared the hole, Rattlesnake bit the boy on the foot, and the boy died. The other runners leaped over the dead boy and crossed the finish line. An anguished Coyote found his son, took him to the whirlpool that Earth Maker had previously created to resurrect the dead, and threw him in. It did no good. Coyote went to the captain and said, "Cousin, that water will not work. I threw my son in, and he has not come to life yet." The captain replied, "Well, you wanted everybody to die so you could have a good time crying and burning. Why don't you bury the boy?" The captain took out a mahogany stick and dug a grave for Coyote's son.

The captain then picked up Coyote's son's body and unceremoniously threw him into the grave. "This is what you wanted," the captain told Coyote.[44]

The events surrounding death were related to the social activities that punctuate the People's lives. Communities hosted a big time to celebrate "first fruit" or first harvests, such as the onset of the acorn-picking season or the first salmon caught during the fishing season. In the fall Concows held a big time called wē'da, "a big burning for the dead." The deceased's friends and family gathered and cried all night for those who had passed away. They attached personal possessions, such as fish, deer meat, clothing, baskets, fish nets, and rope, to poles, then broke the poles and tossed them into a fire. Leaders also used big times to demonstrate their generosity and leadership ability. The hosting community provided all the food for the event. People from surrounding communities also brought food and gifts to the host community's event. Gambling games, such as grass game or the Paiute game naiü'gua, and dances were popular at big times. The People also competed against one another in athletic events. Big times functioned as an important mechanism for cross-cultural exchange. People shared religious and social knowledge with each other at these events.[45]

Indigenous Californians used traditional narratives to describe their economies. Concow Austin McLaine explained that Coyote asked Earth Maker, "What shall I do for my People to eat?" Earth Maker then planted a tree, which bore a variety of acorns.[46] The Yuki creator Taikomol' put different foods in the Yuki homeland for them to acquire: acorns, pepper nuts, hazel nuts, buckeyes, sugar pine nuts, Manzanita berries, wild oats, Indian sunflower seeds, fish, eel, deer, rabbits, and squirrels.[47] With plants and animals prepared for humans to consume, the People developed ways to gather these important resources. Creators established the gendered division of labor that undergirded Indigenous economies. After creating women, Earth Maker said, "I am going to sow a seed for pinole and all the other things to eat, and the women can gather them." Coyote queried, "How are we to get our game, such as deer and all other meat?" Earth Maker then made two guns—one from a rock and one from a stick—and offered them to Coyote. Coyote chose the wooden gun because it was lighter and a better tool with which to hunt.[48] Meanwhile First Man gave a bow and arrow to Paiute males and baskets to Paiute women in which they could gather taboose and other plants. Paiute women received three baskets at creation. First, the women had wā'nü, a cone-shaped basket made from willows with which to make pine nuts. Second, the women had tu'wü, an oval-shaped basket also made from willows. This basket had a tight weave and women used it to sift pine nuts for flour. Finally, women had pătsā, another oval-shaped basket.

This one had a coarse weave, and women used it to harvest *cūzā'vi*, also *cūt'za*, a small shrimp that lived in Mono Lake.[49]

After placing the People on the land, creation narratives described the People's social, political, economic, and cultural practices. The People's lifeways came about after a series of conversations between the Creator (Earth Maker, Taikomol', First Man) and Coyote that occurred at the center of the world. Creator figures established marriage, childbirth, and death practices. Creator figures hosted the first big time, made the People's laws, and gave them food as well as the implements to acquire that food. Creation stories informed listeners who the People were in 1935. Dobey and Weyland explicitly made this point when they connected the People in stories to the Wailackis and Paiutes of the 1930s. California Indians were still a People for whom kinship mattered. They were still a People who intermarried with People outside of their community. They were still a People who held cries and other mourning rituals. They still attended big times.[50] They still went to the sweathouse or roundhouse for religious, social, and political gatherings.[51] They still practiced a gendered division of labor, which emphasized men hunting and women harvesting acorns. They still followed their leaders' advice. These vital aspects of culture, given to the People at creation, still defined who the People were in the throes of the Great Depression. In 1935 these practices sustained California Indians as they engaged in a battle for identity and land in history books and colonial courts.

In the late nineteenth and early twentieth century pioneer societies and amateur historians created their own creation stories about California. The time was ripe to do so. The United States had forced Indian nations onto reservations, railroads knit the nation together, and the East salivated over the West's bountiful resources. Now that the American West appeared safe for Settlers, boosters composed histories to attract tourists and eastern capital. Settlers fashioned two, sometimes antagonistic California creation myths. In southern California writer Helen Hunt Jackson and Los Angeles journalist Charles Fletcher Lummis identified 1769 as the year and the Spanish missions and Mexican *ranchos* as the sites of California's origins. The so-called Spanish fantasy past featured beneficent Franciscan missionaries, comely señoritas, and dashing social bandits. In hopes of attracting tourists, health seekers, land speculators, and permanent residents, the southern California creation story emphasized the region's Spanish roots and slower pace of life, as opposed to the hustle and bustle of northern California's urban and industrial development.[52] In northern California the year 1849 and the Gold Rush represented the moment and San Francisco the site of California's creation. Amateur and professional historians, such as John and Theodore Hittell, Josiah Royce, and Hubert Howe Bancroft, and historical organizations, such as the Native Sons of the Golden West, located the roots of California's greatness in those hardy pioneers and miners who sloshed dirt and water around in pans in the search for gold. For these writers the Gold Rush tamed the wilderness and produced modern capitalism. The miners demonstrated the core pioneer virtues necessary to lead the state into the future: bravery, nobility, and sacrifice for the common good.[53]

The two California stories marginalized California Indians in the state's creation story. Settlers argued that California Indians represented a socially, culturally, and racially inferior caste. In *The Curse of Capistrano*, the first novel in the popular Zorro series, published as a weekly serial in 1919, writer Johnston McCulley described California Indians as "red renegades" (racially degraded criminals, usually horse thieves) and "helpless" servants, in need of the paternal hand of Spanish missionaries, wealthy dons, or popular social bandits.[54] Other parts of the California creation story chastised Indigenous People for failing to modernize the state. Rather than scour mountain streams for gold or develop California's agricultural bounty, California Indians seemed content to live by hunting and gathering before the Spanish or Americans arrived. Bancroft wrote, "We do not know why . . . with such fair surroundings [California Indians] were made so much lower in the scale of intelligence than their neighbors."[55]

Settler writers argued that California Indians failed to put in the work of civilization, and so it was best that Settlers wrested control of the state from them.[56] According to the southern California story, Franciscan priests, led by Fray Junípero Serra, found a wilderness populated by uncivilized, child-like Indians. Missionaries believed that California Indians were lazy and forced them to work in the missions. Convinced that California Indians lacked religion, missionaries baptized them and coerced them to attend church in the mission. Some California Indians failed to understand the mission's benefits and ran away. Franciscans and Spanish soldiers went after the absconding neophytes and returned them to the mission. Writers depicted mission secularization after Mexican Independence as a mixed blessing for California Indians, who regressed into sloth without the kind and guiding hand of their padre. In northern California some writers criticized post–Gold Rush violence. Bancroft opined, "It was one of the last human hunts of civilization, and the basest and most brutal of them all."[57] However, writers believed, Indians were disappearing anyway. Miners and other California Settlers merely accelerated the process. From a Settler perspective, California's creation required that non-Indians exterminate the state's Indigenous population through assimilation in the missions or outright genocide.[58]

California Indians countered this California story with their creation stories. Rather than subscribe to the idea that California was created in 1769 or 1849, California Indians advanced the idea that California was ancient. Rather than look to the Spanish missions or San Francisco as the location of California's creation, California Indians offered local places, such as Chico and Inyo County's Round Valley. Rather than the laid-back culture of the Mexican *rancho* or the nascent forms of industrial capitalism that arose in San Francisco, California Indians argued that California's culture resulted from the contested negotiations between kin. Not only were California Indians the state's first Peoples, but their ways of being remained relevant during the Great Depression, especially when discussing land and identity.

Creation stories subverted orthodox understandings of the state's past and engaged political and legal struggles occurring in Native communities. In 1851 three Indian agents (later called commissioners, when their orders changed during their mission to California) signed eighteen treaties with California Indians, which recognized Indian title to more than eight million acres of land. Charles Wright, Austin McLaine, and Annie Feliz were the descendants of the Concows who signed the Rancho Chico Treaty. California Settlers opposed the treaties, and the U.S. Senate refused to ratify the contracts. Instead the federal government moved Native People to reservations, carved out of the public domain. Many California Indians refused to relocate to reservations, preferring to live on the fringes of Settler society. In 1904 two Senate clerks inadvertently found the treaties and reported their discovery to the Senate. In January 1905 the U.S. Senate removed the injunction of secrecy on the treaties and they became public knowledge. That same year San Jose attorney Charles Kelsey investigated the living conditions of off-reservation California Indians. Kelsey's report convinced the United States to create the California *rancheria* system and provide relief for California Indians.[59]

In 1926 the Commonwealth Club, a nonpartisan public affairs organization founded in 1903, published a report on California Indians, which raised the issue of the unratified treaties and federal responsibility to California Indians. But California Indians had few legal recourses to regain land. Federal law required the U.S. Senate to consent to American Indians filing land claims. Certainly legal procedures were stacked against American Indians, but some American Indian nations, such as the Lakotas in South Dakota, Hualapais in Arizona, and Tlingits in Alaska, filed land claims in the nineteenth and twentieth century, although not all emerged victorious. Persistent lobbying by the Commonwealth Club and other organizations, such as the California Indian Brotherhood, led by Pomos Stephen Knight and Albert James, bore fruit. In 1927 California's attorney general U. S. Webb filed a land claim against the United States on behalf of California Indians. The following year Representative Clarence Lea of Lake County introduced Resolution 491, later called the California Indian Jurisdiction Act, to the U.S. House of Representatives, which authorized the state of California to bring a lawsuit against the United States for its failure to ratify the treaties and compensate California Indians for lost lands.[60]

Although it might appear that the land claims were in California Indians' best interests, problems existed. The first involved Indian identity. The California Indian Jurisdiction Act defined "Indians of California" as "all Indians who were residing in the State of California on June 1, 1852, and their descendants living on May 18, 1928." In a sense, then, Settlers believed that Concows were the same as Yukis, Wailackis, Pomos, and Paiutes. The sovereign political communities that signed the treaties in 1851 did not bring individual claims against the United States. In order to discern who was an "Indian of California" and subject to the claim, the Department of Interior ordered a census. By creating a racialized and homogenized identity of "Indians of California," the claims case was one of many assimilation policies that began with the allotment of the 1880s and culminated with the termination policies of the 1950s. The federal government, and some state governments, attempted to destroy the corporate, tribal identity of Native People and create an individual identity.[61]

In addition to compromising Indigenous identity, the claim denied California Indian sovereignty. Rupert Costo (Cahuilla) railed, "[The term] 'Indians of California,' in the lawsuit, ignor[es] the tribal nature of the people, the tribal rights of the Indians and the culture and governance of the natives." For many decades Settlers argued that California Indians were a stateless and apolitical People. In 1851, for instance, California governor Peter Burnett declared, "The various small tribes upon the confines of California have no political organization, and no regular government among them." In the early twentieth century anthropologists perpetuated the idea that California Indians lacked sovereignty. Alfred Kroeber argued that before the arrival of Euro-Americans, California Indians lived in "tribelets," "groups of small size, definitely owning a restricted territory, nameless except for their tract of its best known spot, speaking usually a dialect identical with that of several of their neighbors, but wholly autonomous." The term *tribelet* suggested that California Indians were excessively primitive and lacked political structures.[62]

California Indians' creation stories established the foundations of identity and tribal sovereignty, situating law and leadership at the moment of creation. First Man became the Wailackis' first captain or chief. Wailacki Nancy Dobey stated, "He seemed to have the power to rule these people." Captains fulfilled many roles in Indigenous communities, such as establishing law and order. Dobey continued, "At that time they were strict in the laws they believed in being [applied] to people." If a Wailacki killed another person, the community asked the murderer to leave. Dobey explained, "They didn't believe in having a bad party around."[63] Roundhouses served as a symbol of a captain's authority. "The beginning of the law," Dobey explained, "was made in the sweathouse they built."[64] Taikomol', the Yuki creator, established Yuki law. Taikomol' ensured that "everything under the sun and all the animals" were the Yukis' food. Yukis followed strict guidelines or faced dire consequences. "If they broke these laws," Taikomol' informed Yukis, "they shall die because they did not obey my word and they shall get into darkness and also shall they get into hell forever and ever." If Yukis adhered to the law, of course, good things followed. "If they believe my word," Taikomol' explained, "they shall be happy and no sickness shall befall them and . . . you must be happy and to have a clear mind."[65] California Indian sovereignty dated to the moment of creation and rested upon the authority of the creators.

Perhaps just as fundamental as homogenizing Indigenous identities and denying Indigenous sovereignty, the claim determined what constituted Indian land. Throughout California history Settlers ignored California Indian land rights. The Doctrine of Discovery, an international legal principle that granted European nations and the United States economic and legal rights to North America, held that American Indians possessed only a use right to the land, not fee title.[66] In California the federal government denied any kind of Indigenous land rights. In the 1840s American Settlers arrived in California and claimed what appeared to be unused land or evicted Indians from desirable mining and agricultural areas. In 1851 the federal commissioners signed the aforementioned treaties with California, but the U.S. Senate failed to ratify them because of high costs and Settler opposition. Instead the Office of Indian Affairs created land bases for California Indians out of land owned by the federal government.[67] Squatters frequently infringed on reservation borders and defied the federal government's attempts to control and supervise Indian land.[68] The claims process failed to restore Indigenous land title because it enabled Native People to sue only for monetary compensation, not for the return of the actual land. In the twentieth century this nettlesome issue has posed problems for several Indigenous nations, such as the Western Shoshone in Nevada and the Lakota in South Dakota's Black Hills.[69] Federal and state law worked in concert with the California story to divest Native Peoples of their land, sovereignty, and identity.

Yet lawyers, politicians, and anthropologists did not listen to California Indians. The time was not right for People to accept California Indian understandings of identity and land expressed in their creation stories. The California Indian claim, later called case K-344, eventually wound itself through courts and political committees. On December 5, 1944, the Court of Claims ruled in favor of the "Indians of California" to the tune of $17 million for the eighteen reservations allocated in the treaties. However, pursuant to the original Jurisdictional Act, the court deducted offsets of $12 million for government expenses since the 1850s. The remaining $5 million was initially placed in a trust fund for California Indians, but in 1950 the U.S. Congress distributed a per capita payment of $150 to those People and their descendants from the 1928 California Indian roll. California Indians derisively referred to this payment as their TDP money: "television down payment."[70]

California Indians countered Settler histories and laws with an Indigenousness that began at creation. Indigenous creation stories asserted that the Indigenous People of California were not "Indians of California" but Concows, Yukis, Paiutes, and members of other tribal nations. Creators made specific pieces of land for them. Creators placed a special People on that land. There were other People in California, but they spoke a different language and lived in other places. The Creator and Coyote then created the People's distinct cultures. Creation stories also claim Indigenous sovereignty. In their charter histories California Indians defined their citizenship, who were and were not members of their respective nations. They articulated a sense of shared territory. They outlined their political organization by describing their captain's duties. And they argued that they were first on the land, a point that rejected U.S. legal doctrines. California Indians insisted that creators made the land specifically for *them*, thereby defying the legal doctrine of *terra nullis*, which undergirded the Doctrine of Discovery. California Indians used the land that the Creator had given them.

Creation stories served as the beginning of the People's history. They detailed the creation of the California Indian land base, thus tying the People to specific places, and explained the People's physical creation and their cultural underpinnings. Rather than simply reflecting on the past, creation stories instructed California Indians how to deal with legal cases in the 1930s. California Indian creation narratives challenged the legal mechanisms that threatened Native identity, undermined tribal sovereignty, and destroyed Indigenous land rights. Creation stories, perhaps implicitly at times, critiqued American colonialism. Another contested narrative in 1930s California involved the naming of California's landscape.

CHAPTER 2

Naming

CALIFORNIA INDIANS UNDERSTOOD THEMSELVES AS A PEOPLE OF A place. Creators made the world for a certain People and a unique People for a specific place. Languages and identities reinforced the significance of place. Owens Valley Paiutes knew the people who lived near the modern-day town of Benton as *ütü'ütü witü*, or Hot Place, and named those who inhabited Inyo County's Round Valley *kwina patü*, or North Place. Yukis too linked identity to place. The people who live in Mendocino County's Round Valley called themselves Ukomnom, People of the Valley. The Ukomnom identified their linguistic relatives who lived to the west as Huchnom, which means People of the Outside. Yukis marked Sherwood Valley Pomos as Onpotílnom, which means Ground Dust People.[1] Place and place-names structured how California Indians told their histories as well as how they understood one's identity. Stories might begin with a place-name or refer to a specific location. Jake Gilbert, a sixty-year-old Mono Paiute man from Lee Vining, started a story, "This happened at Grant Lake."[2] Similarly Billy Rice, an eighty-year-old Pomo man from Ukiah, told Pomo Edgar Jackson, "This story takes place on the ridge [on the] south side of Eel River or north of Potter Valley, Calif[ornia]."[3] At the end of the story, storytellers often returned to a named or specific place. Concow Austin McLaine, an eighty-one-year-old Concow man from the Round Valley Reservation, concluded a story about a young man who went north to gamble, "The[re is a] hole in the rock and each foot print on each side of the hole. This can be seen today on the east side of the valley, in Butte County about 10 or 15 miles east of Durham and after he had killed the deer he took the heart out and took it home and he destroyed it and since then there has been no more evil deer. This ends the story."[4] Oral narratives followed topographic markers, not chronological ones as in Settler histories; historical events proceed from place to place, not date to date.

During the Great Depression oral narratives featuring specific place-names countered and challenged Settler understandings of California history.[5] Between 1820 and 1935 Settlers renamed many of California's landmarks. Settler place-naming, or renaming, was a "discovery ritual" by which Settlers colonized Indigenous land and economies. When American fur traders entered California in the 1820s and 1830s, they assumed that the land was *terra nullis* and named landmarks.[6] These acts of what Ojibwe historian Jean O'Brien calls "firsting" helped Settlers claim to be indigenous to California.[7] By naming places—both in English and in Indigenous languages—California Indians contested attempts to erase their place-names and the historical meanings embedded in the landscape.[8] Oral narratives with specific place-names told an older history of California, refuting the notion that, in the nineteenth century, Mendocino County, Sacramento Valley, and Owens Valley were empty lands. California Indians set stories with place-names deep in time and featured Indigenous historical figures who traveled across the known landscape, created lakes, and captured fire.[9] These stories chartered the People's history and engaged with the history and politics of the 1930s. Place-naming depended on Indigenous People's social, political, economic, and cultural circumstances and respective histories with U.S. colonialism. Pomo history and place-names reinterpreted the history of the American West and California. Owens Valley and Mono Paiutes incorporated settler place-names into their narratives in order to use this colonized landscape to find common cause with Settlers. Concows anchored themselves in a homeland from which the United States had removed them but established a path for future Concow people to follow.

In 1935 Susie Wathen, a sixty-four-year-old Pomo woman from Ukiah, told Clarence Campbell of Pinoleville a story about how a doctor created Mot ti coy, now known as Blue Lake, and Hu se lell, now known as Mud Lake. Both bodies of water sit west of Clear Lake, alongside modern-day Highway 20. A family—a couple and their two daughters—lived on a flat, arid plain. The young girls became desperately thirsty and asked their father to create water. The father dug a hole in the ground and waited for four days. On the fourth day the father, a powerful healer, turned into a dragon, created Mot ti coy, and sank to the bottom of the lake. One of the daughters joined her father at the bottom of Mot ti coy. The other daughter and the mother walked around Mot ti coy and discovered Hu se lell, where the mother and daughter sank to the bottom of the lake.[10]

John McWhinney, a seventy-nine-year-old Pomo man from Ukiah, told Lawrence Allen a story common among Pomos, if not all California Indians, about Fawns and Bear. McWhinney began the story, "Besha' mätä (Deer) and her husband Lemä betä (Bear) lived with Besha' mätä's children—Dē-yas and his two sisters—at Chaum chä pö we (Coyote Valley)." Lemä betä killed Besha' mätä and attempted to hide the crime from the fawns. But Dē-yas discovered what happened to his mother. He took his mother's baskets and threw them in a river, so Lemä betä would not find them. Then Dē-yas waited until Lemä beta went to sleep, and he burned down the house, which was at Mä pō me nä. Dē-yas and his sisters traveled to Shä pä lä mel', now known as Willits Hill, at which point a flood covered the world except for Shä pä lä mel' and Shä kä' bā, "a mountain twenty-five miles south and east."[11]

Place-names in Wathen's and McWhinney's stories served several purposes. For one, they establish the veracity of Pomo histories and oral narratives. Anthropologist Sally McLendon explains, "One of the most elemental narrative presuppositions involved in the performance of Eastern Pomo myths must be that they are true, that they describe events and activities that once really took place, the proof of which is that these events and activities always take place in real, named geographical locations familiar to the Eastern Pomo."[12] From Wathen's and McWhinney's perspective, the events that happened at Mot ti coy and Chaum chä pö are true because the authors and listeners knew the places mentioned in the stories. This was an important statement for Pomos to make. Up to the 1930s scholars dismissed oral narratives as possessing any kind of historical veracity.[13] Wathen and McWhinney argued that their ways of knowing persisted into the Great Depression.

Pomo traditional narratives, with specific place-names, emphasized Pomo ways of understanding the world. Wathen established a relationship between the actors in the stories and those Pomos who lived in the 1930s. On the fifth day, according to Wathen, the daughters returned to where their father created water. Their father had turned into an enormous, multicolored dragon, in another story called Bagi'l, and, with his *mush sam* (a dreamer's staff made out of hickory), sat on the bottom of the lake. The dragon said to his daughters, "This is my water, my four days of hard labor, my very perspiration and my mourning tears." The dragon had many powers. He raised the mountains that now surround the lakes, where he placed an abundance of angelica, which represented his body.[14] In the 1930s, Pomos depended on Bagi'l's goodwill. His tears and perspiration turned into a lake, and he gave the Pomos important medicine. Whenever Pomos harvest angelica in the mountains surrounding Mot ti coy, they remember Bagi'l's sacrifice.[15]

Storytellers also explained how places assumed their modern appearances. According to McWhinney, after Lemä betä killed Besha' mätä, the ever-vigilant

Dē-yas waited until Lemä betä had fallen asleep, then he and his sisters went to the house and set it on fire. "To this day," McWhinney explained, "the hill is red in the vicinity of this den. Called Mä pō me nä."[16] Regarding Hu se lell, Wathen explained the youngest daughter took the round basket full of acorn mush and went to the opposite side of Mot ti coy. She continued on the east side of the lake until she came to Hu se lell, where she threw the basket of acorn mush as far as she could toward the lake's center. Thus Hu se lell is brown, the color of acorn mush. She then reached the south end of Hu se lell, where *bu tae* (a tule reed) grows. This particular stand of *bu tae* represents the young girl's hair. "To this very day," Wathen explained, "if one notices closely can be seen strands of black hair floating about beneath the bu tae."[17] The lakes and valleys on the Pomo landscape possess distinctive physical features, which the figures in Pomo oral narratives created. When Pomos visited or passed by these places in the 1930s, they could recall the oral narratives as well as the meanings those stories conveyed.

Language reinforced Pomo interpretations of place. Throughout the story Wathen called the lake Mot ti coy. "Blue Lake" is a Settler name and refers to the lake's "appearance under certain atmospheric conditions."[18] Wathen also presented Pomo religious objects in the Pomo language first and English second. Thus she called the dreamer's staff a *mush sum* and then described it as a "cane made out of dried hickory."

The places Pomos mentioned in their oral narratives were important landmarks. Pomos believe that springs, lakes, and other bodies of water were a portal to the supernatural world. Doctors and healers bathed in water to supplement their powers. After a healer's death powerful objects would be immersed in water in order to control their power.[19] Many Pomos were wary of Mot ti coy. "To this day," Wathen explained, "the Pomo are very superstitious about the Blue Lakes and are never seen around there." At the end of the story she reiterated Pomo concerns about the lakes: "Strange sights have been seen on these lakes, and many fish have been seen of different types. People have lost their lives there. The Pomo Indians will not stop when passing by these lakes."[20] Pomos who ventured too close to the lakeshore could still see the remnants of the family floating in the lake's blue waters. Wathen enunciated the power of the place when she linked the story to death. After the doctor turned into a dragon, the mother made *way ya* (a doctored bread, likely made from acorn flour). Then Wathen discussed taboos associated with death. The living should not go near the place where a person had died, but were supposed to place *way ya* in the lake. The mourners, like the mother and youngest daughter in the story, then took worldly possessions, in the form of acorn flour and a *ba toll ba ca* (a round pinole basket, also described as big), and disposed of them in the lake.[21]

These oral narratives enlarged the world in which Pomos lived. Both stories featured historical figures traveling across the known Pomo landscape. Their actions created space between places in the Pomo world. Wathen's story of Mot ti coy told of the way Pomo land changed from a flat, arid plain to the lakes, wetlands, and mountains that now dominate the area. The story explained how Pomos enlarged their world to include Mot ti coy and Hu se lell. The mother and younger daughter act as Pomo explorers, traversing opposite sides of the Mot ti coy and discovering Hu se lell. McWhinney detailed how Dē-yas traveled from Chaum chä pö we (Coyote Valley) to Mä pö me nä and finally to Shä pä lä wel', now known as Willits Hill. Wathen and McWhinney knew an expansive and large Pomo world, one in which their ancestors had named.

Pomos have maintained a long relationship with the places they discovered in their deep history. Sometime in the past, Bagi'l created Mot ti coy and Dē-yas and his siblings taunted and evaded Lemä betä near Chaum chä pö we. These places continued to possess meaning in the 1930s. Mot ti coy, Wathen explained, sat "on the old Indian travel trail, and it still to this day is a camp overnight stopping place."[22] Throughout Wathen and her ancestors' lives, Pomos passed by Mot ti coy in order to engage in economic activities. A trade route ran along Clear Lake's northern shores, linking people on the Pacific Coast with central California and beyond. Pomos produced and traded clamshell disk beads, which Native peoples used as currency, with Patwins of central California. In the nineteenth and twentieth century Pomos passed by Mot ti coy on their way to work in the Ukiah Valley's hop fields, in the Sacramento Valley, or on their way to Lake County to participate in social events with other Pomos. Movement and mobility allowed Pomos to connect with these places and the stories that explained them.[23]

Wathen deployed this story to challenge and reframe California and western history. As with Lucy Young, from the introduction, Wathen demonstrated that she was aware of how Settler histories ignored Pomo historical interpretations. At the end of the story the youngest girl said, "We are the makers of trails, in our footsteps a civilization follows over our once silent paths. The traffic of a nation moves."[24] By 1935 it was easier for Pomos and non-Pomos to travel by Mot ti coy. The state of California completed Highway 20, which linked Ukiah with Tahoe, and followed a preexisting Pomo trade route that connected Ukiah to the Sacramento Valley. According to Wathen, Settler society and civilization followed that of Pomos. After establishing Pomo civilization, the youngest girl in the story said, "We were the *pioneer* or even *frontier*."[25] Wathen modernized this story and co-opted two of the most powerful phrases in western history: *frontier* and *pioneer*. Frederick Jackson Turner saw the frontier as the line where savagery met civilization. It always moved west. Wathen indigenized the frontier. Rather than Pomos representing savagery, they symbolized civilization. Pomos, not American Settlers, had transformed the land by planting seeds and harvesting grains. Pomo civilization followed in the footsteps of Pomo pioneers, who came to be near Mot ti coy and kept the howling wolves at bay with their fires. Along the well-trod footpaths on Mot ti coy's shores, Pomo commerce flourished, trafficking baskets, shell beads, and religious beliefs inland to exchange with their Patwin neighbors. Wathen anticipated the ways later scholars flipped the geographical perspective of Turner's frontier. In the 1950s and 1960s American Indian scholars asked others to reframe our understanding of the frontier from the outer edge of Anglo-American settlement to complex interethnic contact zones. This discussion has produced counternarratives, whereby scholars should "face east" rather than west.[26] In addition Wathen presaged those recent scholars who argue that U.S. colonialism and expansion followed in the footsteps of Indigenous expansion.[27]

Wathen also co-opted frontier history by claiming that Pomos were pioneers. Settlers depicted pioneers as hardy white people indigenous or first to a given area. They tamed the wilderness and prepared it for the eventual white civilization. Settler historians often suggested that Indigenous people and pioneers did not live together. Wathen, though, argued that Pomos were the original pioneers, who cleared the land, planted seeds, harvested crops, and beat back wild animals.[28]

In Pomo country place-names served several important functions. A named place, such as Mot ti coy, verified Pomo knowledge; since Pomos knew the place, they knew the story was true. Place-names also asserted a deep Pomo history on the land. Their ancestors had created Mot ti coy and made it look as it did in the 1930s; their ancestors passed by the lake to trade with Patwins, and Pomos continued to move by the lake as they worked in Mendocino and Lake counties. And place-names enabled Pomos to reinterpret California and western history. Wathen purposefully deployed terms such as *frontier* and *pioneer* to indigenize understandings of these terms and California history. Pomos, then, used their named landscape to counter colonial systems in their homeland and claim the land on which they lived. Paiutes in the Owens Valley also lived on the land, but used place-names for a different purpose.

In 1935 Paiute Jake Gilbert lived at Lee Vining, California. The father of at least three children, Gilbert was in his sixties when he told several stories to an unnamed Paiute SERA worker.[29] Gilbert recounted the tale of a large fish, which was dissatisfied with the body of water in which it lived because it was too small. Fish moved to June Lake. Fish then went to Gull Lake but remained unsatisfied. He went to Silver Lake and then to Grant Lake. All of these lakes displeased Fish, so he traveled down the mountains via Rush Creek. As he moved along, Coyote barked at Fish. Afraid, Fish hurried on his way. A Paiute attempted to impede Fish's progress by creating a dam out of rocks from the mountain. Fish could not remain still with Coyote barking. Fish broke through the dam and came to Cū'tza üp, or Mono Lake. Fish found Cū'tza üp too small; the lake's water did not cover his large body. Fish again tried to move, and the Paiute repeated his effort to block Fish's path. The Paiute took land from Benton, California, and covered Fish. However, the slippery Fish went around the land. The Paiute built a third dam, this time from land from the mountains, but Fish knocked the land off and kept going. As the Paiute made a fourth attempt to block Fish's movement, Fish said, "This is my skin, this my people, you can have, this is now called cutzavi [the pupae of *Ephydra hians*, the Mono Lake alkali fly]." After sacrificing his flesh to the People, Fish journeyed to Walker Lake, which was also too small. Finally Fish came to Lake Tahoe. He let out a low whistle and said, before slipping into the deep blue water, "This is the water I'm look[ing] for."[30]

Place-names structured Paiute oral narratives. Rather than adhering to a chronological narrative, Gilbert's story followed a topographical one. He began the story by referring to a specific place: June Lake. Valleys provided the spaces in which Fish moved, and the narrative's action occurred at the various lakes—natural and man-made—along the present-day June Lake Loop or California Highway 158, concluding at Lake Tahoe in Washoe territory.[31]

As in Pomo oral tradition, Paiute place-names signified power. All places possess *puha*, power or "a force or energy."[32] *Puha* can have both positive and harmful effects, in that it can be a generative force in the People's lives or it can be destructive. Paiutes associated high places with positive manifestations of *puha*, such as the place from which Fish began his journey. Benevolent spirits live on top of mountains; doctors travel to the tops of mountains to seek visions and *puha* itself. In the late 1920s Jack Stewart, a Paiute from Bishop, stated that his power came from the Birch Mountains, the towering peaks midway between Mono Lake and Owens Lake. Mount Dana, which overlooks the path that Fish took from June Lake to Lake Tahoe, also possesses *puha*.[33]

On the opposite end of Owens Valley's topography were dangerous low-lying areas. Another of Gilbert's stories, entitled "Water Baby," begins at Grant Lake, Fish's third stopping point. A woman was gathering wild sunflowers. She became thirsty, so she left her gathering basket and took her baby to get a drink at a nearby spring. When she arrived at the spring, she lay her baby down so it could sleep and she started to drink. While she drank a water baby—a sprite that lived in water—came and swallowed her child. After consuming the infant, the water baby crawled into the woman's basket and started to cry. When the mother heard the cries of what she assumed was her child, she came over, picked it up, and began to nurse the water baby. After feeding for a while, the water baby started to swallow the woman. The woman became frightened. Just then a little bird, perhaps Hummingbird, flew around them. The bird told the woman to pinch the water baby's finger. The woman pinched the water baby's finger so hard that he let go of the women's breast. As soon as the water baby loosened its grip, the woman ran away and told her friends. The women fled the place as soon as they could with their food in tow.[34] The low-lying Grant Lake served as a lesson for Paiute women and children, informing them of the very real dangers the People faced if they played or let their children play too close to the water's edge: the water baby might come up and swallow them.

Paiutes understood the intimate links between people, places, and animals. Bridgeport Tom, an eighty-five-year-old man from Bishop, told Luella Turner about the animals gathered on the shores of Mono Lake. From the west, Padwa (Bear) came. From the south, Esha (Coyote) trotted to Mono Lake. Togoqua, Rattlesnake, slithered from the north. Many other animals attended the conference, but these three, Bridgeport Tom explained, were the most important. The animals discussed the jobs that each would perform in the world. They appointed Hummingbird to be the king of the air. The animals told Padwa to protect the woods. They asked Deer to keep peace in the land and Pogue (Fish) to keep the streams pure. Esha, of course, ruled the Paiutes as their father, and the animals made Togoqua the king of the land, sun, and moon. This was an extremely powerful gift—too powerful, in fact. The animals gave Togoqua so much power that it turned to poison and went to his head. "So as a result," Tom said, "the snake is a dangerous but dumb creature." Rattlesnake, "calling himself the devil," became a powerful enemy to the Paiutes. Yet Rattlesnake required proper respect and handling in order to maintain balance in the world. The "old Paiutes," Tom explained, believed that no one should kill or burn a rattlesnake. Instead one should capture Rattlesnake and return him to his home in the hills.[35]

As the story of the animals at Mono Lake illustrates, everything in the world needed to operate in unison. Paiutes understood that different beings and peoples had specific roles in the world, often for peace and protection, and violating those roles had significant consequences. Failing to pay the proper respect to Rattlesnake threatens to create an imbalance in the natural world. Rattlesnake will cause the weather to turn extremely and uncomfortably hot, and no one who lives in the Great Basin or Mojave Desert wants that.

Mono Lake taught Paiutes proper social etiquette as well as the consequences of failing to adhere to social norms. Paiutes who come to Mono Lake and know Bridgeport Tom's story will be reminded of the consequences of hubris. Togoqua's arrogance transformed into poison, a negative manifestation of *puha*. Tom also stated that one should pay proper respect to rattlesnakes, a different perspective than that held by Settlers, who treated rattlesnakes as they treated wolves and coyotes, as a threat, and killed them on the spot.[36] Tom suggested that there are consequences to improperly treating Togoqua; such actions will cause extreme heat, an unpleasant prospect in the already scorching Mojave Desert. People should respect Togoqua's power and move him to a place where he might not harm the People.

Place-names also disclosed the resources Paiutes used to survive in the Owens Valley. In the summer months Paiutes journeyed to fishing villages, such as June Lake, dotted throughout the Sierra Nevadas to fish for *tsōnī'ta*, a native minnow, and huwa *ădăpü'ü*, a suckerfish. A district leader organized the fishing and divided the catch equally among all participants. Paiutes frequently came to Mono Lake to harvest *cutzavi*, which Fish gave to them, for food and trade. Paiutes dried the pupae and removed the outer shell, which left behind a yellow kernel.[37] Gilbert's story challenged understandings of the Great Basin's economic bounty. People consider the region a desert, a land void of food and water. Anthropologist Don Laylander suggests that Paiutes told this and similar stories to explain the absence of fish in saline lakes like Mono Lake.[38] On the contrary, this story details the presence of a vital economic resource in the Paiute world. Paiutes knew that the lakes contained important food sources that they could exploit at appropriate times of the year.

Gilbert and Bridgeport Tom's narratives established a deep history in the Owens Valley. Fish accomplished the same work as Coyote in Paiute creation stories; he enlarged the world Paiutes know. Fish traveled the present-day California Highway 158. References to Walker Lake and Lake Tahoe revealed Paiutes' trade networks and interethnic encounters with their neighbors. Owens Valley Paiutes called the Northern Paiutes who occupied Walker Lake *agai dika*, or fish eaters. Paiutes followed a path that left Mono Lake and cut eastward across the Anchorite Hills through what is known as Whiskey Flat to Walker Lake, where they visited Walker Lake Paiutes in order to trade, hold ceremonies, and establish kinship connections.[39] Lake Tahoe sat at the center of the Washoe homeland. Washoes called Lake Tahoe Daowaya and spent springs and summers on the Lake's shores.[40] Paiute traditional narratives revealed that they lived not in a circumscribed but an enormous world, which they traveled over and knew quite well.

In the early nineteenth century Settlers contested Paiute place-names in the Owens Valley. For most of the nineteenth century the Owens Valley was situated in a space historian Natale Zappia calls an "interior world," a place where Indigenous trading and raiding practices determined the region's society, economics, and politics.[41] Beginning in the 1820s, American fur trappers ventured into the Paiute homeland. Peter Skene Ogden probably traveled through the valley in 1829 and 1830, and Joe Walker periodically entered the Valley between 1830 and 1846. These travelers made little contact with Paiutes, but they left behind broken wagons and other debris, which Paiutes transformed into usable items. In 1845 John C. Frémont's third exploratory mission likely ventured into the valley. Frémont named the Owens Valley after Richard Owens, a fur trader who joined Frémont's 1844 expedition and testified to Congress on Frémont's behalf. In the 1850s mining operations appeared north of Mono Lake. By the beginning of the American Civil War, ranching and farming enterprises enclosed the valley in order to feed the miners.[42]

By naming the valleys, lakes, and mountains, Settlers transformed what they perceived as space into a place for colonization. Seters considered the Great Basin and eastern California a void. Spanish missionaries never established missions there, as they had on the coast. Mexican *rancheros* failed to penetrate the Sierra Nevada range and establish landholdings in the Owens Valley. In the mid-nineteenth century Settlers used the Great Basin and eastern California as a corridor of travel, not an area to inhabit. Overland emigrants hurried across the seemingly barren Basin in order to avoid being trapped on the Sierra Nevadas, like the ill-fated Donner party. Mexican caravans, laden with serapes, ambled from Taos to Los Angeles in order to acquire horses. Upon their return these caravans drove large herds of horses from oasis to oasis in the Mojave Desert. Sometimes illicit activity occurred along the desert thoroughfares. Utes, Americans, and Mexicans drove stolen livestock at a breakneck pace through the maze of mountains and desert from Los Angeles to Utah Lake.[43] In the mid-nineteenth century many Settlers traveled across the Great Basin, but few paused there. Naming the Owens Valley changed how Settlers perceived this part of the Great Basin. A valley is a low-lying area surrounded by higher ground, usually featuring a river or stream running through it. The presence of water in the Great Basin was an important discovery. By naming the area the Owens Valley, Frémont revealed to people in the East that not all parts of the Great Basin were arid. There was hope of transplanting Settler practices to the Basin.

Frémont's naming of the Valley also asserted U.S. right of discovery on the area. Settlers frequently named places after their Anglo-American "discoverer."

Of course, Frémont was not the first person to enter the Owens Valley. Paiutes had lived there for centuries. Frémont was not even the first Anglo-American to arrive in the valley. Historian Irving Richman suggested that Joe Walker traveled through the Valley in 1833, while Hubert Howe Bancroft later argued that fur trader Jedediah Smith ventured into the valley four years before Walker.[44] Americans connected discovery to the legal process of colonizing North America and other Indigenous areas on the globe. The Doctrine of Discovery granted legal rights to the land and trade with Indigenous Peoples to the discoverers of a place. The Corps of Discovery, led by Meriwether Lewis and William Clark, claimed discovery rights on their expedition from Missouri to the Pacific. The Corps marked cliffs, branded trees, mapped the terrain, and named places in order to demonstrate that they were the first Settlers in the American West. Frémont, perhaps as well known as Lewis and Clark as explorers of the American West, with his sobriquet of "Pathfinder," followed in his predecessors' path. Naming the Owens Valley attracted American Settlers and functioned as a legal claim to blunt Mexican expansion from the west or south. Anglo-American "discovery" attempted to erase Paiutes' presence. The Doctrine of Discovery held that Native people possessed only a use right to the land, not fee title. Native People could subsequently be removed at any moment after discovery. Furthermore the Doctrine denied Native sovereignty. The Doctrine prevented Native people from entering into diplomatic negotiations with, selling land to, or trading with nations other than the discoverer's, although the politics of the sixteenth, seventeenth, eighteenth, and nineteenth centuries precluded strict enforcement of this provision.[45]

The writing of history aided and abetted discovery and dispossession. As in New England, local historians narrated the "California Story." These writers denied that Paiutes had occupied the valley for ages. William Chalfant wrote histories of the Owens Valley and Inyo County at roughly the same time that Jake Gilbert and other Paiutes recounted their narratives. William's father, Pleasant, arrived in the Owens Valley in the 1870s and owned the *Inyo Register*, the local newspaper. William followed in his father's footsteps as a journalist and writer. He constructed a usable past for Owens Valley Settlers that glorified American westward expansion. He dedicated his book on Inyo County "to the pioneers" and to his father, a "Pioneer of Inyo and [a] pioneer in endeavor[ing] for her moral as well as material growth."[46] Chalfant proceeded to deny a Paiute history in the Owens Valley. He offered two chapters on Paiute cultural practices; in the process he froze Paiutes in the time in which they encountered Anglo Settlers in the mid-nineteenth century. Then he argued that no one, not even Paiutes, had occupied the Valley before Anglo-Americans arrived.

The artists who made rock paintings were interlopers in the Owens Valley and did not live there. Archaeological remains were the products of a "wandering warrior from some other region," not indicative of a long Paiute occupation.[47] The Owens Valley, then, was open to discovery and occupation by the pioneers of the area, like his father.

If Chalfant and other local historians denied Paiutes' indigenousness, Paiute narratives made the opposite argument. Narratives like the one of the animals congregating on Mono Lake's shores, reveal the long history of Paiute occupation of Mono Lake and the Owens Valley. Rather than interlopers, Paiutes had lived in and used the lands around Mono Lake and in the Owens Valley for centuries. They knew the proper way to interact with the animals and land of the region. They knew how the world in which they lived was organized. Paiute narratives also undermined the legal doctrines that dispossessed them. Paiutes asserted much more than a use right to land; they expressed an indigenous right to land. This right was not vested in fifteenth-century papal bulls or nineteenth-century Supreme Court decisions; rather it was assigned at the moment the animals gathered on the shores of Lake Mono to give each other a job, in the moment Fish made its circuitous trip from Gull Lake to Lake Tahoe. Paiutes retraced the journeys of these Myth People throughout their time in Owens Valley. They traveled from their home villages on the shores of Mono Lake to the small lakes of the mountains to procure necessary resources. They returned to Mono Lake to harvest pupae. Paiutes traded these items with their distant kin who lived near lakes. Paiute sovereignty was conferred in their history, actions, and oral traditions.

The Paiutes' place-making and -naming was more than a simple recitation of names and places. It was a political project that sought to deal with the forces of colonization that affected them on a daily basis. Paiute narratives occurred in a colonized landscape. Reconsider Gilbert's story of Fish. The story begins at the eponymous June Lake, which may have been named for a Settler woman who lived in the region. Fish then moved to Gull Lake, likely named for the presence of aquatic birds. After Gull Lake Fish arrived at Silver Lake, so named because the lake had a silvery appearance from a distance, or it might have referred to the importance of mining in the Sierra Nevadas. Fish eventually moved on to Walker Lake, named for William Walker, who settled on the land adjoining the lake in 1880, and the famous Lake Tahoe.[48] Settlers, not Paiutes, named these. The place-names commemorate Settler people and how they incorporated the American West's natural resources into a global economy. Yet Paiutes insisted on investing meaning in these places and place-names.

By the 1930s Paiutes had integrated Settler place-names into their narratives. It seems Paiutes created a place world cocreated with the Settlers. Paiutes and Settlers shared Owens Valley place-names for several reasons. In 1862 Settlers and the U.S. Army removed Paiutes from the Owens Valley. During the next decade Paiutes returned to the Owens Valley only to find it overrun by Settlers. Paiutes made lives for themselves as wage workers in the valley. In 1873 the Office of Indian Affairs again suggested removing the Paiutes, but this time Settlers lobbied for them to remain because they needed Paiute labor. By the 1930s some Paiutes may have believed that they shared the Owens Valley landscape with their Settler neighbors; after all, Paiute work transformed the landscape from a Paiute one to an agricultural and pastoral one, and Settlers had attempted to prevent another Paiute removal.[49]

Paiutes and Settlers not only lived in the same place; in the 1930s they faced a common foe. Beginning in the early twentieth century, representatives of the Los Angeles Department of Water and Power, under dubious circumstances, purchased the land and water rights in the Owens Valley, constructed the waterway, and funneled Owens Valley's water two hundred miles to Los Angeles. The Water Wars have been a popular topic of study in California's history. Several books and the film *Chinatown*, starring Jack Nicholson, have used the Owens Valley saga to discuss the environmental and economic causes and consequences of the Water Wars.[50] In too many of these stories, authors ignore the Indigenous inhabitants of the Owens Valley. Paiutes may appear as static first inhabitants, but then they disappear, allegedly conquered by Owens Valley pioneers. They are portrayed as having little at stake in the Owens Valley Water Wars, but the conflict over this precious resource was on their minds.[51] By the 1930s Paiutes and Settlers faced the threat of lost land and dwindling economic opportunities because Los Angeles was draining the valley of its water. Paiutes and Settlers had to unite in order to stave off this powerful being that entered the valley and stole the water. As we shall see, Paiutes effectively used oral traditions, history, and place-names to remain in their homeland.

Although Paiutes used Settler place-names in their oral traditions, it did not mean that they understood their past in the same was as Settlers. In the 1930s Paiute place-names fulfilled several political projects. They marked the boundaries within which they lived; they demonstrated familiarity with lakes, rivers, and peoples in eastern California, stretching from the Owens Valley to Mono Lake to Lake Tahoe; and they identified important economic resources in Paiutes' homeland. Rather than a vacant land ready for Settler colonization, the Paiute homeland was rich with resources. In this way Paiute place-names defied the Doctrine of Discovery and other legal mechanisms that had been used to divest Indigenous people of land in North America. Paiutes' narratives and place-names created common ground with their Settler neighbors.

Unlike Paiutes, Settlers successfully removed Concows from their named places. Yet Concows oral histories reconnected them to their old spaces. Consider Concow Austin McLaine's story "How the Coyote Tried to Hold Fire." Lizard and a group of children were swimming near a sandbar. The other children taunted and threw sand in Lizard's eyes. She walked to the river to wash the sand out of her eyes and, as she looked up, saw smoke on top of West Mountain, an English translation of the Concow place-name Táyyamanim or Tájjàni, also known as Lassen Peak. Lizard ran home and told her parents about the smoke. Lizard's parents did not believe her, so she took them to a place with a good view of West Mountain. As the sun set behind West Mountain, Lizard and her parents saw the smoke. Lizard's father hurried away and convened a meeting. The community pondered how it might acquire the fire. Eagle kept the fire hidden from others and vowed to exact revenge if anyone took it. The council enlisted the fastest animals to steal fire: Deer, Fox, Wildcat, Buffalo, Hummingbird, Sparrow Hawk, Chicken Hawk, and Kingfisher. The animals did not choose Coyote because his clumsy paws could not hold the fire. Mouse strolled to the meeting and asked Lizard's father what they were discussing. When Mouse heard of the animals' predicament, he asked to help. Someone was skeptical: "What can Mr. Mouse do? He is so small. He cannot do nothing." Mouse volunteered to go ahead of the others and chew on Eagle's feather so that the People could see the fire better and signal the fast runners to begin their journey. Mouse then suggested that the fleet animals line themselves along a route in order to pass the fire, baton-like, from person to person. "You put the fastest runner next to the fire," Mouse instructed the captain. As Mouse journeyed to West Mountain, the captain decided on the runners' order. Hummingbird waited next to the fire and, in order, Sparrow Hawk, Chicken Hawk, Kingfisher, Deer, Buffalo, Fox, and Wildcat followed.

Mouse ambled to Eagle's home and chewed on his feathers. The captain went to the top of the sweathouse, looked to West Mountain, and saw the fire blazing. He ordered the fast runners to begin their journey. Hummingbird arrived at Eagle's house and met Mouse. "At the time Lizard saw the smoke," Mouse explained, "it was inside of the stick, and the time Lizard had first seen it, it was only smoking a bit. Now it burns and makes fire bright at night and it may burn through at any time and we want to hurry and get home as soon as you can." Mouse handed the stick to Hummingbird, who fled Eagle's home with alacrity. Hummingbird carried the smoldering stick as far as he could and then passed it to Sparrow Hawk. As the animals participated in the relay, the embers burned through the stick. When Fox received the stick, it had nearly burned through. He yelled to Wildcat that he was about to throw the stick. After Fox threw the stick, Coyote jumped in between Fox and Wildcat and grabbed the fire. Coyote ran as fast as he could, but he fumbled the fire onto the Plains. "The whole world was going to burn," McLaine said, "and people from every direction came to help. What is now the Sacramento Valley is where the fire spread to. At that time the country was all mountains and the fire spread and burned up all of the hills. This ends this story of how the world was destroyed by fire."[52]

McLaine's story offers us a vantage point, much like Lizard's sandbar or the captain's roundhouse, from which to see how Concows transformed the space of their creation into a known and experienced place. Place-names structured the way McLaine told his history of West Mountain. Events in the story moved from place to place, from a sandbar to a village to West Mountain and then onto the Plains. Other stories also link Concow mountain and valley environments. Concow Annie Feliz elaborated on the fire story. After the fire began and covered the entire world, Mole visited his family, who lived in a cave on Table Mountain, overlooking present-day Oroville. As the other Myth People attempted to suppress the fire, the sky became cloudy, and by the time Mole arrived as his home rain began to sprinkle. The storm intensified and scared Mole. The thunder startled him so much that he threw up his hands and declared, "Oh God!" Mole remains that way today and has yet to straighten his arms. Meanwhile the rest of the Myth People fought the fire and built new mountains in the Concow world.[53] In Concow oral tradition the Myth People traveled in a downhill direction, from the mountains into the valleys. This narrative structure reinforced the experiential nature of Concow knowledge. Depending on the season, Concows lived in different ecological zones, where they carried on distinct seasonal economic activities and performed unique ceremonies. In the summer they escaped the scorching Sacramento Valley for the cooler Sierra Nevada mountains; every fall they returned to the more temperate valleys. Whenever Concows descended the mountains for the valleys they followed in the footsteps of Lizard, Mouse and Mole.

Place-names demonstrated the historical process by which Concows invested meanings in their landscapes. McLaine's story of West Mountain mentioned several unnamed spaces: Lizard and her friends swim in an unnamed river; Lizard and her friends play on an unnamed sandbar; and the animals live in an unnamed village with a captain and a sweathouse. The river, sandbar, and village were areas where the Myth People moved. The Myth People and storytellers paused, saw, and invested meaning in West Mountain, alluding to the process that occurred sometime after Concow creation, when they transformed West Mountain into a landmark.

That West Mountain figures in a Concow oral tradition is unremarkable; it is a prominent feature on northern California's landscape. With its gray sides flecked with snow, West Mountain juts more than 10,000 feet into the air. Its triangular peak points to the area from which Earth Maker descended in order to create the world. Like Coyote, West Mountain possesses the power to change shape and defy nature. Visit West Mountain in the winter and you will understand why Concows considered it a shape-shifter; it is a geological wonder. West Mountain is the southernmost lava dome along the Cascade Volcanic Arc—its last eruption occurred in 1915. Even when the snowpack is six feet, multicolored sulfuric creeks, bubbling brown water, and venting steam expose the earth as though it were summer. West Mountain literally stands out as a geographic and geological feature to the many people who came to the Sacramento valley.[54]

Oral histories point out that Concows have associated with West Mountain for a long time. Concows set the fire origin story deep in time, well before the period of human beings, when Myth People made the world hospitable for the People. The origin of fire story might be one of the oldest stories among California, Nevada, and Oregon People. Fire was the forge in which human beings were created. It is essential for all aspects of human life, and its use is one way Indigenous people experienced and shaped the environments in which they lived. People use fire to cook and warm themselves, dance around fire during ceremonies, sit around fire and tell their tales. People used fire to hunt. Selective burns made the landscape more productive and easier to traverse. Fire is one of the most important tools in world history. For the Concow, fire was a gift from Lizard and Mouse.[55]

It is possible that there is a literal aspect to the story, recalling when West Mountain erupted. Lizard spotting smoke coming from West Mountain may reference the devastation wrought by the volcanic explosion, which, as the story states, burned up several hills in what is now the Sacramento Valley and flattened the area. When driving to Lassen National Park today, one passes fields of reddish volcanic rocks, thrown onto the landscape by an ancient eruption. We may not know when West Mountain exploded, but we know from Indigenous sources that it did and that the Concows' ancestors were around to see it and observe how it destroyed part of the landscape.[56]

As a landmark West Mountain is integral to Concow understandings of the world, and place-names insert the listener into the center of that space. The place-name West Mountain possesses a directional component that positions Concows south and east of the mountain. The narrative reinforces West Mountain's position on the Concow topography. Lizard and her parents saw the sun set behind West Mountain. The Myth People traveled from their roundhouse toward the setting sun to steal the fire from Eagle.[57] Looking toward West Mountain, as Lizard did in the story, Concows understood their "spaces of control."

West Mountain also marked the limit of the territory within which they could safely travel, hunt, and harvest, representing where their lands ended and others' began. West Mountain is one of four landmarks, along with Honey Lake, Kit Carson Pass, south of Lake Tahoe, and the confluence of the Sacramento and American rivers, that bound the Concow world.[58]

Places such as West Mountain were not merely borders; they were borderlands, the boundaries between political domains.[59] Concows shared West Mountain with their Yana, Achumawi, and Atsugewi neighbors. Yanas, who lived on the other side of West Mountain, named the landmark Wa'gunú'pa (Waxgunuup'a), which means "Little Mount Shasta." Yanas understood Lassen Peak in relation to its larger relative, Mount Shasta—unlike Concows, who understood the landmark as a boundary marker.[60]

Esto Jamáni, Middle Mountain or Sutter's Buttes, was another Concow borderland. Much like West Mountain, Esto Jamáni is an ideal landmark. It is a topographic wonder, a defunct volcano that erupts from the Sacramento Valley. Its seven peaks represented a boundary between Concows and Patwins, a contested place where neither Patwins nor Concows felt safe to tarry for long. Neither People lived at Esto Jamáni permanently, but both groups temporarily hunted and fished there.[61] Yet borderlands were zones where People produced culture and communicated as much as zones where People were in conflict. For example, Concows and Patwins shared the Kuksu religion. Nomlacki Charles Wathen noted, "All the [Concow] songs and dances started in the Marysville Buttes (Esto Jamáni—Middle Mountain)."[62]

Esto Jamáni represented a spiritual as well as a physical borderland. Concow Austin McLaine continued his extended narrative of Concow creation, establishing Esto Jamáni as a borderland between life on earth and an afterlife. After the captain interred Coyote's son, killed by Rattlesnake during a footrace at creation, he decided to leave the world. He buried his drum and walked toward Esto Jamáni. Coyote looked for the captain but did not see him in his home. He tracked the captain to a sweathouse at Esto Jamáni. When Coyote peered inside, he saw his son and the captain sitting by the center post. They had lots of food, and Coyote wanted to rush in and eat it. "Stay back," the captain cautioned Coyote. "You are not dead, you cannot eat that." The captain gave Coyote some food suitable for the living and instructed him, "You eat that food and go back and tell the people around you that you have seen your son and they cannot come here and eat this food until they die." Coyote returned to his people and told them that no one can go to the sweathouse at Esto Jamáni until they die.

After Coyote left Esto Jamáni, a feather rope descended from the sky to the sweathouse, and the captain and Coyote's son climbed the rope to heaven.

"That place," McLaine explained, "was vacant since." Saddened by the loss of his son, Coyote climbed a tree so that he could see his son and the captain. As Coyote reached the top, the branches broke and Coyote fell and broke his neck.[63] In part no one lived near Esto Jamáni because Patwins and Concows contested ownership of the area and because Esto Jamáni sits on the border between life and death.

Esto Jamáni contained both destructive and regenerative powers. Concow Annie Feliz told a story in which the Myth People played grass game near Eschew lâm sýmí, or Deer Creek, which is located in modern-day Nevada County, California, and cuts through Nevada City. One of the players suggested that they play for their eyes and everyone agreed. When one side lost the game, the winners rushed over and dug out the losers' eyes. Then someone suggested that they play for their hearts and everyone agreed. After one side lost the game, the winners rushed over and took out the losers' hearts. They continued to gamble until few remained. Old Man Coyote was one of the few players left on the winning side.[64] He gathered all the eyes and hearts and carried them to Esto Jamáni. Old Man Coyote's grandmother stayed at home and sang, "Bring my people back, bring my people back." Old Man Coyote reached Esto Jamáni and found an abandoned village. Everything was untouched, as if the people had only recently left. Old Man Coyote took the eyes and hearts to a nearby lake and threw them in the water. He returned to the village and spent the night. The next morning, Old Man Coyote awoke and heard hundreds of people singing. However he could not see anyone. According to Feliz, these were "strange people, believe[d] to be the Indian race today." The people paired off into husbands and wives and spread across the earth, inhabiting the mountains, valleys, and "everyplace to make their way in life."[65] When one of these people died, his or her heart or soul returned to Esto Jamáni, the conduit to the afterlife.[66] Esto Jamáni is the place where the dead climb the rope of feathers to the afterlife, thus reversing the story of creation, when Earth Maker descended a rope of feathers to board the raft.

Beginning in the 1820s Settlers renamed the Concow place world. When fur traders and other agents of colonialism invaded California, they identified their own landmarks, some in which California Indians had already invested meaning.[67] In 1827 fur trader Jedediah Smith applied the name Mount Joseph to the range of lava domes in the northern Sacramento Valley, which includes West Mountain. For Smith, renaming West Mountain "Mount Joseph" was an act of firsting, of claiming to be indigenous to the place. Smith assumed that West Mountain lacked a name, so he performed a discovery ritual by giving it one. In 1841 explorer Charles Wilkes added "St.," and the appellation Mount

St. Joseph endured into the next decade. In the 1850s Settlers named West Mountain after Peter Lassen, a Danish explorer who guided overland emigrants into the northern Sacramento Valley; the name stuck. In 1864 the state of California designated the area surrounding the peak Lassen County. Much like planting flags and crosses or engraving names on trees or rocks, naming a landmark signified the "first" Euro-American in an area and a symbolic claim on the land. Firsting and other discovery rituals assumed that no one before had named or claimed the land, that the area Settlers named was *terra nullis*, open to Settlers.[68]

Settlers continued to rename West Mountain in the twentieth century. In 1907 President Theodore Roosevelt signed the law that made Lassen Peak a National Forest, and in 1916 President Woodrow Wilson designated the area a National Park. The creation of a National Forest and Park established West Mountain as a wilderness. These place-names assumed that no one had ever lived in West Mountain and that the area needed to limit human contact for conservation and preservation. As in other parts of the American West, the creation of National Parks and Forests divorced Indigenous Peoples from places and resources.[69]

Concow place-names, and the narratives associated with them, contested Settler colonialism and ideas of Settler progress. Feliz noted that after creation, Concows were wary of a lake located near Esto Jamáni, which "was red like blood" and had an oak tree on its bank, "very tall and straight, great outstretched limbs, like arms reaching for the skies." Maidus, relatives of Concow People, informed anthropologist Roland Dixon that this was the first acorn tree, planted near Durham.[70] After Settlers arrived in the area, Feliz explained, they cleared the land for farming and cut down this oak tree. "In cutting into this tree with their ax," she said, "there flowed out some liquid red like blood, which scared the white men very much." The Settlers then left the tree alone, and it stood there for many years, until it withered and died.[71] Esto Jamáni contained a narrative that described the changes in the land that occurred when Settlers invaded the Sacramento Valley, a historical interpretation that challenged notions of westward expansion and progress. Settlers cut down trees, cleared lands, and drained lakes. At the time that Feliz told this story, American historians glorified Settler actions; the activities that attended settler colonialism ostensibly ushered in progress. Feliz pointed out that Settler colonialism perpetrated violence against the Sacramento Valley's land, causing it to bleed.

Unlike in the Owens Valley, Concows and Settlers did not share central California landmarks nor the place-names associated with them. West Mountain is not a calque, or shared place-name.[72] Settlers did not translate the Concow word into English and thus name the peak. Rather the name Lassen Peak represents a Settler attempt to erase Indigenous meanings from the state's topography. By telling the history of West Mountain, Concows claimed the mountain as an Indigenous place. Concows insisted that their place-names and histories still resonated and had meaning during the Great Depression.

Claiming West Mountain was slightly surprising, for in the 1930s McLaine and Feliz did not live near Esto Jamáni or West Mountain. The sun no longer set behind West Mountain, no longer illuminating the pillar of smoke for Lizard to see more clearly. McLaine, Feliz, and other Concows could not go to Table Mountain to take flint and look toward Esto Jamáni and think of the dead who had already climbed Earth Maker's rope of feathers. Neither McLaine nor Feliz could see Esto Jamáni or West Mountain, for during the Civil War the U.S. Army had forcibly removed Concows beyond their borders, into the utterly unknown territory beyond West Mountain and Esto Jamáni. McLaine and Feliz probably only dimly remembered places like West Mountain, Table Mountain, or Esto Jamáni. Oral tradition, though, brought them back to the homeland, back to the place of creation while expanding the world in which they lived.

Oral tradition provided a lesson for future Concows. The story of West Mountain highlights two diminutive if not powerless figures: Lizard and Mouse. Lizard's peers bully her; Myth People in the roundhouse openly doubt whether Mouse can help in such a dangerous endeavor as stealing fire. Yet these ostensibly weak characters possessed rare power. Lizard is the first one to see fire; no one even believes her. Mouse uses his skills to evade Eagle's detection. These Myth People, at first outside the norms of community, transform Concow culture and history. In the 1930s Concows could heed these lessons. No matter how bleak the situation or how powerless others considered them to be, Concows envisioned a world where there were opportunities to maintain connections to place and land.

Place and place-names undergirded California Indian understandings of their past. After creation the People occupied a homeland. In the process of living on the land, they named salient landmarks and invested meanings in the mountains and lakes. Place-names structured the People's narratives; they began the story, provided anchors for listeners to understand the narrative's arc, and concluded the story. These place-names evoked and argued for a deep historical process whereby they invested particularistic meanings in the land. These place-names also asserted Native sovereignty over the land, identifying the People's borders, borderlands, and precious economic resources. Yet these place-names, and associated meanings, were contested in the 1930s. Settlers had renamed West Mountain and Mot ti coy, providing the Settler names Lassen Peak, Blue Lakes, and Mono Lake. Indigenous place-names thus restored Concow, Paiute, and Pomo understandings to California's land and history.

CHAPTER 3

Discovering

IN 1935 CALIFORNIA INDIANS IN MENDOCINO COUNTY TOLD ORAL narratives in which religious leaders prophesied the moment Indigenous People discovered Settlers. In these stories the prophets fell asleep and had a vision about Settlers and their societies. After waking, the prophets shared their dream with their followers, concluding that the newcomers would turn Indigenous worlds upside down and impose new living circumstances on Native people. On one hand, prophecies may have been the product of hindsight. California Indian religious leaders may not have predicted the arrival of American Settlers; rather California Indians discussed and interpreted Settler society after the fact and integrated those understandings into their oral traditions. On the other hand, prophetic oral traditions may be the residue of rumors that traveled along trade networks. California Indians could have picked up information they acquired via direct and down-the-line trade rather than possessing visions of the first cultural encounter. But whether these stories were the product of ex post facto understandings of contact, gossip, or actual predictions of the arrival of newcomers, California Indians continued to tell them into the twentieth century. Mendocino County Indians told and interpreted California history through their prophecies.[1]

For Indigenous People and Settlers, narratives about first contact emphasize the opening of a new historical epoch and the joining of two distinct histories. Yet Indigenous People and Settlers disagreed about how contact occurred and what it meant. In 1927 Gertrude Atherton, the author of fifty books, many set in California, depicted Spanish and Indian contact in southern California. After Spanish soldiers and priests waded ashore at present-day San Diego, they held the first Mass in California. "The Indians, who were hidden behind every rock," Atherton wrote, "ignored the invitation [to participate in Mass], but felt sufficient awe of the impressive ceremonies to remain passive." Rather than join the

Mass, California Indians hid behind "every rock" and bled into the landscape, which also included the "incessant and horrible racket" of seals on the beach.[2] Atherton understood contact and discovery as an "anticonquest."[3] She argued that the Spanish, with their animals, ceremonies, and technology, dumbfounded California Indians, who hid from the newcomers. These child-like Indians, Atherton suggested, needed the vestiges of Settler power—the nation-state (military) and the church (Franciscan priests)—in order to survive. Accordingly California required a Settler society to uplift docile Indians and mute the wild soundscape.

Prophets and storytellers interpreted contact and discovery within Indigenous frames of reference. Throughout North American Indian history, prophets have appeared at moments of cultural, economic, political, and social stress. After seeing the future, prophets have argued that by following certain protocols, Indigenous People could regain power over their lives. Although influenced by Euro-Americans, prophecies gained authority within Indigenous ways of knowing.[4] During the Great Depression storytellers—among them Yuki Little Toby, Concow Annie Feliz, and Lassik Lucy Young—used internal methods, such as age, to validate the prophet's credibility and the story's veracity. They also placed prophecies in a cultural and religious context influenced by both the older Kuksu and more recent Dreamer beliefs. Prophecies contributed to a larger context of religious ceremonies and beliefs that guided California Indian people in the nineteenth and twentieth century.

California Indians drew upon their older oral traditions and beliefs to explain their circumstances in the 1930s. Their prophets challenged the notion that the settlement of California was an anticonquest. Rather settler colonialism was a part of the longue durée of California Indian history. Settlers arrived with new ideologies, plants, animals, and technologies that colonized California. The joined history of Indigenous People and Settlers after contact meant colonialism, not progress. Yet prophecies also offered a hopeful message for the present and future of northern California Indian communities. By linking contact to Indigenous ways of knowing, prophets and storytellers restored continuity to California Indian lives and asserted control over the events that occurred between 1840 and 1935. Prophecies empowered Native People to take control of their lives during the Great Depression.

Yuki Little Toby had never experienced a life without American Settlers. Toby listed his age as seventy-five, so he was probably born in 1860, six years after Settlers invaded Yuki lands. Despite being born after contact with Americans, Toby possessed and shared knowledge that predated the Yukis' discovery of Americans.

This Indian was a great prophet, but before he could tell the future he had to sleep so many days and nights. On this occasion, he slept four days and four nights and on awakening on the morning of the fifth, he called them to build a big sweathouse and cook up something to eat and they would have a big feast before he would tell them what he saw and heard in his dreams. After these things were completed and the feast was over, he says to his people, "I am going to tell you something the spirit has spoken and show[n] me in my dreams. You can believe me or not but watch and see if what I tell you is true. I see people in east coming. They are of the same stature as we are. They have hands, legs, and arms, just as we have, only they are white. They are getting ready to come to our country.

"These people have something they are eating it is an object about the size of our fist. It is round and is red in color (tomato). They have something red, which they drink. After they drink this stuff some become helpless, others fight, other becomes happy. They are bringing this to our country.

"They are bringing some sort of an animal that has a shell of some kind on his feet. He has a head, large round eyes, ears and tail with a large body. They are bringing another kind of an animal that has split feet and is something similar to the other animal but this one has horns on his head besides the ears. Then there is another kind of an animal that is black in color with short legs and long nose and this animal is rooting up the ground as they come. They have a bird that holler in the morning and through the day and these birds produce an object that is small and white. These people break this, cook and eat the substance that's in them.

"There are men and women in this bunch of people with children. These people that are coming is going to rule this country. They are going to take our hunting grounds away from us. Our streams where we catch fish will be guarded. We will not claim this land anymore. We will not hunt and fish as we do now. They are going to have our kind of women. They are going to raise families from these women of ours. They are going to take our children. They will show them how to make marks on paper or board, which will have a meaning we don't understand.

"These white people are going to clean us out. They have something about four feet long and out of this will come smoke and this they will make a noise like thunder. This will kill us. These things I am telling you will happen, so watch my people and believe. My spirit told me when I was asleep that at the end of four years from now I will die and one year after I am dead the white people will be in this country."

After he had completed his prophecy, the Indians said, "What shall we do with this man. Shall we kill him?" But the majority of them said, "No. He may be telling the truth. He may be a prophet." All these things has happened as he said.[5]

While Little Toby provided a Yuki perspective on contact, Concow Annie Feliz shared a prophecy about the Concows' discovery of Settlers. Born perhaps in 1875, Feliz lived her entire life on the Round Valley Reservation. She told Concow Frank Britton the following story:

> There was a man who layed down and slept and he dreamed that there would be a nation of people to come and they would come from the south. The leader of these people would ride a big dog with long ears and he would have a string in this dog's mouth to guide him with. That his hair would be the color of dry grass and his eyes would be blue and his face the color of ashes, and he said I believe it will be the devil. So when this did eventually happen, the white people were called the devil.[6]

Lassik Lucy Young provided the third prophecy. Older than Toby and Feliz, the ninety-year-old Young was a prolific storyteller. Throughout the early twentieth century anthropologists and Indian reformers sought her out for oral traditions and information on Lassik plant use.[7] She told her husband, Sam Young, a Native man from Hayfork:

> They seem to have been regular prophets in the early days for they told of many things that would happen. One old fellow told his people of the white man coming and told of the cattle, sheep, and horses. And this was quite a while before the white people came to this part of the country. The old fellow even told as best he could [about] the fire arms. He described it as a stick and holding it to his shoulder and said smoke would come out of the end and it would kill anything and would make big noise. And he even told of the wagons. Of course he did not call it a wagon, but he said like a canoe but run on dry land. And the one that smoked and run very fast and would hollow land. I suppose this was the railroads.
>
> He said that after while the white rabbit would eat all the grass and spoil the water and so on. I suppose this was sheep. Then what looked like elk but had smooth horns, which was cattle of course. This old fellow was so old that none of the old Indians knew even when he was a young man. So he must have been over a hundred years old. They had to carry him about in a large basket made on purpose for to carry him in. This old man was all doubled up and could not straighten himself out. To save himself his knees sit alongside of

his face. His youngest son carried him about all the time and he even told the people how he would die. He said that he would not suffer when he passed away but would fall over like an old stump and he did as he said he would. He called the white man Saultoo, that as near as he could call them. He also told his People that the Saultoo would kill nearly all his People and so they did. All that this old man prophesied came to pass.[8]

Toby, Feliz, and Young offered Indigenous perspectives on the first contact between their People and American Settlers. But rather than telling of the first moment that their People encountered Settlers, as Atherton did to open her book on California, California Indian storytellers discussed contact via a prophecy. These stories were set in the historical moment before they had ever laid eyes on an American. California Indians discovered Settlers before Settlers discovered them.

Certain powerful California Indians possessed the ability to see into the future, and some of them saw the Settlers' arrival. Although listeners doubted the prophet, the storytellers established the prophet's credibility. Toby, for instance, began simply, "This Indian was a great prophet." Yet Toby never defined what constituted a "great prophet."[9] In part he did not have to elaborate. Listeners, such as the fifty-six-year-old Yuki-Nomlacki George Moore, who interpreted and recorded Toby's stories, had been raised in Yuki oral tradition, and knew that the prophets had either the requisite training or a vision that granted them access to their powers. For Young, age established the Lassik prophet's criteria. Age, an "old fellow," refers not so much to a specific number of years spent on earth as the role of elderly men and women in California Indian communities. In an oral culture elderly people possessed scarce cultural and social information that their years on earth enabled them to accumulate. They knew the best hunting territories and the proper way to perform ceremonies. Elders were the primary teachers and instructors in Indigenous communities. Not only did the elderly possess wisdom, but they understood how and when to use it in social and ceremonial settings. Wise men and women spent their lives developing and honing mental acuity and dexterity. They learned and remembered the oral traditions, knew the places associated with those oral traditions, and understood when to employ that wisdom.[10] Young's "old fellow" possessed the power to see into the future, the wisdom to interpret the vision, and the social and cultural knowledge to deploy the story at the appropriate moment with the intended effect.

All three storytellers situated their prophets in a deep body of knowledge, which rested upon the older Kuksu and newer Dreamer religions. In the early nineteenth century northern California Indians practiced a variant of the Kuksu religion, which featured boys and girls (usually between ten and twelve years of age) who were initiated and trained into distinct religious societies. The initiation lasted for as short as four days and as long as several months. During the ceremony, prospective initiates died and were reborn. After their rebirth, older society members taught the initiates the People's creation story and aspects of social decorum and prepared for them to become one of several categories of healer. An initiate might one day become a sucking doctor, a bear doctor, or a poisoner.[11]

In the 1870s Native Californians altered their religious beliefs because of disease, Settler violence, and federal Indian policy. Native communities lost volumes of oral knowledge when elders perished either from disease, massacres, or forced relocation. Older ceremonies failed to protect the People when Americans invaded California. Hill Patwins and Pomos merged the Kuksu and the Paiute Ghost Dance into the Dreamer, or Bole Maru (from the Hill Patwin word *bo le*, which means "spirit," and Eastern Pomo *ma rú*, which means "dreamers"), religion.[12] The Bole Maru featured individual dreamers who could see the future. The *ma rú*, or dreamers, did not learn their knowledge, as in the older Kuksu religion, but acquired it through individual contact with spirits via a vision. Dreamers conducted ceremonies, recited the traditional stories and dreams that undergirded the religion, and assumed the healing and poisoning duties of older doctors. The Bole Maru resembled other religious revivals in North American history, Indigenous and non-Indigenous, in which individuals connected with supernatural forces rather than relying on a hierarchical religious structure. The Bole Maru supported Native People through the late nineteenth century. The religion endured in California Indian communities well into the twentieth century; one of its most famous practitioners was Pomo Mabel McKay.[13]

The Kuksu and Dreamer beliefs resonated throughout the prophecies. Young and Feliz included the prophecies within a longer discussion of California Indian religious beliefs. Young, for instance, began her interview, "In starting this writing, [I] will begin with the old time religion."[14] She then proceeded to explain how Lassiks transmitted knowledge within oral tradition and the Kuksu's initiation procedures before telling of the prophet. Little Toby likewise situated his prophecy within Yuki ceremonial protocol. After awaking from his four-night sleep, the Yuki prophet asked the People to build a sweathouse and prepare a feast. The prophet waited to share his vision until after the People had followed these ritual proscriptions. The creation of a sweathouse and the holding of a feast were significant events in the Yuki ritual cycle.

When the People founded new towns, they first built a roundhouse. If People disbanded a town or changed religious practices, they burned down the roundhouse. Feasts likewise structured Yuki beliefs. Yukis held "first fruits" or "first catch" ceremonies, which featured ceremonial consumption of the year's first acorn crop or the season's first salmon. Creation stories, such as the Concow story in chapter 1, also featured roundhouses and feasts. Older religious beliefs framed Yuki, Concow, and Lassik prophecies, from the prophet's credibility to how storytellers distributed their knowledge and the manner in which action occurred in the story.[15]

The storytellers drew on that corpus of knowledge to revise their prophecies for a contemporary audience. The Yuki prophet described the newcomers using nineteenth- and twentieth-century ideas about skin color and race: "They are of the same stature as we are. They have hands, legs, and arms, just as we have, only they are white." Later the Yuki prophet said, "These white people are going to clean us out."[16] Toby interjected a 1930s ideology into a story set before contact with Americans. Describing someone by skin color would have been unheard of in early nineteenth-century California Indian communities, presumably the time that this prophecy took place. Before contact with American Settlers, California Indians used place, kinship, and language, not skin color, to distinguish between people. Yukis marked people as kin and strangers, not Indians and whites.[17] Maidus utilized the cardinal directions and place to describe other Peoples. The Maidu word for Concow is *tájim májdy*, which translates into "west person." The Maidu word for Nisenan is *tánkym májdy*, which means "southerner person." *Kóm májdy*, or "snow people," refers to Atsugewis, who lived north of West Mountain.[18] As in other contact zones, Yukis, Concows, and Lassiks used their own frames of reference rather than skin color and race to differentiate themselves from Settlers.[19] Toby's 1930s audience, though, knew and understood Settler racial ideologies and their consequences, and so it made more sense to use skin color rather than language as a marker of difference.[20]

In the early nineteenth century Americans created racial ideologies to explain the enslavement of African Americans and the elimination of Indigenous Peoples. The alleged superiority of white, Anglo-Saxon Americans and the supposed inferiority of African Americans, Mexicans, and Indigenous People justified American territorial and economic expansion.[21] Between 1848 and 1900 Settlers applied these ideas to California, consigning California Indians to the lowest level of humanity, racializing them as savage and heathen obstacles to Settler societies. Historians then reinforced these ideas. Hubert Howe Bancroft's *Wild Tribes* supported the idea that all American Indians were savages. Regarding California Indians, Bancroft wrote "[They] wear no clothes, they build no houses, do not cultivate the soil, they have no boats, nor do they hunt to any considerable extent; they have no moral nor any religion worth calling such."[22] Settlers constructed a racial binary—white versus Indian—to justify policies of genocide and ethnic cleansing that opened the land.[23] "This vast and lovely tract, with soils as rich as the minerals within her," Atherton wrote, "was peopled by a few Indian tribes, so stupid that they rarely learned another's language, so lethargic that they rarely fought. The squaws did what work was done; the bucks basked in the sun for eight months in the year, and during the winter sweated out their always negligible energies in the *temescals*."[24] In the 1930s California Indians were quite aware of the consequences of racial constructions and the binary Little Toby described in his history of Indian-Settler contact.

In addition to race, prophets identified how ecological imperialism attended American colonization of California.[25] The Yuki prophet predicted that the newcomers "have something they are eating, it is an object about the size of our fist. It is round and is red in color."[26] Older Yuki ideas shaped how the prophet described this plant. The prophet, and Toby, used analogues comfortable for a precontact Yuki audience; the shape, size, and color of a tomato made sense within older Yuki frames of reference. Then Toby interjected the contemporary understanding of the item, naming it a tomato, into the oral narrative.

That a tomato signified ecological imperialism demonstrates the contingent nature of cultural encounters as well as how Californian Indian were connected to the "Red Atlantic."[27] As early as 500 ce Indigenous People in South America domesticated the tomato. Gradually cultivation of the fruit moved north, into Central America. In 1544 Spanish observers first mentioned the tomato in print, and soon Italians consumed *pomi d'oro* (golden apples).[28] Although indigenous to the Western Hemisphere, the tomato signified Settler society and federal Indian policy to Yukis as it traveled from South America to Europe and then to North America. At Round Valley government officials endeavored to teach Indians how to farm. Indians worked on a communal farm, perhaps growing tomatoes, and received a portion of the proceeds in the form of rations. Reservation agents and other government officials believed that agriculture lifted Indians from their supposed savage and degraded state and facilitated their entrance into American society. Policymakers also argued that farming represented a more efficient use of land than hunting and harvesting. The United States could then acquire Natives' "excess" land and sell it to American Settlers.[29] From a Yuki perspective, tomatoes went hand in hand with land loss and economic change.

Domesticated livestock accompanied tomatoes as emblems of colonialism and federal Indian policy. The Yuki prophet described cattle: "They are bringing another kind of an animal that has split feet and . . . has horns on his head besides the ears." The prophet also mentioned the arrival of pigs: "Then there is another kind of an animal that is black in color with short legs and long nose and this animal is rooting up the ground as they come."[30] Settlers considered livestock essential for economic survival. Pigs, cattle, and sheep provided colonists with food, labor power, and a means of transportation. When invading an area, Settlers practiced mixed husbandry, in which they grazed livestock on communal lands and raised an assortment of grain crops. Domesticated livestock also possessed a cultural value for colonists. Mixed husbandry changed the way North America looked, from what Settlers considered a wilderness to a tamed land. The same applied to American Indians, as government officials considered livestock raising as a way to assimilate Indigenous peoples.[31]

Domesticated livestock clashed with Indigenous economies. Pigs unearthed acorn caches that Indigenous People stored for the winter. Recall that the Yuki prophet observed pigs "rooting" around in the ground, perhaps in pursuit of those food storage areas. Cattle scared deer away from hunting areas. Domesticated livestock also changed the land. The Yuki prophet, for instance, described horse hooves as "a shell of some kind" and cattle with "split feet." Horse and cattle hooves are distinctive (dissimilar from deer, bear, or coyote) and impacted the land in different ways. The ungulates weighed more than deer or other cloven-hoofed animals and tore up the ground around watering holes, rivers, and creeks. The Lassik prophet said, "After a while the white rabbit would eat all the grass and spoil the water and so on. I suppose this was sheep."[32] After the Civil War, Settlers introduced sheep to Mendocino County in order to offset losses in the cattle industry and take advantage of high wool prices. But, as the prophet predicted, blanket grazing of sheep eroded soil, ruined streams, and destroyed areas in which Native People harvested indigenous plants.[33] Cattle and pigs changed the way California looked and transformed the state from an Indigenous to a Settler ecology.

Domesticated livestock also challenged Indigenous sovereignty. As in colonial-era New England and Virginia, Settler fencing practices inhibited Indigenous People's ability to resist the arrival of domesticated livestock. Under American laws, Native People had to fence in their fields, but Settlers did not have to fence in their free-grazing animals.[34] Even if Indians erected fences, Settlers sometimes destroyed them. Into the 1870s Settlers flaunted federal power by tearing down the reservation's fences and herding their cattle, pigs, and sheep onto the reservation.[35]

Horses too altered power relations in northern California. American Settlers in Round Valley and Mendocino County largely came from southern or border states, where horseback riding provided visual cues to class status. Sitting astride a horse elevated a plantation owner above slaves, commoners, and other plantation owners. To go about on foot led to being considered a man of low social standing. Horsemanship, proper care and treatment of animals, and fleet horses represented badges of social honor and status.[36] Southern men who migrated to northern California replicated these beliefs and enforced these social codes among Indians. Horses also provided American Settlers with military power. Previously California Indians conducted warfare on foot. Opposing sides walked to prearranged battle sites, conducted surprise attacks, or launched pedestrian invasions of an enemy's resource sites. In the 1850s Settler militias and the U.S. Army used horses to conduct campaigns against Indigenous People. An illustration from the 1850s, entitled *Protecting the Settlers*, features six Settlers, one on horseback, firing into an Indian town. Horses provided Settlers with a tactical advantage on the battlefield and increased mobility, which Settlers used to gain access to previously inaccessible Indigenous communities.

California Indian prophets anticipated the items those militiamen used to "protect" themselves. The Yuki prophet foretold, "They have something about four feet long and out of this will come smoke and this they will make a noise like thunder. This will kill us. . . . These white people are going to clean us out."[37] The Lassik prophet similarly interpreted firearms' impact: "The old fellow even told as best he could [about] the fire arms. He described it as a stick and holding it to his shoulder and said smoke would come out of the end and it would kill anything and make big noise."[38] Guns and horses shifted the balance of power in northern California. Settlers used guns to lay siege to Native communities and commit atrocities, which some histories argue constituted the war crimes of genocide and ethnic cleansing.[39]

Guns not only perpetrated violence against Indians; they altered Indians' sensory experiences. Both prophets mentioned the sights ("smoke") and sounds ("like thunder" and "big noise") that accompanied the arrival of Settlers and their technology. In other colonial contexts Americans and Europeans used sound as a tool to colonize North America. The spoken word paved the way for Spanish colonialism of the Southwest and Southeast; English farmers replaced an Indigenous soundscape with a more "civilized" one; and new sounds on the Overland Trail ushered in a new social and political order in the American West.[40] In northern California the crack of a firearm symbolized a violent and disorienting new order. Both the sight of smoke and the noise of thunder caused confusion: smoke obscures clear vision; loud noises can befuddle a person. From a California Indian perspective, prophets anticipated a confusing and tumultuous arrival of newcomers.

California Indian prophets predicted that the ideologies, plants and animals, and technologies portended what we now call settler colonialism. "These people that are coming," the Yuki prophet predicted, "is going to rule this country." The Yuki prophet anticipated that American power manifested in different ways. Land was at the center of the conflict between Indigenous People and Settlers. The Yuki prophet said, "They are going to take our hunting grounds away from us. Our streams where we catch fish will be guarded. We will not claim this land anymore. We will not hunt and fish as we do now."[41] Before the arrival of Settlers, California Indians had created an efficient hunting and harvesting economy. They hunted for deer and other animals, they fished the streams for salmon, and they harvested Indigenous plants for food, medicine, and spiritual power. Americans considered these land use patterns crude, inefficient, and lazy. Settlers ignored the precision with which California Indian men prepared for the hunt and fishing or how California Indian women tenderly cared for the ecosystems from which they took basket-making materials. California, Settlers argued, offered a natural bounty that could sustain Anglo-American land use systems of extractive industries (such as mining and logging), pastoralism, and agriculture. These land use systems attempted to erase Indigenous ones. Mining destroyed salmon habitats. Miners used guns to keep California Indians away from their fishing spaces. Cattle, horses, pigs, and sheep competed with deer and other animals for forage as well as grazing on Indigenous plants and tromped through basket-gathering material sites on their way to waterholes.[42]

Prophets predicated how colonialism would affect American Indian families. The Yuki prophet said, "They are going to raise families from these women of ours."[43] Beginning with the North American fur trade, Euro-American men married into Indigenous communities, following the Settler colonial logic of replacing Indigenous People and families with Settlers. In some instances Indigenous women sought out such unions in order to gain access to European trade goods and military alliances. Euro-American men sought Native wives for similar purposes. In some cases Native women, their Euro-American husbands, and Métis offspring positioned themselves in prominent economic and political roles. Métis children often had access to Euro-American languages as well as kinship ties and trade connections to American Indian communities and served as go-betweens, traveling from their Indigenous communities to Euro-American ones for trade and diplomacy. As Anglo-Americans invaded the American West in the nineteenth century, however, Setter societies marginalized and racialized Métis, their Native mothers, and their Euro-American fathers.[44] Yukis understood that these changing family circumstances undermined their power and authority in their homeland.

In addition to changing family dynamics, Settlers threatened California Indian children: "They will show them how to make marks on paper or board, which will have a meaning we don't understand."[45] The education process itself assisted in the process of colonialism. Beginning in the late nineteenth century, federal officials removed Indian children from their homes and placed them in off-reservation boarding schools in order to eliminate the Indigenous population and acquire land. The California Indians who told these prophecy narratives knew all too well the pain of losing one's child to the boarding school system. Children spent between three and five years at off-reservation boarding schools. Some never returned, succumbing to disease. If they returned, children and young adults experienced difficulties readjusting to reservation life.[46] Additionally "marks on paper or board" erased California Indian histories. Settler models of history were predicated upon written, not oral sources. This meant that American Indians, who usually lacked written sources, lacked a "history" and, because they lacked writers, did not have historians. It was up to Anglo-American writers relying on the documents produced by Euro-Americans to write about the Indigenous past.[47]

Despite the prophecies' pessimistic tone, they empowered Indigenous communities. Although prophets mentioned the way ecological imperialism threatened Indigenous communities, they also pointed to how California Indians used colonial tools for themselves. If the tomato represented how the nation-state intruded in Native lives, it also symbolized a survival strategy. In addition to the communal farms, Round Valley Indians cultivated small private gardens. Reservation rations were notoriously small and inadequate. Round Valley Indians developed a multisource economy to eke out a living in northern California. Gardens, and the tomatoes that grew there, were one such strategy. Much like the tomato, domesticated livestock offered opportunities to Indigenous Californians. As Settlers undermined Indigenous economies, Indigenous People gravitated to wage work in order to survive. In northern California, Indigenous workers found jobs as cowboys, shepherds, and sheep shearers. Although plants and animals reshaped Indigenous lives, Indigenous people could use those same plants and animals to survive their changing circumstances.[48]

Native prophets insisted that their ways of history and knowing were correct. Before telling his prophecy, the Yuki prophet said to his audience, "I am going to tell you something the spirit has spoken and show[n] me in my dreams. You can believe me or not but watch and see if what I tell you is true. I see people in east coming." The Yuki prophet declared, "These things I am telling you will happen, so watch my people and believe. My spirit told me when I was asleep that at the end of four years from now I will die and one year after I am dead the white people will be in this country." Yukis listened closely to the prophet and could not decide who was more dangerous: the newcomers or the man who saw into the future. Toby explained, "After he had completed his prophecy, the Indians said, 'What shall we do with [the prophet]. Shall we kill him?' But the majority of them said no. He may be telling the truth." Colonialism, for all of its negative implications, validated Indigenous knowledge: "All these things has happened as [the prophet] said."[49] That Settler colonialism was carried out exactly as prophets predicted proved that these men had seen the future and knew what was coming.

Prophets established order and continuity in Indigenous lives. The prophets anticipated that the arrival of new technology would introduce disorienting sights and sounds to Native communities. Domesticated livestock threatened to devour the countryside. The newcomers would turn Indigenous worlds upside down. Yet these events possessed meaning within Yuki, Concow, and Lassik contexts. In the Yuki and Concow sense, contact was a local experience. The Yuki prophet predicted that the newcomers would arrive from the east, while the Concow prophet saw Settlers coming from the south. Contact, then, was not a universal experience but a particular one that varied according to time and place. Furthermore the prophets used Indigenous analogues to describe the newcomers. The Concow prophet said, "The leader of these people would ride a big dog with long ears and he would have a string in this dog's mouth to guide him with."[50] Concows, like Plains and Columbia River Indians, equated horses with a familiar domesticated animal: the dog. In a manner similar to the Concow prophet, Saukamappee, a Cree man, described horses as "Big Dog."[51] In Lakota *šung*, or *šúnka* translates into "a horse, the four-footed animal that becomes as familiar as does a dog."[52] Dogs and horses fulfilled similar functions, in that they carried supplies and people and provided companionship. Settlers certainly disrupted Indigenous society after discovery, but prophets and the analogues they used established a continuity of meaning over the events. Indigenous ways of knowing persisted, even though colonialism transformed Indigenous worlds.

Looking backward, California Indians used their prophecy narratives to interpret how encounters affected Indigenous People. Colonialism permeated every aspect of Indigenous lives. Indigenous People found themselves marginalized in the racial and social contexts of California. Settlers destroyed their economies and disrupted their households. Prophecy narratives also suggest, though, that Native People developed ways to deal with these new aspects of their lives. They adapted to federal Indian policy by planting tomatoes in gardens. They rode horses to herd cattle and visited sheep ranches as herders and shearers. Prophecy narratives indicate that Native People knew of the Columbian Exchange before it arrived in their communities. They had the power of Native knowledge and ways of life to blunt the worst aspects of ecological imperialism.

California Indian histories of discovering Settlers make no allusions of that event's benign nature. Rather prophecies foretell the grave consequences of contact on empowered California Indian communities in the 1930s. Historians like Atherton wrote that the California Indians were kept in awe of Europeans and were a part of the natural landscape, and the prophets and their audiences did exhibit uncertainty about the newcomers. The Concow prophet noted that the "[the newcomer's] hair would be the color of dry grass and his eyes would be blue and his face the color of ashes, and he said, 'I believe it will be the devil.' So when this did eventually happen, the white people were called the devil."[53] To the Concows "white people" were no saviors or saints; they were the cause of destruction and, eventually, the people who forced them to leave the center of the world. This was made abundantly true when California Indians described the Indian Wars of the nineteenth century.

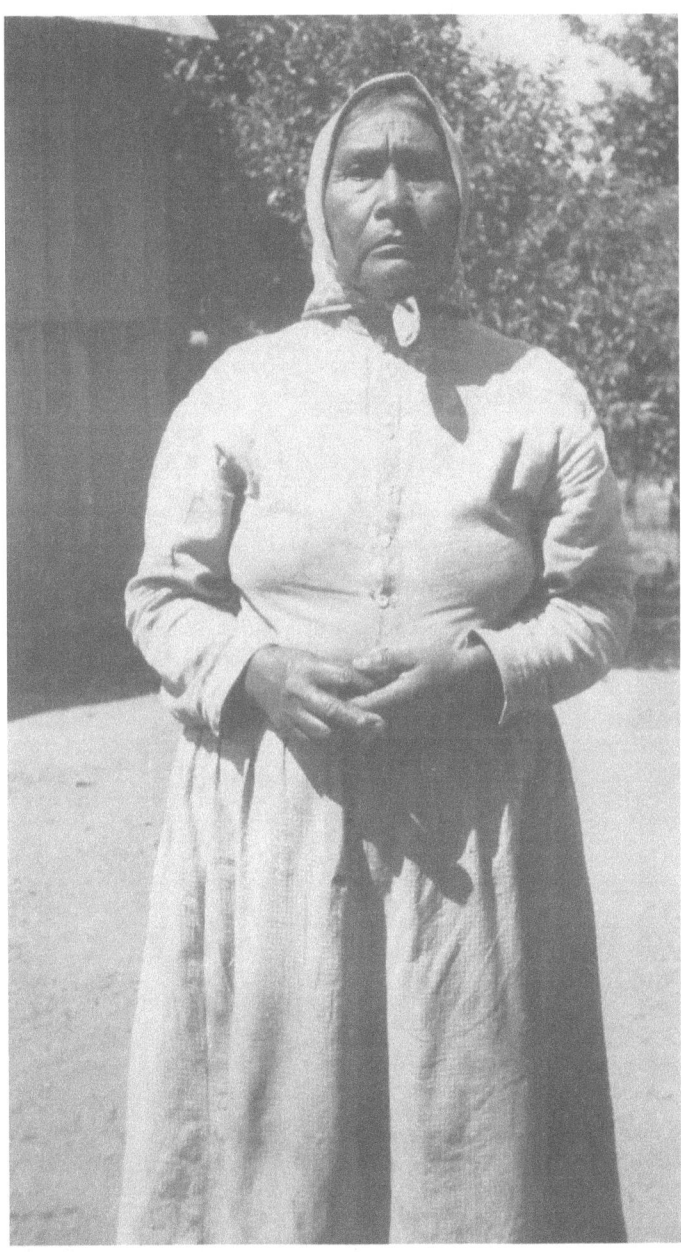

FIG 1. Mrs. Lucy Young, Zenia, Calif. July 1, 1922. Young was a prominent Lassik storyteller who worked with several anthropologists and ethnologists to record Lassik traditional stories. C. Hart Merriam Collection of Native American Photographs, BANC PIC 1978.008, Bancroft Library, University of California, Berkeley. Reprinted by permission of the Bancroft Library.

FIG 2. Owens Valley Paiutes participate in a gambling contest. Paiutes used special gambling songs to ensure good luck in these games. Series 1, Album A, Grace Nicholson Photograph Collection, Huntington Library, San Marino, CA. Reprinted by permission of the Huntington Library.

FIG 3. Mot ti coy. Deep in Pomo history, a healer created Mot ti coy (Blue Lakes) turned into a dragon and sank to the bottom of the lake. His daughter later joined him. In the background are mountains that Dragon created and where he placed angelica, a plant used in healing practices. Photo by author.

FIG 4. Paiute Mack "Bridgeport" Tom was a healer and storyteller in the Mono Lake region. He and his family spent part of the year living in the Yosemite Valley. Tom married sisters Leanna Tom and Louisa Tom, who became well-known basket makers. His daughter, Lucy Telles, was also a highly regarded basket maker in the Yosemite region. Yosemite Research Library 17840. Photo courtesy of Mrs. John Telles. Reprinted by permission of the Yosemite Research Library.

FIG 5. Mono Lake. A long time ago Fish traveled through Rush Creek and ended up at Mono Lake. However, a Paiute man attempted to prevent Fish's movement. Fish sloughed off his skin and gave it to the man in the form of cutzavi, the pupae of *Ephydra hians*, the Mono Lake alkali fly. Fish continued his journey, eventually ending up at Lake Tahoe. Photo by author.

FIG 6. The Myth People stole fire from Eagle, who lived here, at West Mountain (Lassen Peak). Lassen Peak as seen from Lake Helen, Lassen Volcanic National Park, CA. Photo by Daniel Schwen. https://commons.wikimedia.org/wiki/File:USA_Lassen_Peak_CA.jpg (accessed September 25, 2015).

FIG 7. After a fire burned the Sacramento Valley, Mole came to visit his family here at Table Mountain. Looking west, one can see the snow-covered North Coast Range and Tieyamunne (Anthony Peak). In the deep past Old Man and Coyote walked between these two places in order to find fire and hunt quail. Before the United States ethnically cleansed the Concows, their ancestors had walked that path many times. Photo by author.

FIG 8. Esto Jamáni, looking north, is a borderland between horizontal and vertical planes of existence. Coyote found his dead son and Earth Maker in a sweathouse on this mountain. Earth Maker then took Coyote's son to the afterlife. The mountain also marks the boundary between Concow and Patwin territory. Photo by author.

FIG 9. *Protecting the Settlers*, J. Ross Browne. Browne criticizes settlers who claim they protected others by attacking Indian women and children in an ambush at dawn. Art and Picture Collection, the New York Public Library, New York Public Library Digital Collections, http://digitalcollections.nypl.org/items/510d47e1–170a a3d9-e040-e00a18064a99 (accessed September 20, 2015).

FIG 10. Camp Independence in 1871, Owens Valley, eastern California. This place was the site of U.S. Army maneuvers and several peace councils between Paiutes and the United States. Record Group 106: Records of the Smithsonian Institution, 1871–1952, Geographic Explorations and Surveys West of the 100th Meridian, compiled 1871–1874, NWDNS-106-WB-54.

FIG 11. Concow Valley, now flooded because of the Feather River Dam. Concows recalled that they engaged with Settlers here and that this was the beginning point of their ethnic cleansing. Photo by author.

FIG 12. Concows participate in the 2013 Nome Cult Walk, just below Tieyamunne (Anthony Peak). Photo by author.

FIG 14. The Alabama Hills of western Owens Valley, where the Giant began his journey, with the Sierra Nevada range in the background. Photo by author.

FIG 13. Pomo Stephen Knight, along with Pomo Albert James, led the California Indian Brotherhood, an all-Indian welfare and intertribal organization. In the 1920s Knight led the effort to depose Lucy Keenan as the field matron in Ukiah. Series 1, Album C, Grace Nicholson Photograph Collection, the Huntington Library, San Marino, CA. Reprinted by permission of the Huntington Library.

FIG 15. A now dry part of Owens Lake. A giant began his journey to the north here, picking up people and placing them in a bag, and it was here where a water baby captured the giant and pulled him under the water. Photo placed in the public domain by author, https://commons.wikimedia.org/wiki/File:Owen%27s_lake.jpg (accessed April 30, 2015).

FIG 16. The Owens River Gorge, looking north near the outlet close to Hot Creek. It was here, according to some oral narratives, that Coyote placed the original Owens Valley Paiutes. Photo by Jet Lowe. Library of Congress, Prints and Photographs Division, HAER, Reproduction number CA-298-H-2.

CHAPTER 4

Fighting

AS WE SAW IN CHAPTER 3, CALIFORNIA INDIAN PROPHECIES ANTICIpated the violence of Settler contact and colonization. The Yuki and Lassik prophets predicted the arrival of guns and described how they upset Indigenous worlds. Of course violence and fighting were not new to California Indians. Oral histories featured stories of skirmishes, battles, and warfare. In northern California neighboring Pomo polities fought with each other for several reasons, such as violating another's territory, demonstrating improper visiting protocol, and surprise attacks. When a People decided on a battle, the participants adhered to the proper ritual protocols. As the prophets noted, though, warfare in California changed after the arrival of Settlers. Owens Valley Paiutes told their version of the Owens Valley War of 1862 and 1863. They highlighted the long-standing grievances between Indigenous people and invading Settlers and the experiences of women and children as well as men. Although they told of different violent moments in their past, both Pomos and Paiutes narrated their history of Indian wars as lived experiences.

One of the most prolific genres of frontier and western American history is the story of the "Indian Wars." Settler historians have used the conflicts between Euro-Americans and Indians to define American identity, assert American innocence, and avoid the consequences of frontier violence. Settler histories ignored the causes of the conflict, arguing instead that American Indians savagely attacked Settlers, who gained appropriate revenge, even though they sometimes employed ruthless methods.[1] In California, Settler writers shaped their accounts of the state's Indian Wars to meet colonialism's varied demands. Some California writers depicted California Indians as timid, placid, and incapable of starting or finishing a fight. Author Gertrude Atherton wrote, "California's historic period began very late. When New England was burning witches on the green, and the South was dancing the minuet, and New York was founding an aristocracy out of Dutch burghers, this vast and lovely tract, with a soil as rich as the minerals within her, was peopled by a few Indian tribes, so stupid that they rarely learned one another's language, so lethargic that they rarely fought."[2] Other writers depicted California Indians as violent savages. Historian A. A. Gray wrote of Modocs "brutally butchering" Oregon emigrants who traveled to the California mines and "murdering" captives.[3] By portraying California Indians as simultaneously docile and savage, Settler historians transformed the violence of the 1850s and 1860s into a narrative of anticonquest. Either California Indians timidly surrendered California to American Settlers by failing to put up a fight, or they started the conflict with American Settlers, who were justified in cleansing the contact zone.[4]

By telling stories in the 1930s of warfare and violence, California Indians accomplished three things. First, Pomos and Paiutes challenged the idea that they were docile. Pomos narrated a long tradition of warfare that began deep in time and continued into the mid-nineteenth century. Paiutes, meanwhile, emphasized their martial abilities in their battles against Settlers and the U.S. Army. Second, Pomos and Paiutes confronted the manner in which historians interpreted the Indian Wars. Rather than conveniently explaining westward expansion or justifying Settler genocide, California Indians understood warfare as set in a web of kinship relationships and firmly rooted in place. Third, Pomos and Paiutes told the history of the Indian Wars as lived experiences. The storytellers had endured the California Indian Wars as children and used the moment of the Great Depression to tell their life histories.

Some settlers and scholars believed that California Indians were docile and tractable. Anthropologist Alfred Kroeber wrote of Wailacki warfare, "The miniature pitched battles, the long-range shooting and incessant dodging of flying arrows, the occasional invulnerable armor, the slight losses, the immediate mourning, the cremation of those slain away from home, and the lack of all idea of organization [was] typical of the fighting of the Wailaki and their neighbors."[5] Kroeber portrayed California Indian warfare in a manner similar to the way he described their social organization: California Indians were so primitive they practiced nothing that could be considered true warfare, just as they lived in "tribelets," a social organization below nations and tribes. These explanations of California Indians provided a self-fulfilling prophecy for Settlers, wherein California Indians failed to defend themselves and allowed whites to take the state.

According to Pomo oral tradition, however, warfare and violence had been present a long time. Conflicts arose when one People trespassed on another's territory. Pomo Tony Francisco, who lived at Habematolel in Lake County, told a war story entitled "K'e bāy Cho k'lal Rancheria" (perhaps either Kabe'lal [Edge of the Rocks] or Kabedile [Among the Rocks], northern Pomo towns located in the Sherwood Valley). One day the People from K'e bāy Cho k'lal went to K'ŏ̆,ŭl-K'ŏy (probably Kulakau [Tree Left Alone]) to harvest "grain," likely indigenous oats or ryes, in order to make pinole. The People from the town of P'hŏ,ŏl, K'ŏy (Balo Kai, "Oat Valley," located in modern-day Potter Valley) observed the K'e bāy People harvesting grain at K'ŏ̆,ŭl-K'ŏy and attacked because the K'e bāy People had not asked for permission.[6] Pomos possessed a finely tuned sense of their territory's limits. In the right circumstances borders could be fluid. It was not unheard of for People to ask for approval to use resources within another group's territory. If one did not ask for clearance or offer a payment, as appears to have occurred in Francisco's story, violence and conflict followed.

Violence also occurred when People failed to follow proper social protocol. Coast Pomo Steve Parrish was fifty-six years old when he worked on the SERA project; two years later he was elected chairman of the Manchester Pomo Community Council and signed their Indian Reorganization Act constitution. He told of an old man named Cabbacal (Kabekel), who left his home at Molala, near present-day Sea Lion Rock, to visit a friend at Cardalaow (Kodalau), now Anchor Bay. Cabbacal led the town of Pdahau, one of the Bokeya Pomos' principal towns, located near modern-day Point Arena.[7] When Cabbacal arrived at Cardalaow, his friend was not home. The townspeople told the old man to enter his friend's house. When Cabbacal's friend returned, the man informed Cabbacal, "I didn't know that I had a relative living around here. I am almost starved." Then the friend ordered the People of Cardalaow to steal Cabbacal's beads and kill him. Cabbacal lost his beads but escaped the village with his life.[8]

In early California, Pomos frequently visited other communities; such trips dated back to creation stories. Communities exchanged goods, information, and marriage partners during these visits. As with hunting and harvesting in another's territory, visitors needed to follow proper social protocols. Parrish suggests that some visitors failed to do so. For instance, the People of Cardalaow did not invite Cabbacal to visit. Indeed Cabbacal's "friend" denied a kinship connection with him and asserted that Cabbacal failed to provide food to his host. Cabbacal took it upon himself to visit unannounced. Kin should know better than to arrive without the proper authorization.

Surprise attacks also initiated wars and violence. Pomo Billy Rice, an eighty-year-old from Ukiah, told Edgar Jackson that the People who lived at Coyote's Knee Rancheria were harvesting oats when they heard cries coming from their town. The People raced back to their home to find "their Sacramento enemies" had attacked. Although the People joined the battle, "all their heavy force was unable to conquer the enemy. Nearly all their people was killed and their homes and property destroyed." Bear Lady hid in the brush and was the only survivor of the attack. Lonely, she put a nut from a pine cone and sugar from a sugar pine into a basket and placed that basket under dripping water. The next morning a boy appeared from the basket. He grew up in only four days. On the fourth day he went to gather pine nuts. He climbed a pine tree and, while atop, he saw enemies from the Sacramento Valley returning. A "devil dreamer," "a person who can foretell and see ahead what's going to happen or begin," accompanied the invaders. This "devil dreamer" discovered the boy in the tree. The enemies fired arrows at the boy, but because he was made of stone they glanced off him and struck the attackers. After this skirmish the boy went to his brothers, the fence lizards, who taught him how to fire a bow and arrow. The next day one thousand enemies from the Sacramento Valley attacked, and the boy fended them off.[9] Surprise attacks featured prominently in Pomo war stories, as well as those of other California Indians. It is unclear if the Pomos at Yassisoma had failed to adhere to proper social conventions when they interacted with "their Sacramento enemies," but it is certainly clear that the enemies did. Yet the story did not dwell on the massacre; the narrative shifted quickly to how the survivors rebuilt their lives and defended their town from subsequent attacks.

The beginning of these war stories illustrated Pomo understandings of their history. Pomos situated their war stories in specific places in their known landscape. Place, not time, structured these histories. We do not know when Cabbacal (Kabekel) went visiting, but we know that he left his home at Molala for Cardalaow (Kodalau). Rice's and Francisco's stories illustrate the place-based way of knowing as well. Their war stories featured well-known communities, such as Coyote's Knee Rancheria, that inhabited Pomos' landscape. As we saw in previous chapters, specific place-names verify Pomo understandings of the past; Pomos know the stories are true because they know the places where the stories occurred. In addition to place, human relationships organized these stories. Pomos participated in warfare because someone failed to sustain the proper relationships with their neighbors. Kinship relationships guided Indigenous systems of knowledge and social relationships. Harvesting pinole in someone else's territory without permission, visiting a neighbor unannounced, and, most vividly, launching a surprise attack indicated that social relations had broken down.

Once a community decided to attack another, combatants prepared for battle. Warfare required tapping into the appropriate forms of power. After the People of Cardalaow (Kodalau) stole Cabbacal's (Kabekel's) beads, Parrish explained, the People of Molala invited two warriors from a village at the mouth of Brush Creek to instigate the battle. These two brave men traveled to Molala and held a "war dance" all night. They fixed their bows and arrows for the impending battle, painted their faces and bodies, and put up their hair to "show they are going to fight."[10]

Pomo Jeff Joaquin, an eighty-nine-year-old from Hopland, told the story of six boys from the village of Katomal, also known as Canel, located one mile east of present-day Hopland, who visited the town of Yomuch, a Makamotcemei Pomo town near modern-day Cloverdale. "That's the place," Joaquin explained, "where they don't like outside visitors." The People of Yomuch killed one of the Katomel boys, and the remaining five ran home without rescuing their friend's body. The People of Katomel traveled for four days to attack the town of Yomuch. On the first night one hundred Katomel men, armed with bows and arrows, held a war dance. The next day they traveled to Carbayo (Kabeyo), a fishing camp and dance ground, where they again danced. On the third night they stopped and danced at Shapada (Shepda or Cepda, "Cut Grass Creek"), near the entry of Wise Creek, south of present-day Hopland. Finally, on the fourth night, the warriors danced at Mochu toca bayo (Kcakaleyo). After that dance the warriors ascended a hill and saw the fires of a fishing camp below belonging to the People from Yomuch.[11] Rituals, a series of war dances, and place-names structure Parrish's and Joaquin's stories. Combatants needed to perform the proper ceremonies in order to ensure that the following battle would succeed. These rituals served as the necessary prologue to the battle.

When the wars began, Pomos fought with escalating ferocity. The People from Molala, Parrish said, killed nearly all the people at Cardalaow—five women escaped—and reclaimed Cabbacal's beads.[12] Coast Pomo Andrew White, a forty-five-year-old who lived in Point Arena, told the story of Cha-boos (Cabus) from the town of Kauca, who sought revenge for his uncle, whom the People of Buldam, located near the mouth of Big River and present-day Mendocino, poisoned.[13] Cha-boos and another of his uncles invaded Buldam territory. "Whether they were to return alive," White said, "was a matter of luck and they knew their chances were very slim." When the duo came to Buldam "they made their movements very carefully under cover. As sly as a fox, they moved toward the settlement, crawling and walking." Nevertheless a Buldam watchman spotted the duo and sounded the alarm. "The story seems strange here." White paused. "How the Bull-das knew the early mission of the two Cow-shas [Kauca] meant a blood skirmish. Perhaps superstition." Both sides possessed ritual power. Yet Cha-boos was "a great man in strength, a powerfully built man. He was known to have done super human acts of many different kinds." Cha-boos drew his arrows and let them fly. In the middle of the battle Cha-boos's uncle died, and Cha-boos "became much braver." The steeled Cha-boos killed eighty People with eighty arrows.

With his ammunition spent and facing only a score of people, Cha-boos fled the battlefield. He ran south toward the ocean. The Buldam Pomos had prepared for this eventuality and attempted to drive him toward the water, probably Mendocino Bay. Cha-boos reached the edge of the bay and "made a wild leap into the ocean." The Buldam Pomos continued to fire at him as he "dove under water for about hundred to hundred and fifty yards at a time." The arrows zipped through the water, but they did not hit Cha-boos. "Luck with him all throughout," White said, and Cha-boos resurfaced on the other side of the bay. After returning to his home, Cha-boos decided he must exact revenge for his second fallen uncle. This time he took several men with him, and "they went to wipe out the entire tribe." In the middle of the night Cha-boos and his men snuck into Buldam and killed all but one man. White said, "What remained fled for their lives and no fight in them. Neither did they poison another Cow-sha [Kauca] for pleasure."[14] Pomo war stories disputed their image as a docile people. They defended their territories, expected visitors to follow the proper social decorum, and avenged covert attacks. Pomos possessed their own protocols for warfare and appropriate forms of power. In battle Pomos fought with bravery and ferocity. These were not small, pitched battles, but rather large assaults that took many lives. Pomos were a fighting people.

While Pomo war stories described events that occurred before the arrival of Settlers in their territory, they also resonated with the storytellers' life experiences. Francisco, Rice, and Joaquin were born between 1845 and 1858, a period of conflict between Pomos and Settlers. The most well-known battle in Pomo country was the so-called Bloody Island Massacre. In 1850 a group of Pomos killed their employers, Charles Stone and Andrew Kelsey, for which the town of Kelseyville is named.[15] The U.S. Army and Settler volunteers attacked the Pomos in a predawn raid and killed between sixty and one hundred at a place known as Bloody Island.[16] Many of the tactics and actions described in oral narratives were similar to those of the Indian Wars the storytellers told. Settlers attacked Native communities after the men had left to hunt, harvest, or engage in wage labor, as Ukiah Pomo Billy Rice remembered in the story of Coyote's Knee Rancheria. It is likely that every California Indian community has a memory of a Settler surprise attack. The listeners of Rice's account of Coyote's Knee Rancheria no doubt remembered something very similar to how Rice described the unexpected attack: "The band of wild men came rushing out of the brush."[17] Pomos also recalled the massacre's aftermath. It was not out of the realm of possibility that elderly women, like Bear Lady at Coyote's Knee Rancheria, emerged from some hiding place after witnessing the carnage of a Settler attack.[18]

Unlike Settler histories of the Indian Wars, Pomo war stories empowered their communities. Settler histories used the Indian Wars to chart Native destruction. Scholar Sherburne Cook depicted California history as a story in which an allegedly superior white race encountered and conquered an inferior Indian race. Once Indians lost this conflict, they disappeared from the state. Between 1769 and 1900, Cook estimated, the number of California Indians decreased from 310,000 to about 22,000. By the time Rice and other Pomos told their stories, the number of California Indians had not appreciably increased. The 1928 California Indian census counted 23,585 People.[19] Pomo war stories reminded Pomos and non-Indians that Pomos remained and that the state's history was not the a fatalistic race war that Cook described. Rather California Indians were thriving and persisting. As Rice described the ambush at Coyote's Knee Rancheria, "The boy being fearless rushed out in the center of the field, there they surrounded him and shot at him, but he could never be shot, the arrows that glanced off of him and hit one of their own men."[20] Here a Pomo cultural hero was impervious to his attackers.

Other Pomos also used stories about violence and warfare to narrate a positive story of survival and persistence. Pomo Emily Siegel told a story of the Bloody Island Massacre's aftermath. The story begins with Pomos fleeing the massacre site to hide in the mountains. Four old people could not keep up with the others and decided to stay behind. That night the quartet built a fire and went to sleep. Later an old bear came into the camp and sat down by the fire. The old people woke up and were quite startled to see the bear warming itself. One woman grabbed a stick, put it in the fire, and used it to light the bear's fur on fire. The bear screamed like a human, went out of the camp, and rolled on the ground until he put out the fire. Despite the commotion, the soldiers never found these old people, and once the soldiers left, the Pomos returned to their home.[21] Pomo war stories were not racial struggles leading to Native Peoples' disappearance. Rather they featured otherworldly powers; for instance, the bear (likely a Bear doctor) protected the old people from the soldiers and Pomos did not vanish in the aftermath of their battle but returned to their homeland. Pomos insisted they could fight, they could win, and they persisted.

In contrast to Pomos, who told a history of warfare that was set before the arrival of Settlers, Owens Valley Paiutes narrated a history of a specific conflict with Settlers. In 1862 and 1863 Paiutes battled Settlers and California

Volunteers in an event called the Owens Valley War, one of several Civil War–era battles between American Indian nations and the United States.[22] Settler histories of the Owens Valley War begin with California's disastrous winter of 1861 and 1862. A particularly wet winter flooded Sacramento, Los Angeles, and San Diego and washed away the Klamath Indian Reservation. Beginning on Christmas Day 1861, the Owens Valley received rain or snow for fifty-four consecutive days. The wet and cold winter exacerbated the cattle industry's impact on the Owens Valley. Earlier that year Nevada and California ranchers had brought livestock to the valley to provide food for miners. The grazing cattle destroyed areas where Paiutes harvested food, and Settlers and miners cut wood and scared off game. Facing food shortages, Paiutes killed cattle. Cowboys, entrusted to protect the herds in the Owens Valley, attacked Paiutes whom they suspected of killing stock. In January 1862, Al Thompson, a cowboy, killed a Paiute who was butchering a steer. In February Settlers killed four Paiutes who were looking for their horses. Paiute leader Captain George and Joaquin Jim, a Yokuts from the San Joaquin Valley, retaliated with attacks on Settlers. In April 1862 a unit of the California Volunteers under the command of Lieutenant George Evans arrived in the Owens Valley with orders to "chastise [the Paiutes] severely." That summer Captain George moved to Camp Independence, where he signed a peace treaty with the army, but Joaquin Jim continued to harass Settlers.[23]

Captain George's surrender failed to secure peace. Soldiers stationed at Camp Independence raped Paiute women, and the United States failed to provide for the incarcerated Paiutes. In March 1863 Captain George fled Camp Independence and, with Joaquin Jim, renewed attacks on Owens Valley Settlers. On March 19 the California Volunteers and Settlers massacred about forty Paiutes at Owens Lake and, later, thirty-five Tubatulabals and Paiutes on the Kern River. In May Captain Moses McLaughlin, now commanding the Volunteers, waged total war against Paiutes by destroying their food caches and imprisoning and shooting the People. Captain George again surrendered at Camp Independence, this time with about one thousand Paiute men, women, and children. In July the United States marched the Paiutes to the San Sebastian Reservation, near Fort Tejon.[24]

Local historians swaddled the history of the Owens Valley War of 1862 and 1863 in the "California story" and American innocence. William Chalfant, local historian and journalist, devoted several chapters of his history of Inyo County to the Owens Valley War. Chalfant extolled Settler bravery. At a battle on Bishop Creek in 1862, he estimated, 500 to 1,500 Paiutes fought a group of fifty to sixty-three cowboys and ranchers. The cowboys fought with valor and honor; they stood their ground and threatened anyone in their number with death who retreated. Chalfant wrote, "[Charles] Anderson, knowing that if that were done the whole party would be exterminated, said he would shoot the first man who left them to run. [Dr. A. H.] Mitchell then bravely proclaimed his own intention of taking a shot at any one who would exhibit such miserable cowardice." The cowboys remained on the battlefield until that night, when they escaped to Big Pine. Chalfant had little good to say about Paiutes. Since they outnumbered the Settlers by about ten to one, the Paiutes should have carried the day: "Had Paiutes possessed any marked degree of courage they could have wiped out the little company of white men, though of course it would have been at a heavy cost to themselves."[25] According to Chalfant, the Paiutes' perceived racial deficiencies and Settler bravery, not Paiute military acumen (perhaps perceiving that when one's opponents are better armed, making a frontal assault is foolhardy), permitted the Settlers to retreat and determine the battle's outcome. Paiute histories and interpretations of the Owens Valley War, however, differed from Chalfant's.

For Paiutes the war began not in the short-term context of the winter of 1861–62 but in the longer history of invasion and settler colonialism. Hank Hunter, a ninety-five year old man from Independence, was one of several Paiutes who remembered the Owens Valley War.[26] Surveyors, he noted, "sent out by the United States Government to stake out homesteads in the valley for the settlers," arrived in the Owens Valley. Paiutes preemptively struck against the surveyors, and the invaders "began to lose their horses, equipment, and their instruments."[27] Surveyors and mapmakers were the vanguard of the U.S. colonization of the West. They transformed a wilderness into a landscape legible to a settler colonial society.[28] Hunter argued that Paiutes understood this aspect of settler colonialism from the beginning; far from being compliant with it, his People resisted the invaders from the outset. The small thefts attempted to dissuade the surveyors from staying.

Although Paiutes contested the Settlers' invasion, agents of settler colonialism continued to arrive in the Owens Valley. Hunter remarked, "Then the day came when the settlers began to arrive." He recalled that Paiutes treated the Settlers the same as the surveyors: "As the settlers arrived, they were plundered of their belongings, they lost their horses and their cattle."[29]

Quickly Paiutes felt the brunt of the U.S. invasion of their homeland. Jennie Cashbaugh, a seventy-year-old woman from Bishop, also remembered the events leading up to the Owens Valley War: "There were times when we scarcely had anything to eat, when especially the white men never knew or stopped to realize that it was our land that they settled themselves on and when we went to gather food that we thought was ours, the white man did not want us to disturb his land which produced our only means of living and would chase us away, brutally hurt our Indian members and trouble would begin or one of our men may chance to hurt them." The American invasion and settler colonialism undermined Paiute economies. As Cashbaugh noted, there was little food available after Settlers arrived in the valley, which affected Paiute women and children. After Settlers drove Paiutes off their hunting and harvesting areas, Cashbaugh recalled, Paiute men led everyone to the mountains: "While out there we had many a sleepless night. I heard hungry babies crying."[30] Jim Jones, a 100-year-old Paiute man from Long Valley, said, "As the Red man had their food just about eaten up, the children were very hungry. So they ate whatever they could find."[31]

The invasion of Settler society upended Indigenous women and children's world. As Cashbaugh noted, Settlers prevented women from harvesting food in customary areas, and the resulting scarcities impacted the women, as providers, and their children. Cashbaugh and Jones focused on the experience of children because these events occurred within their lived history. Cashbaugh was likely a toddler and Jones was perhaps a teenager when the Owens Valley Wars began. The hunger and pain associated with war and invasion were not abstract to Jones and Cashbaugh, who had experienced the suffering themselves.

Paiute storytellers placed their People's next actions within their ritual complex. Jones recalled that "Indians from all over the land" met in Round Valley and held a dance. Paiutes at the ceremony expressed concern about a possible Settler attack. The People went "without sleep for they were afraid of the white people." Paiutes decided to defend their home.[32] Round Valley was a significant place for Paiute People since it was where Coyote initially encountered First Woman. From the war's outset, Paiutes, like Pomos, sought access to proper forms of power. After the dance in Round Valley, Jones said, "the whites went on up after them." Settlers shot a Paiute man in the stomach and his intestines fell out.[33] In another battle Paiutes and Settlers squared off "just north of Greek George's place." Settlers had harassed the Paiutes, but "only a few in number as the men, most of them, had been killed." The Paiutes performed a mourning ceremony in which "cries rent the air," Cashbaugh recalled.[34] Paiutes thus linked warfare to creation (Round Valley) and death. Beginning with the dance in Round Valley, Paiutes interpreted the war's beginning through their ritual cycle. Paiutes intended dances at the outset of a battle to activate the proper forms of power and ensure a victory. Mourning ceremonies, like the one Cashbaugh described after the battle near "Greek George's place," ushered the dead into the afterlife.

The war began poorly for Paiutes. Cashbaugh explained, "One white man laid in wait for our Indian men to come over and peep over a cliff to see if there was no more. But each time, they never came back, death claim[ed] them all." Paiutes attempted to rectify the situation. They sent a young woman as an emissary of peace. The young woman walked to the top of the ridge and "hollered so loud, so the mountains will hear her cries for mercy." A storm then barreled down off the Sierra Nevadas. Cashbaugh explained, "We considered [the storm] a help to scare the white men back to their homes and also to get their powder wet so they wouldn't be able to shoot at us, to kill us."[35] Across North America, the presence of Indigenous women signified peace.[36] By bringing a storm, this young woman demonstrated the Paiutes' effort to maintain goodwill in the Owens Valley and she possessed impressive power.

In addition to the storm, the woman brought Settlers to the bargaining table. Since "certain settlers knew that the Indians outnumbered them," Hunter said, "it was then decided that a peace should be made with the Indians." Paiutes and Settlers entered into several councils "for the purpose of having all the Indians forget their hatred for the settlers and make peace."[37] Hunter continued, "The Indians being well convinced decided [peace] was a good thing until some agitators among the tribe again stirred up troubles and hatred. After these agitators worked among the Indians, the settlers began to lose their cattle and horses and the settlers again tried hard to make their peace among the Indians but [with] no success."[38] At this point Paiutes argued that they possessed more power than the Settlers. After all, they outnumbered the Settlers. The Settlers begged for peace. Such expressions of Paiute power certainly empowered Paiute People in the 1860s and the 1930s. Yet Paiutes were not of one mind. Some "agitators" did not believe peace was possible with the invading Settlers and raided the most visible symbols of settler colonialism: cattle and horses.

Paiutes and Settlers interpreted the renewal of violence differently. Maggie Earl, an eighty-year-old Paiute woman from Independence, recalled that "it was while she lived [near Independence] that she saw for the first time her father and it was also to be the last time for he was killed that same day she had seen [him]." Earl's father and a group of Paiutes were looking for their horses, which grazed east of the town. Settlers encountered and killed Earl's father and three other men.[39] In Chalfant's telling, in February 1862 a group of cowboys named Barton, John, and Taylor McGee, Allen Van Fleet, James Harness, Tom Hubbard, Tom Passmore, Pete Wilson, and "Nigger" Charley Tyler rode near the Putnam Ranch, when they saw four Paiutes walking toward some cattle. The cowboys approached the Paiutes and asked where they were going. The Paiutes replied that they were looking for their horses. The cowboys said the men could continue but they would have to leave their weapons. According to Chalfant, the Paiutes refused, thus becoming the "savage" aggressors. Van Fleet claimed one of the Paiutes shot him with an arrow and another Paiute shot Harness in the arm. The cowboys returned fire and killed all four Paiutes, including a Paiute leader named Shondow.[40] Earl and Chalfant agreed on one aspect of the story: the Paiutes were looking for their horses. Yet they disagreed on the presence of weapons. Moreover Earl understood this event as a lived experience. She had seen her father that day and never again. For her, the Owens Valley War signified the loss of an important family member.

Earl and Chalfant also agreed that the killing of the four Paiutes sparked more violence in the Valley. After the death of her father, Earl and other Paiutes "fled during the night and went north [from Independence] into the mountains." Paiutes hid during the day and traveled at night, until they reached Keough Hot Springs, about twelve miles south of Bishop.[41] Jones recalled that the Paiutes' captain decided the People should move from Round Valley to Long Valley, a distance of about thirty miles. The captain and a group of Paiute men left early to scout the rugged terrain ahead. The remaining Paiutes stayed for a few nights longer to prepare for the trek. On the first day of the trip, Jones recalled, his parents carried him because "he was a small boy." The trip was extremely difficult for the children. "As they were on Sherwin Hill, he and some of the children were tired and hungry as they had been almost with nothing so their parents roasted some kind of roots for them. Some plant like rhubarb or asparagus." The next day the group traveled to McGee Creek, which feeds Lake Crowley, where they once again rested. The next morning the Paiutes discovered that the Settlers still pursued them. "As the Indians saw them coming," Jones remembered, "they fled and left one woman who was a cripple and the whites come, they saw her, was going to shoot her as she raised and waved her hand." The Settlers did not kill the woman; instead they burned the Paiutes' homes and gave the woman food, clothing, and beads that the Paiutes had left behind.[42] Earl and Jones understood the Owens Valley War as a lived experience. They had traveled the rough paths through the foothills of the Owens Valley. They had endured hunger and thirst while being pursued by Settlers. Their stories were true because they had lived the war. They also linked the war to a distinctive Paiute place-world, one they saw in the 1930s.

The arrival of the U.S. Army exacerbated relations between Paiutes and Settlers. Earl explained, "The Indians had been mistreated by the soldiers, especially the women. The soldiers, where they saw an Indian woman, would take her by force and use her whether she wanted to or not, and it got so the soldiers would hunt for the Indian woman and to protect themselves that had gathered on that hill and the government soldiers were beaten off, which goes to show that they did not want to fight an organized Indian." Paiutes held the army accountable for this violence. Earl criticized the soldiers: "Such cowardice displayed by the soldiers and the mistreatment of the Indian women at their hands had aroused the Indians as it would any other nation."[43] The army represented the third prong of the U.S. invasion of the Owens Valley. This invasion was no less violent than that of the surveyors and Settlers. As was true of those earlier invasions, women and children suffered greatly. But Earl added a twist to this aspect of the war: she emphasized Paiute nationhood and sovereignty by drawing an equivalence between "Indians" and "any other nation."

Despite the army's and Settlers' violence toward Paiutes, storytellers argued that the story of the Owens Valley War was an empowering one. Paiutes claimed they had the upper hand in conflicts with the soldiers. Earl described the first encounter between Paiutes and the soldiers at Keough Hot Springs: "It was while they were [at the Hot Springs south of Bishop] that the soldiers came upon them. The soldiers were riding horses and they saw the Indians on the hills and started after them." In the ensuing fight Paiutes killed a "few of them" and the soldiers fled. "The soldiers left everything they had. They left their wagons and everything in it. The Indians had gathered there to fight the government, [and the] army and the soldiers had fled when they saw an opposition."[44] Hunter remembered another time when Paiutes successfully engaged the U.S. Army: "Indians from all parts of the valley attend[ed] this main council [at Taboose Ranch, north of Aberdeen]. There the Paiutes declared war on the soldiers. The next day the Paiutes left Taboose Ranch and traveled toward Independence. Upon hearing that the army marched toward them, the Paiutes decided to "lay in wait" in the lava fields west of Aberdeen. They dispatched a scout to see when the soldiers would arrive. The scout reported that the soldiers advanced, and some Paiutes counseled that they should lay an ambush at Dawson Creek. The Paiute men hurried to the creek, set up their positions, and once again dispatched a scout. This time the soldiers saw the scout and knew the Paiutes hid in the willows near the creek. The soldiers trooped toward the creek on foot, but the Paiutes had the element of surprise. "The Indians with yells got up from their hiding places, ran to meet the enemy at the same time shooting their arrows," Hunter related. The swift Paiute attack startled the soldiers, who ran for their horses and retreated to Camp Independence. Rather than pursuing the soldiers, the Paiutes paused at Thibaut Creek, held a council, and "decided to go back to Taboose Ranch and forget the battle and once more peace reigned."[45]

This peace, like the earlier one, was short-lived. Soon Paiutes and Settlers backed by soldiers fought at Big Pine. Hunter said the Paiutes possessed inferior weapons: "The bows and arrows did no damage as the range of the weapon is only fifty yards to make a kill." However, Paiutes used their knowledge of the land and superior tactics to fight this battle: "For this reason the Indians always picked a rocky place to battle in." No Paiutes died at Big Pine because "[the] Indians [were] up in the hills and behind rocks." After the Big Pine fight Paiutes and Settlers fought at Bishop, where "a few Indians [died] and two soldiers." The battle at Bishop occurred in the late fall, and with winter setting in, Paiutes retreated to Round Valley. A snowfall blanketed the Valley; "the Indians could not get out of Round Valley" and soldiers refrained from invading. During the winter "the Indians managed to thrive."[46]

Paiutes continued to emphasize their strengths as the war continued. "It was agreed," Hunter explained, "that the soldiers go to Round Valley and make peace with the Indians. Also give them rations." Eight men as well as a cook and his field kitchen left Camp Independence for Round Valley. When they got close, the soldiers left the cook and field kitchen behind and, on foot, took a trail near Rock Quarry, where Coyote saw First Woman, into Round Valley. Paiute scouts spotted the soldiers and "decided to ambush these eight men." The Paiutes hid in the rocks above the quarry and, when the soldiers appeared, opened fire with guns. They shot one soldier in the side. The soldiers grabbed their fallen comrade and retreated to a canyon. There, hidden behind rocks, the soldiers set up a "fort." Paiutes surrounded the soldiers, who appeared doomed. That night, however, the soldiers experienced two fortuitous events. First, a Paiute with an elaborate head ornament stuck his head out from behind a rock, and a solider shot him through the nose from a long distance. Second, the soldiers escaped the canyon under cover of darkness. They met with the cook and left the field kitchen behind. The pursuing Paiutes "got the rations and field kitchen." After this battle "the Indians disbanded from Round Valley, went to their respective homes with battles forgotten. Once more, peace was in the air. The Indians at their disbandment agreed to leave the settlers alone and make friends."[47]

Place figured prominently in how Paiutes interpreted the Owens Valley War. It is unclear *when* these battles took place. Indeed it mattered little how many people fought or died. Settler histories mention that the California Volunteers arrived in Owens Valley in April 1862, established Camp Independence that July, and continued to fight with Paiutes into 1863, when the army removed the Paiutes to Fort Tejon. The battles that Hunter described could have occurred then. Battles at Division Creek and Black Rocks occurred in January 1865, and the war continued until March 1867, with a final battle at Rainy Springs Canyon. Hunter did not dwell on dates; he mentioned places. He and his listeners knew the exact location of battles. Knowledge of land and place gave Paiutes an advantage in the Owens Valley War. They compensated for their lack of technology with their understanding of the land. In Hunter's telling, the U.S. Army lost one battle after another, and soldiers had to travel to Paiute camps to sue for peace and offer gifts of food to end the war.

In the 1930s oral histories of the Owens Valley War galvanized Paiutes as they prepared to again battle outsiders. Earl thought about the Owens Valley *Indian* War in the context of the Owens Valley *Water* War: "The Indians had gathered there to fight the government, [and the] army and the soldiers had fled when they saw an opposition."[48] As they had in the 1860s, Paiutes in the 1930s were battling government forces for control of the Owens Valley. In the past, Paiutes insisted, the outsiders asked the Paiutes for peace. Since the Paiutes successfully fought the government in the 1860s, they again prepared to put up a fight.

The outcome of the Owens Valley War, however, was not quite so clean. The California Volunteers marched one thousand Paiutes from the Owens Valley to the San Sebastian Reservation, near Fort Tejon. Many Paiutes, including Maggie Earl, returned to the Owens Valley after removal. In the 1930s, though, the City of Los Angeles recommended that the federal government remove the Paiutes again. Memories of successfully fighting soldiers and Settlers galvanized the Paiutes, who once again faced the threat of removal.

During the Great Depression, Pomos and Paiutes narrated histories of the Indian Wars. To combat the notion that they were a docile People, Pomos described battles that occurred between Native Peoples in northern California. Instead they possessed a long history of warfare in California, in which they claimed territories and insisted on the proper protocol between People. These war stories documented the survival and persistence of Indigenous People, not their decline. Paiutes revised understandings of the Owens Valley War, fought during the American Civil War. Paiutes, Settlers, and California Volunteers clashed in the Owens Valley. Paiutes insisted that they possessed martial abilities comparable to those of the United States, and reconciliation, not conflict, resulted from the war.

CHAPTER 5

Cleansing

AT THE CONCLUSION OF CALIFORNIA'S INDIAN WARS, THE U.S. ARMY rounded up Native People and marched them to reservations, sometimes far away from their homelands. Between 1860 and 1863 the United States forcibly removed Concows from West Mountain to the short-lived Mendocino Reservation, on the Pacific Coast near modern-day Fort Bragg, and, finally, to the Round Valley Reservation. After the Owens Valley War, Settlers made the Paiutes leave the Owens River, where Coyote placed them, for the Tejon and Tule River Reservations. These acts of ethnic cleansing have been seared into California Indians' telling of the state's history. Paiute Hank Hunter, a ninety-five-year-old man from Independence, said, "The people telling or remembering these incidents cannot forget these dreadful pasts."[1]

U.S. history is a story of removal. Enter the Opera House off Disneyland's Main Street and find the cavernous theater that features "Great Moments with Mr. Lincoln." The audio-animatronic Abraham Lincoln delivers a speech based on a letter he wrote to a friend. Lincoln declares his father "removed from Kentucky to what is now Spencer County, Indiana, in my eighth year [ca. 1815]." In Lincoln's case, and that of many nineteenth-century Americans, removal meant to simply pick up one's belongings and move to another residence, which promised new opportunities. Lincoln described early nineteenth-century Indiana as a "wild region, with many bears and other wild animals, still in the woods."[2] With hard work he and his father tamed the frontier.

At the same time that the Lincolns hewed a home out of the wilderness, the United States developed a policy of ethnically cleansing American Indians who lived east of the Mississippi River. Beginning in 1803 President Thomas Jefferson suggested that eastern Indians should move across the Mississippi River.[3] In 1824 President James Monroe (a Jefferson protégé) and Secretary of War John Calhoun devised a voluntary removal program, whereby southeastern

Indians could exchange lands in the east for lands in the newly formed Arkansas and Indian Territories. In 1830 President Andrew Jackson signed the Indian Removal Act, which enabled the United States to forcibly remove Indians from the eastern United States to the area west of the Mississippi River. In 1838 and 1839 the U.S. Army marched more than 20,000 Cherokees and their slaves from their homelands in Georgia and North Carolina to Indian Territory. Indian removal came at an extraordinarily high cost of Cherokee lives, as anywhere from 4,000 to 5,000 people died en route.[4]

Lincoln's and the Cherokees' removals were related in the project of settler colonialism. One could not have occurred without the other. Early nineteenth-century politicians believed that the nation's economic development needed Indian and Settler removal. Jefferson, Monroe, and Jackson advocated Indian removal in order to acquire land for western Settlers, like the Lincoln family, whose removal resulted from that of the Miamis and Shawnees after the War of 1812. In the Southeast the displacement of the Cherokees led to the cotton boom and the spread of the market economy.[5] U.S. presidents justified removal as a humanitarian effort to protect Indian nations from land-hungry settlers. They argued that moving Indians west of the Mississippi would give them enough time to become civilized. Subsequent historians depicted removal as a story of anticonquest. Francis Paul Prucha argued that removal was a humane decision; rather than advocating extermination, President Jackson supported removal in order to save Native Peoples from violent Anglo-Americans. Robert Remini, one of Jackson's biographers, shared Prucha's assessment of Indian removal as a beneficent act for southeastern Indians that stopped short of genocide.[6]

In the 1850s and 1860s California Settlers advocated Indian removal. After the United States acquired the American Southwest, Settlers breached the frontier line that separated Indians from whites. U.S. Indian policy shifted from removing Indigenous Peoples west to concentrating them on remote reservations. Still concentration required the federal government to remove Indians. In 1859 Settlers suggested relocating California Indians to Nevada or Baja California. The *San Diego Herald* believed that removal would ensure peace between Indigenous People and Anglo-Americans and allow California Indians to live safely.[7] In 1863 the United States removed Concows from present-day Butte County to the Round Valley Reservation; 460 Concows set out from Chico, California, but only 270 survived the 110-mile trip because of illness and malnourishment.[8] That same year the United States forced 1,000 Paiutes from the Owens Valley to the Tejon Reservation, a distance of about 220 miles, but 250 escaped en route.[9]

California Indians understood the history of Indian removal differently than Settler politicians and historians. California Indians incorporated ethnic cleansing into their histories as a travel narrative, a vein of oral literature that Native Peoples used to assert landownership and invest meanings into places.[10] Indigenous People described the origins of conflict between themselves and Settlers, the impact of ethnic cleansing on women and children, and the violence of Indian removal. Like stories of warfare, the history of removal was based on storytellers' lived experiences. For instance, Hank Hunter survived ethnic cleansing to tell its brutal history. The story of ethnic cleansing was not relegated to the past; it was relevant during the Great Depression. As in their prophecy narratives, Concows explained that their cultural heroes had already taken the trip to the Round Valley area some time in the deep past. Furthermore Concows reinterpreted ethnic cleansing as a narrative of ethnogenesis, whereby the People re-created themselves in a new place. Owens Valley Paiutes, on the other hand, built their removal stories on the strength and resiliency of kinship relationships. Regarding the Paiutes' march to Fort Tejon, Jennie Cashbaugh, an elderly Paiute woman from Bishop, recalled, "I clung to my little brother who was a year or so younger, watching and waiting for a chance that the four of us may take to freedom."[11] Kinship remained important, for in the 1930s Paiutes again faced the specter of ethnic cleansing.

In 1859 Settlers in northeastern California demanded that the United States do something about the Native People living in the mountains. In Tehama and Butte counties, agriculture and mining pushed Maidus and Concows into the rugged Mill and Deer Creek canyons, where they allied with the indigenous Yahis. From this remote corner of California, Maidus and Yahis raided farms and ranches, stole horses and cattle, and burned houses and crops in the Sacramento Valley. As in other contact zones, California Indians killed livestock for food and also to send a message to Settlers who trespassed on Indigenous lands. California Settlers meanwhile took these attacks as an affront to their identity. Settler societies saw private property, such as land, domesticated livestock, buildings, and agricultural produce, as fundamental to their sense of self. Many Settlers exacted revenge for these assaults on their property and identity. In 1859, for instance, Harry Lockhart, a ferry operator at Fall River, mixed strychnine with flour and sugar and gave it to Pit Rivers.[12]

Other Settlers used petitions to bring attention to their aggrieved situation and envelop ethnic cleansing in democratic processes. In 1859 Tehama County Settlers complained to Governor John Weller, "The Indians, living in the mountains, . . . have been for many months committing depredations on the white inhabitants of the valleys, by driving off and killing stock of all kinds, and within the last few days have commenced a more fearful and calamitous warfare—that of firing and burning houses at the still hours of night." Some Settlers formed democratically elected militias to hunt down Indians. Weller dispatched General William Kibbe to northeastern California to raise a militia to quell the violence. Kibbe organized a company of about a hundred men, led by William Byrnes, to scour northeastern California's mountains and canyons. These militias did little more than kill Concow, Maidu, and Yahi women and children. Militiaman Elijah Potter recalled in the fog of Settler amnesia, "I will say nothing further on this expedition except to say that we were gone four months and that we brought away more than 1500 Indians." As with many pioneer reminiscences, Potter elided the violence that attended ethnic cleansing.[13]

The odyssey was only beginning for Concows, Yahis, and Pit Rivers. The U.S. Army and Kibbe's Guards marched Concows and Pit Rivers from Fort Crook, established about seven miles from the Fall River ferries, down the Sacramento River, through the Delta to San Francisco. There they put the Indians on a boat and sailed them to the Mendocino Reservation, located near modern-day Fort Bragg.[14] In 1861 the federal government disbanded that reservation and removed the Concows and Pit Rivers to Round Valley. Both groups remained at Round Valley for about a year, when leaders decided that conditions on the reservation could not sustain them. Concow Tome-ya-nem led the Concows from Round Valley to present-day Paskenta, when California Volunteers from Red Bluff intercepted and escorted them to the nearby Nome Lackee Reservation. Concows returned to their homeland at an inopportune time. California Indians had apparently killed a handful of children in the Sacramento Valley, and angry Settlers demanded the army return Concows to Round Valley. In the fall of 1863 the army marched 460 Concows from Paskenta to Round Valley. Only 270 Concows arrived at the reservation; many had died from malaria, and the rest were left behind on the trail.[15]

Settlers used well-worn defenses to justify the removal of Concows and Pit Rivers from the Sacramento Valley. Government officials reasoned that removal was in the best interest of Indians and Settlers. When asked if Pit Rivers could be moved to the Nome Lackee Reservation near Paskenta, Kibbe explained they would be too close to their former homes; they would likely flee the reservation, return to their homeland, and continue to harass Settlers. Mendocino, not Nome Lackee, offered the path to peace.[16] Kibbe argued that the Concow and Pit River removal had a positive effect on the Indians who remained. He explained to Governor Weller, "It is a salutary lesson to the tribes, occupying territory contiguous to the scene of action, which they will not be likely soon to forget. It has taught them the certainty of the punishment which must sooner or later overtake them, for their hostile visitations upon the persons and property of the whites."[17]

Concows and Pit Rivers, who as children experienced removal, offered different understandings of ethnic cleansing. For them the process of removal began when Settlers invaded Indigenous lands. Pit Rivers expressed uncertainty about meeting Settlers. John Heenan, who was eight or nine when he made the trek from the Pit River homeland to the Pacific Coast, explained, "Several years ago, when the white people first came to Fall River Mills, the Indians didn't know what to make of them. They hadn't seen or heard of a white man before."[18] Concows knew to be wary of the newcomers because prophecies had foretold that contact would turn their world upside down. "When the Indians first saw white people they were afraid of them. They called them Devils," Concow Bob Green said, echoing Annie Feliz's earlier prophecy. "When they first saw Negroes, who came also to look for gold, they were all afraid. The young children saw the Negro men, ran and all hid. They called them black bears."[19] As with prophecy narratives, Green's oral history established that Concows knew what to expect from the invaders. He made Concow analogues for the two newcomers. Concow "Devils" possessed harmful spiritual powers and could poison people by injecting them with foreign objects. Concows also referred to the few African American gold miners as "bears," a reference to skin color of course, but also to spiritual power. Concow bear doctors transformed themselves into bears by wearing bear skins and sometimes acted violently. It was best, then, that Concows watch the newcomers.

After the Settlers arrived, Concows and Pit Rivers attempted to establish cordial relations with them. Pit Rivers used language to bring the two people together. Heenan explained, "An Indian by the name of Oregon Jack was the first Indian man to speak the English language. The white man told him that they wanted to make friend with the Indians."[20] Across California learning another's language transformed strangers into friends and possible kin. Oregon Jack made the first effort to integrate Settlers peacefully into Pit River communities. The exchange of goods and work created reciprocal relationships between Concows and Settlers. Green said, "The white people camped out and hired the Indians to work for them, to cut wood and to move them. Then they would pay them with clothing and sometimes money."[21] Concow Polly Anderson added, "Some of the white people made friends with the Indians and they traded beads and things for clothing and food."[22] As in many contact situations Settlers depended upon Indigenous People for their survival. Concows knew that Settlers were unprepared to carve out a living in northern California and attempted to smooth relations by offering their labor and resources. Nowhere, though, did Concows assent to removal or surrender land; rather they allowed the newcomers to live and trade on Concow land, much as they might other strangers who followed the proper protocol.

The Gold Rush damaged Indigenous-Settler relations. Anderson said that Concows and Settlers got along well, but "that was before the white people saw the gold." With the discovery of gold, "the white people first found them and drove the Indians out of [the Concow Valley] because there was gold there. The Indians didn't want to leave that place because it was home to them. They couldn't understand why the white people wanted to drive them away."[23] Settlers introduced livestock to feed the growing mining population, which only worsened relations. Green observed, "The white people brought in a lot of stock and some of the Indians would steal them, so they gathered all the Indians and took them all to Concow Valley."[24] Austin McLaine remembered that soldiers informed the Concows that they had to leave the mountains. Otherwise, the soldiers said, "we will just shoot you down like some wild animals."[25] Concow and Settler understandings about the reason for conflict, and thus removal, diverge here. Settlers argued that they needed to remove Concows and Pit Rivers because Indians had destroyed Settler property. Concows averred that Settlers and livestock invaded their native ground and, despite Concow hospitality, demanded their removal.[26] Settlers were clearly failing to follow the proper social formalities.

Ethnic cleansing took two paths: overland and by water. Green said the army gathered the Concows at Concow Valley, twenty-five miles north of Oroville, and marched them to the Mendocino Reservation, near the Noyo River. Green listed every campsite along the 220-mile route: French Ranch, Mill Ranch, Keeper Ranch, Tehama, Paskenta, Thomas Creek, Mountain House, Log Springs, Government Flat, Round Valley, Eden Valley, Sherwood, Little Valley, Ball Mountain, and, finally, the Mendocino Reservation.[27] Another group of Concows and Pit Rivers made the trip to the Mendocino Reservation via waterways. Concow Polly Anderson said, "When [the soldiers] drove [Concows], they bunched them up like cattle and took them." Anderson's family traveled by steamboat down the Sacramento River to San Francisco and then to the Mendocino Reservation.[28] Pit River John Heenan said soldiers escorted Pit Rivers to Red Bluff, where they loaded the Pit Rivers on a boat. The Pit Rivers sailed down the Sacramento River to the state capital, then embarked for San Francisco, where government officials "unloaded all of the Indians and took them and line[d] them up and also took their picture." Pit Rivers then boarded another boat and sailed out into the Pacific Ocean. Heenan said, "The reason why they did this is because they wanted to turn the Indians around. So when they put them on land they wouldn't try to run away." The ship sailed north for Fort Bragg and the Pit Rivers arrived at their new home.[29]

Whether by land or sea, Concows and Pit Rivers depicted their ethnic cleansing as a traveler's narrative, in which they expanded the world in which they lived. Green remembered every campsite at which he stopped; Anderson and Heenan recalled passing through Sacramento and San Francisco before arriving at Mendocino. These stories reinforced Native ways of history; the history of ethnic cleansing moved from place to place, not date to date, as Settlers told it. Green, Heenan, and Anderson invested meaning in the new places they encountered. The storytellers transformed Sacramento, San Francisco, and other campsites into Indigenous places and reminders of the trip Native People took away from their lands instead of gateways to the Gold Rush and capitalist modernization. Removal, and the travel it entailed, also cut new paths in California. Concows and Pit Rivers had long walked the roads in northeastern California that linked Native communities via war, trade, and intermarriage. Now they traveled new paths, sailing down the Sacramento River or walking over mountains that must have looked like the edge of the world. Concows and Pit Rivers grafted these new places and paths associated with removal onto older ones. The Concow and Pit River world was a more violent and bigger place after ethnic cleansing.

Depending on the route, Concows and Pit Rivers had diverse experiences on their journey. Green said that before making camp each night at the named locations, soldiers went ahead, killed a steer, and fed the hungry and weary travelers. If an elderly person or child tired on the trip, "[the soldiers] would put them in the wagon with the food and haul them." When the Concows reached the South Eel River, "the soldiers would let the old people ride their mules and pack the small children across." Upon reaching the south side of the Eel, an old lady became ill and died. The soldiers allowed her family to stay behind to mourn and probably cremate the body. The Concows and soldiers killed the last steer when they reached Ball Mountain, but severe hunger was not in the offing for they were close to the Mendocino Reservation.[30] Anderson interpreted removal differently than Green. She remembered, "The Indians didn't want to leave and some would try to run off but the white men would shoot them down. They would camp at night and start out the next morning early. Some of the old Indians would be so tired and some sick from the heat or just not able to walk any further and the white men would just knock them in the head and go on."[31] While Green remembered cordial relationships between Concows and Settlers, Anderson recalled a far more violent experience.

It is difficult to assess why Green and Anderson interpreted ethnic cleansing differently. Some historians have suggested that the descendants of removed

Indians invented stories of soldier violence. Perhaps, then, Anderson created stories of soldiers shooting people and killing the elderly.[32] The different understandings of removal may also stem from the different routes Green and Anderson took to the Mendocino Reservation. Much like Cherokees and other southeastern Indians, Concow removal occurred in phases.[33] It may have been that the overland route that Green traveled was easier than the water route that Anderson followed. Despite the different narratives Anderson and Green provided of ethnic cleansing, it is important to note that neither invalidated the other. Neither Anderson nor Green claimed to possess the one and true story of ethnic cleansing. Rather their stories build on and inform each other, providing a richer understanding of this difficult time in Concow history.

Although the People offered different tellings of the trip, Concows and Pit Rivers agreed that the conditions at the Mendocino Reservation were poor. Green said there were houses in which the Concows could sleep, but there was little wood nearby to heat the homes. Concows moved to Pudding Creek, where they built new houses and a sweathouse. Then illness struck the Concows and "quite a few died." Moreover food was limited at the reservation and the Concows had to rely on potatoes from local Settlers.[34]

Neither Pit Rivers nor Concows permanently remained at the Mendocino Reservation. Anderson explained, "They took this bunch to the mouth of Noya also. Here they stopped for about a year. Then the white men saw that there were too many big redwood trees and decided it was too good for them."[35] Anderson used the word *stopped* to interpret removal from Mendocino as a traveler's narrative. Mendocino was temporary and Concows moved later. Anderson also understood ethnic cleansing as a result of the development of extractive capitalism. Earlier she had claimed the discovery of gold imperiled Concows and caused their initial removal. Now the emergence of the Pacific Coast's timber industry and the desire for the giant redwoods initiated another removal. The trip to Round Valley extended the traveler's narrative. Green told the story of the Concows leaving Pudding Creek and arriving at Ten Mile River, Long Valley, and Dos Rios before coming to Round Valley.[36]

Concows and Pit Rivers refused to remain at Round Valley. Known places beckoned both groups. Heenan recalled, "After staying at Round Valley year or two, some of the Indians were out in the mountains gathering food for themself. Some of the hunters spied Mount Shasta several miles away and when they went home, they told the people what they had seen, Mt. Shasta. So finally the people got ready and ran away."[37] Heenan situated the narrative of ethnic cleansing within the Pit River place-world. Pit River landmarks beckoned the People home. Mt. Shasta is an important place in the Pit River world. Pit Rivers believe that spirits inhabit the mountain and that spiritual power drew the Pit River People home.[38]

Told in the 1930s, Concow stories of ethnic cleansing explained their history and maintained their ways of knowing. Kiowa writer N. Scott Momaday calls stories of ethnic cleansing "stories in the blood" or "blood stor[ies]" since they are passed down from generation to generation and are vital to identity and self.[39] Concows used ethnic cleansing to initiate a story of ethnogenesis. In the Concow creation story, Earth Maker informed Concows that when People left the site of creation, they would have to speak a new language and become a new People.[40] After ethnic cleansing, Concows began the difficult process of creating a new People on the Round Valley Reservation. Anderson recalled, "So then they brought them on to Round Valley, they still tried to have their old ways until they all have died except a very few."[41] Some Concows secured lumber and built a sweathouse for tribal ceremonies, mournings, and other events. Building a sweathouse established a sense of permanence in Round Valley and linked Concows to their creation stories. In one version Coyote and Earth Maker created a roundhouse to hold political meetings and ceremonies.

Concows and Pit Rivers then began the work of living on the reservation. Concows Austin McLaine and Annie Feliz explained:

> There they began life anew. They were made to work in the fields, men & women alike, the men do the plowing and cutting the grain, hay, or whatever there was to be done. They were kept busy at all times. They had sawmill, shop, and flour mill. They all took part in working in each. They build schools, churches, and the children attend school and on Sunday all the Indians would attend Church, they were very regular Christians and they were very interested. Now the working men in fact that all had to have some food so the nearest place that they could get their supplies was Noyo and the provisions were brought in on pack mules a whole drove of them say about forty or more mules. The Indians done all of the packing the mules. And for meat, they took quite a few of the Indian men out to the mountains to kill deer for meat and some were busy at all times packing deer meat in for the workhand, besides meat they would issue flour every evening, these stuff would be issued out each family would get enough to last them until the next day.[42]

Work perpetuated the People. McLaine and Feliz continued, "The Concows are very much advanced in civilization, doing all of the business and attending to their own affairs. So there is a Concow tribe of today."[43] In the aftermath of ethnic cleansing, Concows created an empowering narrative. In the context of the Great Depression, they demonstrated both "civilization" and sovereignty by "attending to their own affairs." The latter attribute was vital as Round Valley Indians began to discuss and vote on the Indian Reorganization Act. Additionally the Concow People persisted despite ethnic cleansing. They remained a Concow People in the 1930s (and now) because these storytellers had survived ethnic cleansing and created new identities on the reservation.

As Concows took control of their identity and created a new one of the Round Valley Indian Reservation, they also exerted power over how the People interpreted ethnic cleansing. Concows understood that some time their ancestors and cultural heroes had already made the trip between their homeland, in the Concow Valley, and the Round Valley area. McLaine and Feliz explained that an old man and an old woman lived with their two children, a boy and a girl. One day the old man said to his wife, "I going away for a year and I want you all to stay at home. You have plenty to eat, and whenever you hear anyone coming, why you can sing if you want to." He then told his wife the song: "Nan-tu-tu-um su-su-way-um Nan-tu-tu-um su-su-way-um." ("Bring back the quails, bring back the quails.") The old man found his brother-in-law, Coyote, and the duo began the hard work of hunting quail. They first brought fire to the People and then supplied the quail. The old man and Coyote walked between two sweathouses: one located in present-day Butte County, where the People of the East lived, and one on the other side of Tieyamunne (Anthony Peak) in Round Valley, where the People of the West lived.[44] Ethnic cleaning divided the Concow People into those who lived in the West at Round Valley and those who remained in the East in Butte County. Yet they remained Concows.

McLaine and Feliz's story was important on two counts. First, they purposefully modernized their oral history to include ethnic cleansing. They added new places and new experiences and framed it within the time when their cultural heroes made the world habitable for the People. Second, they argued that ethnic cleansing was a known experience. Their ancestors had made the trip back and forth between the Concow Valley and Round Valley before the 1860s; this journey was a significant part of their identity. The storytellers had then survived ethnic cleansing, remembered and maintained their oral tradition, and re-created their lives on the Round Valley Reservation. Such purposeful modernization and seeking an empowering narrative from ethnic cleansing is an ongoing process. The descendants of all the Concow storytellers in this book now commemorate the Concows' and Pit Rivers' survival of ethnic cleansing with the Nome Cult Walk, held every September.

During the same years the United States removed Concows and Pit Rivers from northeastern California, Owens Valley Paiutes experienced their own forced relocation. At the conclusion of the Owens Valley War, federal and state officials pondered what to do with the thousand or so Paiutes who surrendered at Camp Independence. Some members of the Office of Indian Affairs suggested placing them on a reservation in the Owens Valley, but Settlers opposed the idea, fearing for their livestock and property. Other officials suggested that the government remove the Paiutes to the Nome Lackee Reservation, near Paskenta, more than 400 miles northwest of the Owens Valley and home to some Concows and Pit Rivers. Instead Colonel R. C. Drum ordered the removal of Paiutes and Shoshones from the Owens Valley to the Tejon Indian Reservation, 250 miles to the southwest.[45]

Paiutes experienced many difficulties living at the Tejon Reservation. For one, the reservation's boundaries were unclear. Former California Indian superintendent Edward F. Beale claimed to own part of the land that composed the reservation. For another, the federal government failed to adequately provision the reservation. Paiutes and other Indians at Tejon stole cattle, harvested acorns, and begged the soldiers for food. After a year the U.S. Congress reduced the number of superintendents in California from two to one and the number of reservations to four. Rather than maintain the Tejon Reservation and its contested land boundaries, Superintendent Austin Wiley closed the reservation and moved the Paiutes to the Tule River Reservation.[46] As at Tejon, disease and inadequate food plagued the twice-removed Paiutes at Tule River. Furthermore the local Yokuts considered the Paiutes "roamers" and prevented them from participating in reservation governance. Consequently conditions at Tule River produced another Paiute exodus. In 1873 the federal government moved the Tule River Reservation to Porterville. Many Paiutes used the opportunity to leave the reservation and return to their home.[47]

Paiute histories of ethnic cleansing picked up with the end of the Owens Valley War. Mary Looker and Hank Hunter, both of whom lived in Independence, explained that the soldiers hired two interpreters, Harry Bowers and Jose Chico, to end the war. Throughout Paiute history men and women had functioned as go-betweens, carrying messages of peace and war to the different towns in the Owens Valley.[48] Now Bowers and Chico traveled throughout the valley to invite Paiutes to a peace council. Hunter said Chico's "first destination was Taboose Ranch and there he held a powwow with the chief. From Taboose, he went to Big Pine. From Big Pine, he went to Bishop. At these pow wows, he told the chiefs that a big pow wow was to be held at Taboose Ranch for all the Indians. This pow wow was to be furnished with beef, coffee and other edibles to be furnished by the soldiers." But Chico had lied: "The Indians . . . began to arrive at Taboose by numbers. When all around settled down, the pow wow began, which lasted for two days. As this progressed, the rations donated by the soldiers was eaten. When the last day of the pow wow came, Chico the interpreter called a special meeting to end the day with. At this pow wow, Chico outlined to the Indians that at the soldiers' camp in Independence they will find waiting for them there more rations, which is to be issued to them, when they arrived at the camp."[49] "The unsuspecting Paiutes, thinking it was a peace offering," Looker remembered, moved to Camp Independence.[50] Paiutes interpreted the beginning of ethnic cleansing through the framework of generosity and reciprocity: soldiers provided food and promised peace. The constant movements, however, suggested that relations may not have been what they seemed.

At Camp Independence Paiutes discovered that the soldiers had tricked them. Jennie Cashbaugh, an elderly Paiute woman from Bishop, and her family were among those who set up camp at Independence: "There were lots of little willow huts or just a shade for sun protection. These were to be out houses or something and also there was a fence with one entrance and one house what the man in charge lives in. We were round together in the evening. Every one head of the family were given a small amount of flour and some clothing were given out to the men folk and at the same time order was given."[51] The soldiers distributed the food and supplies to the Paiutes, who enjoyed themselves and went to sleep. Once again the soldiers had acted with proper generosity. The next morning, Hunter explained, "all the Indians waking up were surprised to find that during the night a detail of soldiers had surrounded the Indians." Chico informed the Paiutes that they would not receive their rations that day. Instead the soldiers needed to count them and promised to distribute the rations on the following day. Hunter remembered:

> [Chico told] the Indians, the issue of rations was delayed, they would receive it the next day. . . . He also told the Indians they would have to be counted first before the issue of rations are delivered to them. The counting began at noon and ended nearly sundown. While the counting was going, the army officers were holding secret meetings behind closed doors. At these meetings, it was decided to kill all of the Indians on the grounds. A cannon was made ready, filled with slugs of every description, also extra charge of powder. After the cannon was loaded with such a charge it was then concealed in one of the barracks, which had a door facing the Indians. After the count, the Indians were told to group themselves in a certain formation so the cannon with one

shot would exterminate the most of them and the remaining would be shot by the soldiers. When the plan was ready to be carried through, by some good thought the plan was changed.[52]

Rather than massacre the Paiutes, the U.S. Army removed them from the Owens Valley. Paiutes understood that this act was not as beneficent as some historians have portrayed. Rather Paiutes remembered considerable grief attending ethnic cleansing. Maggie Earl recalled, "They went to the Independence railroad station and after they were gathered and brought to Fort Independence. Indians from all parts of the valley. They were waiting for the feast and other things they would be given them. One morning the Indians were surprised when they were driven south like cattle. Some of the women were crying and especially the children. The soldiers were riding ahead of them, some back of them, and others alongside them."[53] Cashbaugh remembered, "Early next day, they were to move on to their destination promised to them. They were to start real early to walk over the east side mountain of Independence. People cried and didn't want to go. Children & babies cried of hunger & weariness from the long trip. The next day, sure enough, we were well on our way to our new promised home."[54] Paiutes had many reasons to grieve. Coyote and First Woman had created them in the Owens Valley. The People named the landscape. Their ancestors and cultural heroes had walked the land and made it usable for the People. They had defended it from Settlers and the U.S. Army. And now they were moving into the unknown.

Paiutes understood that rather than a benevolent act on the government's part, removal was an act of violence. Paiutes encountered difficulty after difficulty on the march from Independence to the Tejon Indian Reservation. Earl described the discomfort of removal: "After a day's march, through the hot sun and through all the dust made by the Indians, they reached the Lone Pine country."[55] Hunter recalled that water was scarce en route, especially after the caravan passed Olancha.[56] Paiutes remembered marching in fear. Earl said that upon reaching Indian Wells, "It was known somehow by the Indians that they were going to be massacred there." The threat of violence was at every campsite. Hunter mentioned that the soldiers stopped the Paiutes at several places: George Creek, Lone Pine, Olancha, and Cowan Station. At each place the soldiers lined up the Paiutes to kill as many as possible with a concealed cannon, but before the soldiers could execute the Paiutes, a government official saved them. Earl said that a man riding a horse arrived at Indian Wells to stay the execution and ordered the soldiers to march the Paiutes south. Hunter said that a man in a buggy came to Cowan Station in the nick of time and delivered a message to the soldiers' captain, which ordered the soldiers to march the Paiutes to Tejon.[57] Paiutes argued that rather than protecting them, removal meant they traveled under the constant threat of Settler or army violence.

Similar to Concow Bob Green, Hunter and Earl understood removal as a traveler's narrative. Hunter mentioned each campsite, pointing out that Paiutes moved across a known and expanding landscape. Paiutes and soldiers acted in ways that corresponded to Paiute understandings of how events take place in an oral tradition. In two cases soldiers threatened to kill the Paiutes near bodies of water. Commonly, harmful events, such as water babies emerging from the water and abducting women and children, occur near such low-lying topographic features.[58] Yet it is clear too that ethnic cleansing expanded the world Paiutes know. Hunter and Earl incorporated new places into the Paiutes' place-world.

Although the soldiers never massacred the People, Paiutes experienced traumatic violence on the trip. Hunter said, "An old lady, being tired and thirsty seeing a small spring of water along the way stepped out of the caravan toward the spring was shot in the back by one of the soldier guards." The unfortunate woman suffered an ignominious end: "No funeral or anything to the dead woman. She was left there for the coyotes and buzzards."[59] Cashbaugh recalled, "Some were too feeble, weak and fell. I saw them lay down to rest or sit down to rest for want of water or food. I saw the white men with long knives stick the knife into their sides. I know by now the promised land was but a promise of the earthly graves. Our flesh was to pick[ed] up by the hungry birds and coyotes for the while." Indeed such an act occurred to Cashbaugh's grandmother: "[She] sat for just a second. She was thirsty. She wanted water, just then one of the men with the sword saw my grandmother sit down to rest, he was upon her in a little while, he stabbed her through her heart, dead, in a pool of blood layed my grandmother. All alone, cold & stiff."[60] Violence, especially perpetrated against women and the elderly, is deeply engrained in Native memories of ethnic cleansing. Cashbaugh and Hunter possessed similar histories as Concow Polly Anderson, and Dakotas on the Dakota March of 1862 and Dinés on the Long Walk. Telling about ethnic cleansing kept such stories in the blood and reminded listeners of their relatives' sacrifices.[61]

Some Paiutes escaped the march and returned to the Owens Valley. One night, when Mary Harry and her mother left camp to gather firewood, they ran away and fled to the Owens Valley.[62] On another morning Cashbaugh and her brother stole out of camp and hid under some brush. A couple of soldiers tracked the children to their hiding spot. The soldiers then heard Cashbaugh's mother escaping and chased her rather than the children. Another set of tracks again diverted the soldiers, and Cashbaugh and her family successfully evaded the troops and went back to the Owens Valley. The other Paiutes were unfortunate. "God only knows what they did to the Indians they found," Cashbaugh mused. "We heard their cries of agony and disaster."[63]

Those Paiutes who failed to escape found the Tejon Reservation a difficult place to live. Food was scarce. Upon arriving at Tejon, measles swept through the Paiutes. No healing techniques helped. Some Paiutes bathed in the streams near the reserve, but this failed to cure the measles. Anglo-American medicine also failed to alleviate the symptoms of the disease.[64]

After a year the Owens Valley Paiutes experienced another removal. Earl's family heard that the soldiers planned to move them again. "Fearing the hardship of being driven again," Earl remembered, "the Indians made plans to escape." One morning her family fled Tejon and made their way back to Owens Valley.[65] They were some of the 250 Paiutes who escaped the Tejon area and returned to Owens Valley.

Tule River was no better than Tejon. Disease again plagued Paiutes, who lived in small adobe houses in congested conditions. "The Indians never got used to staying in [the adobe houses]," Hunter explained. As with those Paiutes who died en route to Tejon, soldiers treated the Paiute dead with little respect. Soldiers piled dead Paiutes in wagons and dumped the bodies in the hills surrounding the reservation. Rations were poor at Tule River. Hunter noted that Paiutes received only flour, wheat, sweet potatoes, and some game. Meat in other forms was scarce because "the Indians were watched closely at their new reservation to keep them from leaving."[66] Paiutes used stories of ethnic cleansing not only to discuss violence but also to indict Settler society for the federal reservation policy. As with Pit Rivers, Paiutes recalled the terrible conditions that existed at the places to which they were removed. Disease, poor housing, and death existed at the Tejon, Tule River, and Mendocino reservations.

Unlike Concows, Paiutes permanently returned to their homeland. When they arrived back in the Owens Valley, Paiutes met those who had evaded capture, fled the removal, or escaped before them. According to Cashbaugh, the Settler invasion of the Owens Valley and ethnic cleansing scarred the People:

> We lived there since and watched the white man come in and fence the land where we lived and raised our little families and then like all Indians we had to move off the old home grounds that we thought belonged to us. All we can see is "no shooting allowed," "no trespassing," what can we do? Nothing, but hang our heads in shame and sorrow. For once we had lived & roamed the Valley in peace and harmony but today is selfishness and greed, nowhere to gather the seeds and herbs for medicine and good. We have to eat the white

man's food entirely. We get sick the white man's sickness and get white man medicine and our lives is rather short than that of the old time Indians lived. Today Indians live about same as the whites, some very short. I am an old woman now, the white man is better to us now, but just the same we are handicapped by the agent that the white father send to look after us, although not like the men in uniform had done to us.[67]

Stories about ethnic cleansing were not simply locked in the past. Paiutes lived much of their lives under the threat of removal. In 1873 the Office of Indian Affairs proposed to return Paiutes to the Tule River Reservation. However, Paiutes and Settlers, who relied on Paiute labor, prevented another ethnic cleansing. During the Great Depression Settlers again suggested removing Paiutes from the Owens Valley. Beginning in the early twentieth century the City of Los Angeles bought land and water rights in the Owens Valley, depriving Paiutes and Settlers of jobs and natural resources. In the 1930s A. J. Ford, a land agent working on behalf of the Los Angeles Department of Water and Power, suggested removing Paiutes west of the Sierra Nevadas in order to facilitate the city's land and water grab.[68] Officials in the Office of Indian Affairs suggested either Merced, California, or the Walker River Reservation in Nevada as soft landing spots for Owens Valley Paiutes.[69]

In 1935 Paiutes knew they had to resist another removal. They narrated and interpreted removal as a violent event in their lives. They recalled the dangers they faced en route to Tejon, including the dusty conditions, lack of water, and the threat of massacre, and they remembered the loved ones who perished on the trek. Paiutes criticized those Paiutes and Settlers who allowed the U.S. Army to remove the People. Cashbaugh explained that at first Paiutes harvested food, such as taboose, sunflower seeds, and pine nuts; hunted game, which they dried in the sun; and gathered plants for medicine. But after the arrival of Settlers, Paiutes began to work for food or cash, usually earning ten cents per day. Soon the Paiutes received a tract of land "below [where] the flour mill is today." A Paiute man soon saw an opportunity for personal gain. He collected money from other Paiutes, who "just thought it may be for land tax." Soon, however, the Paiutes found themselves landless, and the Settlers no longer wanted the Paiutes around. Without a land base the Paiutes squatted on land or wandered around the valley. Then they took matters into their own hands: "Members of the tribe at last decided to prosecute him [the Paiute man who had collected money from them] for the wrong he has done them. They decided death would be the penalty because he was a bad man." Paiutes accused the man of being a witch. At a gambling event several Paiutes took this man away from the gathering and murdered him. "All because he was a bad man, was no good," Cashbaugh explained. "He would never sell their land no more and collect for the tribes." Cashbaugh then brought the story into the present: "He still had a brother, who it seems the land not sold went to, or they took possession of, and it was sold a few years ago to the city of Los Angeles or to some white people."[70] Cashbaugh linked the historical event of Paiute removal to the current event of the draining of the Owens Valley and the construction of the Los Angeles aqueduct. Both involved Paiutes, perhaps like Chico, betraying their People and creating hardships for other Paiutes in the valley. Indeed some People suffered severe consequences for their role in losing land in the Owens Valley.

Ethnic cleansing signified the false peace at the end of the Owens Valley War. Tricked into moving to Camp Independence, Paiutes endured the violence of ethnic cleansing. Yet the Paiutes returned home and lived with the consequences of settler colonialism. One of those was the specter of removal. In the 1930s Settlers again proposed removing Owens Valley Paiutes. These oral histories served as a reminder of the consequences of ethnic cleansing as well as the power of Indigenous People to return to their homes and reclaim space.

Ethnic cleansing, then, was not necessarily a story of Indigenous defeat. Settler societies are premised on the removal of Indigenous People and replacing them with Settlers. Indigenous People saw their removal differently. Concows made removal part of their ethnogenesis in a new place and the origin story of how they perpetuated themselves as a People. Paiutes narrated a history of return to a place, a changed place but their place of origin nevertheless. Histories revealed how California Indians persisted and thrived in the twentieth century.

CHAPTER 6

Persisting

BY 1935 MANY PEOPLE IN INDIAN COUNTRY RECOGNIZED THAT FEDeral policies needed to change. In 1911 educated American Indians formed the Society of American Indians, which lobbied for American Indian citizenship and to improve reservation conditions. Throughout the 1910s and 1920s Native writers, anthropologists, and artists "talked back to civilization," critiquing the manner in which the United States approached American Indian policy and demanding reform. After the passage of the Indian Citizenship Act in 1924, the SAI disbanded, but American Indian intellectuals continued to lobby for reform. In 1928 their efforts culminated in the Meriam Report, authored by Ho-Chunk Henry Roe Cloud and anthropologist Lewis Meriam. The report concluded that wars, removal, and the policy of confinement and forced assimilation had crippled Indigenous People and harmed their lands. Life expectancy was short. Allotment policies blighted agricultural lands. Many observers proposed a shift in federal Indian policy. Beginning in 1932 Commissioner of Indian Affairs John Collier initiated several reforms.[1]

During the Great Depression Pomos and Paiutes looked around at their communities, People, and land to see the consequences of California's history. The People were ill, suffering from tuberculosis. The land failed to produce the food that nourished the People. Rather than turn to the federal government, both groups relied on their oral traditions to narrate a history by which the People and their knowledge systems persisted into the twentieth century.[2]

In the 1920s and 1930s tuberculosis struck Pomo communities at rates similar to those in the rest of Indian Country. Stories about the poor health in Pomo Country raced across the United States. Government officials believed they had an answer for the Pomo health crisis: the modernization and professionalization of the Indian Health Service. Pomos, on the other hand, "purposefully modernized" their oral traditions to confront the health epidemics that affected their communities.³ Pomo oral histories, featuring biographies of individual healers and autobiographies of those who were healed, demonstrated their healers' ability to diagnose and treat illnesses, drew parallels between Native and non-Native doctors, and confronted projects associated with their bodies.⁴

While Pomos addressed sick individuals, Paiutes recognized that the land was endangered. Paiute George Brierly said the Paiutes from Benton had always harvested tules, which "grew plenty along the creeks of whichever way the water ran." In 1935, however, "[that] kind of tules are seldom seen today." Brierly traced the tules' disappearance to the time when "white settlers" arrived in the Owens Valley.⁵ Paiutes revised their oral histories about water to critique the meanings and consequences of settler colonialism in eastern California. They articulated an alternative narrative of the Owens Valley Water Wars, arguing that the war began at Paiute creation, not in 1905, when Frederick Eaton first purchased land in the Owens Valley. Owens Valley Settlers, rather than the City of Los Angeles, functioned as their stories' antagonists. And the ultimate victors in the wars may not have been the City of Los Angeles but Paiute systems of knowledge and Paiute efforts to reclaim water.

In the late nineteenth and early twentieth century many American Indians faced two related health crises. First, they suffered from near epidemic rates of tuberculosis and trachoma. Poor sanitation on reservations, overcrowding at boarding schools, and the policy of returning ill students to their reservation homes facilitated the spread of these diseases throughout Indian Country. The Office of Indian Affairs (OIA) attempted to resolve these poor health conditions by modernizing the Indian Health Service. The OIA established professional criteria for health officials by requiring field matrons, doctors, and nurses to pass a civil service test and possess advanced degrees. The OIA also emphasized preventative care and improved hygiene in order to thwart the onset of disease. These changes in federal Indian policy produced the second health crisis: the OIA discredited Indigenous ideas about sickness and health. When health professionals offered preventative care or addressed hygiene, they blamed Native People for the poor sanitary conditions that existed on reservations (ignoring the government's role in producing overcrowding) and denounced Native healers as ineffective and antimodern.⁶

In 1929 a sensationalistic news story revealed Pomo Country's health crises. That fall newspapers reported on the "weird and fantastic health cults of the Pomo tribe" and the unfortunate deaths of the Williams sisters. Geraldine Williams, the daughter of Billy Williams, "a well educated, prosperous, and highly respected" Pomo man, died from tuberculosis. Newspapers described

Geraldine as a girl possessing "rare personal beauty," who had represented Pomos at the April 1927 christening of the *Mendocino*, a ferryboat that served San Francisco Bay and was named after the county in which many Pomos live. It was a tragic loss, made more so a week later when Geraldine's sister Catherine came down with the same illness. Catherine's unnamed mother sent for two Pomo healers, Topsy Pettit and Tony Metlock, to cure her seriously ill daughter. Pettit wrapped Catherine in heavy blankets, built an enormous fire, and held a healing ceremony. Afterward Lucy Keenan, Mendocino County's government nurse, observed, "The girl's throat and body were bruised as though she had been bitten about the throat and beaten upon the body." Pettit and Metlock failed to cure Catherine, who soon died. Neither Billy Williams nor his wife blamed the healers for Catherine's death; Billy suggested that his daughter's death resulted from "an evil spell placed on her by an envious member of the tribe."

Keenan, though, held Pettit and Metlock responsible. She contacted Colonel L. A. Dorrington of the Office of Indian Affairs and, with the aid of Reverend Frederic G. Collett, a controversial member of the Indian Board of Cooperation, brought criminal charges against the two Pomos. The case went to the grand jury, which dropped the inquiry against Pettit and Metlock. "After four or five white doctors had been unable to save the child's life," the grand jury concluded, "a squaw [Pettit] was called to suck blood from the throat and chest of the patient, in accordance with tribal custom, but there is no evidence of torture or mistreatment." Although the grand jury considered the matter closed, Pomos did not. Pomo Stephen Knight held a meeting of the Ukiah Council of the Indian Brotherhood of Northern California, which newspapers described as an "intertribal pow-wow" of Pomos, Yukis, and Wailackis. After this meeting Knight and the Brotherhood demanded Keenan's removal from her post as government nurse and that the OIA investigate Collett's role in the grand jury. In 1931 the OIA transferred Keenan to Arizona.[7]

The Williams sisters' unfortunate deaths revealed the interlocking narratives of modernity and colonialism in Pomo lives and health. Media coverage depicted the Pomo healers as antimodern. The story's author highlighted Pettit's and Metlock's efforts to heal Pomos and non-Indians in Mendocino County. During World War I, Metlock healed a man stricken with the flu. The news story quoted Metlock saying, "I'm 88 years old . . . but I'll get up in the middle of the night to treat anybody." The author of the news story added, "Maybe there's a good more precept in that remark for our own physicians who look down on the Indian health cults as 'fanatical superstition.'" Yet the reporter consistently qualified Metlock's and Pettit's healing prowess. First, the writer called Pomo health practices "cults," which suggested that they were abnormal, bizarre, and out of step with modernizing America. The story also featured a picture of an alleged Pomo "hex doctor" holding a duck in his or her left hand and wearing an elaborate mask. Second, the writer placed the word *cures* in scare quotes, suggesting that Metlock and Pettit could not provide help to ill people. Third, the article described Pomos as lacking what historian Pablo Mitchell calls "bodily comportment."[8] Pomo healing ceremonies featured "tribal gyrations," "eerie incantations," and blood sucking. From the newspaper's perspective, Pomo healers were vestiges of a superstitious past, not a modern way of dealing with health problems.

The girls' deaths also highlighted the federal government's efforts to discredit Native healers. In 1891 the OIA instituted a field matron program, whereby non-Indian women went into the field in an effort to prevent diseases and poor health conditions on reservations as well as to oversee sanitary and hygiene conditions.[9] Yet the federal government failed to fund the program, despite the efforts of some white women to lobby for more money. In 1928 the Meriam Report blasted the OIA's failures to provide adequate health conditions for Indians and recommended that field nurses replace matrons in Indian communities. Trained and skilled nurses, the report argued, would provide better care for Native Peoples.[10] Keenan, a government nurse, represented this modern health practitioner in Pomo Country.

Keenan used every instrument at her disposal to undermine Pettit and Metlock. First, she funneled the story about Catherine's death and the inability of Pomo healers to cure her to newspapers. This story quickly raced across the country via wire reports, and interested readers in Detroit and Miami soon read the news of the Pomo girl's death. Second, Keenan directed county courts and the rule of law against Pomo healers. The two Pomos were hauled in front of the grand jury to testify to their abilities.

Pomos resisted the newspapers' narrative and the OIA's directives about health and disease. Some Pomos purposefully modernized their political organizations to meet this challenge. Stephen Knight and the California Indian Brotherhood launched protests against Keenan and the OIA. Other Pomos used oral histories to counter the notion that they were antimodern and that their healing practices lacked efficacy. Edgar Jackson, a Pomo in his twenties who lived in Ukiah, narrated the biography of elderly healer Billy Rice. Rice came to his profession through his kinship connections: "His career as a doctor came to him naturally through his people, that is people on his mother and father's side."[11] After establishing his authority to heal, Rice explained that violating taboos caused illnesses: "According to Indian rules, the father of the born baby is not suppose to do no hunting or no fishing or of no other task that may effect the baby. In this case, it is effect the baby instead of the adult." Another cause of illness was "frightening." Rice explained, "A person may be just walking around or swimming or any place he or she goes. They may be scared by something that they don't even know or remember of. Sometimes it effect them where it happened and sometime when they get home."

Singing and the use of certain items diagnosed, treated, and cured illnesses. Rice described two types of doctors: *soc-ka* (frighten doctor) and rattle. A *soc-ka* owned a willow wood staff, about three feet long and adorned with string and four white feathers, which they "sway[ed]" over an ill person, and sang songs from their expansive repertoire. "There is about fifty song for this type of doctoring," Rice said. "There is a song for everything that can scare a person." Eventually the *soc-ka* found the correct song to heal the patient. "When [the *soc-ka*] does strike the thing that scared [the person], . . . the patient jumps up from this bed and is very hard to calm down." Usually the *soc-ka* needed four days and nights to heal a scared person. The rattle doctor operated in a similar fashion. The healer used a *ka-yo-yo* (rattle) "fill[ed] with tiny rocks from the homes of red ants. Often enough rocks are put in, it is tied to end of an eagle feather and tied on there tight so it cannot come off." When relatives called the rattle doctor to a patient, the healer sang and "rattle[d] his rattles" over the prone body. Eventually the healer found the right combination of singing and rattling, for "the [patient] shakes . . . and then jumps up all tired and sweating" and healed. The patient's family paid the healer if he or she was successful. In earlier times the family paid the healer with beads, but in the twentieth century "money" became the primary choice for compensation.[12]

In one sense it appears that Rice's biography was ethnographic or representative of the "memory culture" method.[13] One might conclude that Rice documented how "traditional" beliefs persisted into the modern era and that a discerning anthropologist could decipher which aspects of cultural contact contaminated Pomo beliefs. However, Rice and Jackson purposefully modernized their stories about healing. For example, they presented the story as Rice's biography. Dipesh Chakrabarty notes that "the biography [and] the autobiography" are two of the "basic genres that help express the modern self."[14] Jackson narrated Rice's story as a third-person account of Rice's origins and healing practices. Additionally Rice and Jackson suggested that Pomo doctors healed as effectively as professional ones. "The [rattle] doctor has his idea just the same as a white doctor," Rice explained, "sometimes he get it right and sometimes wrong, but he tried different ways to pull him or she through." Pomo doctors and white professional doctors both had to diagnose a patient and did so based on prior experience, and sometimes they failed to address ill health. While lambasting American Indian healers, doctors and nurses rarely acknowledged that they themselves failed to provide adequate health services to Native Peoples. "An Indian doctor same as white doctor pulls a patient through or loses it," Rice recognized. "Generally loses too far gone, that when a person dies right there while being doctored." Possibly Rice recalled the Williams sisters' deaths from tuberculosis: despite the hard work and knowledge of both a Pomo and a white doctor, the girls were "too far gone" by the time anyone administered to them. Rice also noted that healing was entrenched in the modern economy. He and other healers earned "money" and sometimes "money or bead[s]" for healing. "An Indian doctor do not ask for pay," Rice allowed, "he get what the patient think he deserves, and is usually large quantity of bead[s] or large sum of money." The forms of payment that existed for Pomo doctors pointed to the coexistence of traditional and modern. Beads and cash, Pomo healers and white doctors, tradition and modernity intermingled in Mendocino County.[15]

Other Pomos gave autobiographical accounts, the other genre of the modern self, of how healers treated them. Pomo John McWhinney's oral history begins with his family living a subsistence lifestyle: "As we made our living mostly from hunting, at a very early age, I became very fond of hunting." As a boy McWhinney pleaded with his father for a gun. Eventually his father relented and bought a .44 rifle for him. Early one morning after acquiring his modern hunting technology, McWhinney awoke and went hunting while the rest of his family slept. Immediately he recognized that something was amiss. "While hunting, I became tired and sat down," he explained, "my ears began ringing and didn't feel any too well." Despite these warnings he persisted. He walked through a deep canyon until he spotted his prey: a large buck. McWhinney raised his new rifle and fired. The deer "didn't move, this caused me some anxiety, and a feeling of fear." McWhinney fired nine more times, and after the final shot the "deer sauntered off as if nothing was happening." McWhinney walked to where the deer had stood and saw blood on the ground. He followed the blood trail to a spring, where he saw a *komshō*, an animal that resembled a porcupine. "This was a bad sign among my people," he noted, "so I immediately hurried home."

On his trip home McWhinney fell down and slept. He experienced a vision in which a little boy appeared and woke him. McWhinney again walked toward home. When he reached the top of a hill, he fell asleep again. Once more the little boy appeared in a vision and said, "Wake up, wake up, what are you laying there for?" The boy explained that he was *kēlābehché* and that he had appeared to McWhinney at the spring. When McWhinney woke up again, he "found [him]self covered with blood." He recalled "how my old people used to tell me of the different rules I should follow before I ever went hunting or fishing." He had failed to adhere to Pomo hunting taboos and was now in trouble. He again started for home and arrived the next morning. Although his family was pleased to see him, fearing that he "was probably killed or hurt," they understood the gravity of the situation. His father put him to bed, where he "then lapsed into unconsciousness." After discovering what happened, McWhinney's father and his two uncles traveled to Lake County and brought back the *käbäkel* (great doctor) and a *dämäyī* (assistant): "This great doctor handled cases for people that got scared." The *käbäkel* and *dämäyī* stayed with McWhinney for one year, at which time he "was able to get up, then a skeleton of my former self."[16]

McWhinney's autobiographical account mixed traditional and modern ideas about health. His family survived on hunting, but had adapted that way of life by using modern technology: guns, not bows and arrows. Still, older hunting taboos possessed meaning in a modern world. McWhinney endangered himself by hunting without following the proper protocols. He should have known this from the beginning, when he quickly tired and his ears "began ringing." Still he trudged ahead and saw his prey. His modern technology failed to kill or even scare the deer. It was not until McWhinney saw the *komshō* at the spring that he realized he was truly in trouble and attempted to go home. His male relatives called upon a healer and an assistant, as Billy Williams had done for his daughter, to treat this traditional illness in a modern context. In this case modern technology—the gun—had alienated McWhinney from participating in the proper hunting ceremonies. Healing this illness was no job for Keenan or government doctors. The *käbäkel* and *dämäyī* successfully treated their patient and left. Even in a modern context with modern tools, Pomo healing practices and systems of knowledge persisted and explained everyday events.

In the 1930s Pomos narrated a history of Indian health that offered an antidote against the attack on Pomo healers and empowered Pomo Peoples and knowledge. As in other Indigenous communities in North America, the onset of a health crisis did not produce "despiritualization" or a crisis of Indigenous systems of knowledge; rather Pomos created new ceremonies, protocols, and stories regarding healing and disease.[17] In the process they engaged in a debate regarding the meaning of modernity in twentieth-century America. Pomos refuted the salacious newspaper articles and federal efforts to stamp out their healing beliefs. They told stories about their experiences with healers that argued that traditional healing practices persisted and thrived during the Great Depression.[18]

In the 1930s People were not the only unhealthy beings. The land too had experienced trauma. Susie Baker, a Paiute women from Big Pine, California, told the following story: A giant approached the Alabama Hills, a range of small hills and protruding rock formations on the southern edge of the Owens Valley. As the giant reached the hills, he screamed at the top of his great voice. Frightened, People scurried from their hiding places. As they fled, the giant picked them up and killed them. He planned to take his victims home for a feast with his wife. When the giant reached Tinemaha, a peak that looms over the Owens Valley, he again screamed at the top of his voice. More People ran from their hiding places, and the giant picked them up too and killed them. He traveled as far north as Tupueseenata (Hammil Valley) and then decided to return home with his prey.

The water baby, a sprite that lives in lakes, grew tired of the giant's screaming, which had frightened him several times. The water baby knew when the giant would pass by his home in the Owens Lake, so he went near the trail, lay down on a rock, and waited. When the giant approached, he saw the water baby lying on the rock. He asked where his mother and father were, but the water baby refused to answer. The giant pressed the water baby's little fingers to see if it would scream, but the water baby said nothing. The giant pressed his little head, but he did not even mumble. Again the giant asked, "Little boy, where is your mother and father?" The water baby said nothing. The giant pinched the water baby's finger, saying, "You have a very little hand and pretty little body." The water baby sat up and seized the giant by the forefinger. The giant exclaimed, "Let me go, you must have thought I was your dad or mother but I am not!" The giant tried to escape with his great strength, but it was useless. The water baby stood up, dragged the giant to the edge of Owens Lake, and threw him into the water. Then the water baby jumped in after the giant and took him down to the bottom. Years later the water baby took the giant's bones and threw them opposite the Alabama Hills, across the Owens River, which drains into the lake. The remains of the giant's bones are still there, Baker informed the young Paiute woman who recorded her story.[19]

Baker used the story to contemplate the history and consequences of a crucial event in California history. She concluded her narrative by saying that the rock on which the water baby waited for the giant still existed, but "it may be destroyed by the Los Angeles aqueduct builders. The waterbaby's home may be still there. I do hope it's there."[20] The aqueduct to which she referred is, of course, the channel that siphoned water from the Owens Valley to Los Angeles and the flashpoint of the Owens Valley Water Wars. Yet in too many histories, scholars ignore the Owens Valley's Indigenous inhabitants. Paiutes may appear as static "first inhabitants" of the Valley, but then they disappear, allegedly conquered by Owens Valley "pioneers."[21] They were thought to have had little at stake in the Owens Valley Water Wars—a sentiment that Baker refuted. The draining of the Owens Valley threatened the relationship between Paiutes and the land itself. Yet Paiute oral tradition articulated a path for Paiutes to follow as they persisted as a people in the Owens Valley.

The connection between Paiutes and water began at creation. Paiutes believe that specific bodies of water are central to their identity. Owens Valley Paiutes call themselves *nuwa paya hup ca'a' otuum*, which roughly translates as "water ditch Coyote children." In a variation of their creation story, Coyote placed the People next to the "water ditch," or the Owens River, that runs through the valley. Paiute ethnogenesis occurred next to a known and specific body of water; they were not "water ditch Coyote children" until Coyote created them next to the Owens River.[22]

After creation, Paiute economies utilized specific bodies of water. Paiutes called the Owens River the "water ditch" because they irrigated the Owens Valley for centuries before Anglo-Americans arrived. At a town named *pitana patü*, near modern-day Bishop, Paiutes used irrigation ditches to increase the growth of indigenous plants, such as *nā'hāvīta* (spike rush). In the spring the town head man announced the beginning of the irrigation season, usually when snow runoff from the southern Sierra caused creeks to rise. Residents of *pitana patü* then elected a *tuvaijü'u*, or irrigator, who led a corps of twenty-five men in building a dam out of rocks, brush, sticks, and mud on Bishop Creek, similar to those structures a Paiute man placed in front of Fish when he came down Rush Creek. After completing the dam, the *tuvaijü'u* directed the water into the ditch, which fed northern and southern fields in alternate years.[23] Stories about the water ditch position Paiutes as those who first purposefully diverted and used the water.

Water is also crucial to how Paiutes understand the world in which they live. All things, especially water, are sentient in Paiute cosmology, possessing human emotions and abilities. In one story a group of women are gathering basket-making materials near a lake at present-day Dyer, Nevada. The women foolishly made fun of the water. Angry, water leaped out of the lake and attempted to sweep them to the bottom.[24] Although the lake failed to take its intended prey, water, like humans, felt insults and attempted to exact revenge. In another traditional story a group of children was playing at Pasasa'a (now known as Casa Diablo Hot Springs and home to a geothermal power plant). An impetuous boy threw rocks into Pasasa'a, despite his peers' warnings. A water baby emerged from the spring, abducted the boy, and took him under the water.[25]

In addition to possessing human-like abilities, water, Paiutes believe, possesses its own *puha*. The most common manifestation of water's *puha* was the water baby. Although we have seen the water baby's destructive capabilities, often taking women and children to the bottom of lakes and drowning them, it also functioned as a spirit helper for some healers. The relationship between *puha* and water is more than just possessing power and spirits. The Paiute word for water, *paya*, sounds like *puha*. A Southern Paiute man from Las Vegas, Nevada, described *puha* in liquid terms: it "flows into and down the sides of mountains."[26]

Water guided Paiute place-naming practices. Consider again the story of the giant. Baker knew the path the giant walked, from the Alabama Hills to Tinemaha to Tupueseenata and then to Owens Lake. She also knew the exact location of the rock on which the water baby waited for the giant. Other stories about water are also clear about where they occurred. We know that the event related in the story of the basket makers took place at Dyer, and the event in the story of the children occurred at Pasasa'a. Specific places in the Owens Valley serve as "anchors of memory" linking human history to place.[27] We do not know when the events in these stories occurred, but they are true from a Paiute perspective because they occurred at places known to historical and contemporary Paiutes.

Topography structured oral narratives. Paiutes associate high places, such as the Alabama Hills and Tinemaha, with positive manifestations of *puha*. Hence *puha* "flows down" from mountains. Benevolent spirits live on mountain peaks; doctors go to the tops of mountains to seek visions and *puha* itself. Low-lying areas, such as Owens Lake, Pasasa'a, and other bodies of water, usually (but not always) have negative manifestations of *puha*. Water babies emerge from water and snatch women and children. In between high and low areas are the plains, or Owens Valley itself, an area of stasis or what geographer Yi-Fu Tuan calls "space."[28] Paiutes structure their oral narratives to replicate this understanding of their topography. The narratives begin in space, either on the plains or at the foot of the hills, and proceed to high or low places. The story of the giant originates at the foot of the Alabama Hills and then moves from named place to named place before the giant meets his end at Owens Lake.[29]

Other oral traditions about water adhere to this topographic narrative structure. Susie Baker told of the Frog sisters, who lived at a spring. Rattlesnake, who lived about one mile or more away, planned to steal the spring away from them. He kept very close watch until he had a chance. One afternoon, when the Frog sisters were fast asleep and no one was around, Rattlesnake came down to the spring and drank as much as he could, holding the rest of the water in his mouth. He took every bit of the water in the spring and started for his home.

He was about a half-mile away when the Frog sisters woke up and to their surprise found no water in their spring. They immediately investigated and guessed what had become of their water. They pursued Rattlesnake and saw him climbing up the hill. The Frog sisters followed him up the hill as fast as they could. Upon seeing the sisters in pursuit, Rattlesnake increased his speed, but as he ascended the mountain, he became tired, coughed, and spat out some of the water. Rattlesnake continued on his journey until the Frog sisters overtook him, stopped him, tickled him, and made him spit out all the water he had in his mouth. The Frog sisters drank the water and took it back to their spring, where they deposited the water in its rightful place.[30]

Baker's story embodies the topographic narrative structure that undergirded Paiute oral culture and history. The story begins with Rattlesnake on the plains, moving down to the spring and stealing the water. Afterward Rattlesnake climbs a hill, where the story's positive resolution occurs. Baker used the Paiute language to map and claim the Owens Valley landscape. She identified the place where Frog sisters lived as *ya qua java joh* (Frog Spring). She called the place where the Frog sisters overtook Rattlesnake *togo wamo cha qua tepu* (Snake Spat Out).[31] The Paiute landscape functioned as a mnemonic device, reminding Paiutes where valuable sources of water exist—essential knowledge in an arid environment. Mattie Bulpitt, a ninety-five-year-old Paiute woman from Inyo County's Round Valley, told a variation of the Frog sisters and Rattlesnake story: "[Frog] owned a spring about five miles out, north of Big Pine and it still is there just below the state highway." She identified the location of Snake Spat Out: "These willows can be seen still to this day near the top of the mountain just off the main state highway."[32] The places mentioned in Paiute traditional stories were not ancient memories; they remained meaningful locations that Paiutes saw on a daily basis and in which they invested meaning.[33]

Paiutes also co-opted Settler place-names for their own purposes. Settler place-naming worked in concert with their economic practices and histories in an attempt to erase Paiute histories and systems of knowledge. In the 1860s Confederate sympathizers living in the Owens Valley named the Alabama Hills after the CSS *Alabama*, which sank the Union ship *Hatteras* off the coast of Texas.[34] Paiutes reclaimed such places by telling their own narratives about them. The Alabama Hills are not significant because they commemorate a Confederate naval victory, Paiutes tell listeners; they are important because they were the place from which the giant began his rampage and where, ultimately, he ended his journey and his exploitation of the People. Thus Paiutes were not interlopers, recent arrivals, or wandering warriors; they had a deep history in the Owens Valley.

Paiutes argued that they had occupied the Owens Valley for a long time and possessed a deep understanding of the area's history through knowledge of places. Although "pioneers" had arrived in the Owens Valley and displaced the Paiutes, the place-names, historical actors, and tellers of history remained. Although neither Susie Baker nor Mattie Bulpitt explicitly referred to the local histories of the Owens Valley and Inyo County, it is likely both knew the meanings Settlers had embedded in the Paiute landscape, which they refuted with their oral histories. The story of Rattlesnake and the Frog sisters reasserted a Paiute landscape, known to them, defiant of American colonialism.

Paiutes understood that their history since 1850 concerned water. In the mid-nineteenth century Anglo-Americans arrived in the Owens Valley, which sparked conflict over natural resources. Jennie Cashbaugh, a seventy-year-old Paiute woman from Bishop, noted, "Trouble arose every now and then as the white people wanted more water."[35] American Settlers established a mining, pastoral, and agricultural economy in the valley that drained water from Paiute communities and resource areas. Conflict ensued as Paiutes clashed with miners, ranchers, and the military. In 1863 the California Volunteers forcibly removed nearly one thousand Paiutes to Fort Tejon. From there federal officials relocated the Paiutes to the Tule River Reservation, near modern-day Porterville, California. By 1873 very few Paiutes remained at Tule River, for they had returned to the Owens Valley. By that time Anglo-American farmers and ranchers had claimed much of the best land and water. Paiutes eked out a living by creating a mixed economy of wage labor and hunting and using the little water available to irrigate gardens and small fields.[36]

In the twentieth century Paiutes observed the consequences of settler colonialism. Baker ended the story of the giant with a reference to a contemporary event: that the rock on which the water baby waited for the giant "may be destroyed by the Los Angeles aqueduct builders." Similarly she concluded the story of Rattlesnake and the Frog sisters, "[*Ya qua java joh* and *togo wamo cha qua tepu*] were springs at one time, but they are now dry."[37] In other words, in 1935 Frog Spring and Snake Spat Out no longer had water. Why not? Simply, someone had entered the valley and drunk all the water.

Paiutes used their oral traditions to address the unique ways the Water Wars affected the People. The disappearance of water particularly harmed Paiute women. When Cashbaugh described the sedge plants Paiutes gathered, she said, "Nā'hāvīta is a taboose class of seed food, [it] cannot be found in the Owens Valley since the Valley went dry. The plant must have all dried up, never to grow again."[38] Settlers developing a mining and pastoral economy in the Owens Valley and Los Angeles's siphoning the valley's water destroyed indigenous food sources, specifically those harvested by Paiute women. Harvesting indigenous plants grounded women's identity. At creation the Paiute Father gave baskets to women in which they could gather plants.[39] Without water, women could not contribute to the family economy. Paiute women found job opportunities as domestic workers and washerwomen, but these occupations were poor substitutes for lost resources.[40]

The Los Angeles aqueduct posed a similar threat to Paiute systems of knowledge. The aqueduct threatened to destroy the places where the events related in Paiute oral histories occurred. Passing the Alabama Hills in the Owens Valley, Paiutes remember that screaming giant. Passing the rock where Water Baby waited for the giant reminds them of Water Baby's unusual service to the People. If those places ceased to exist, the history might disappear. Owens Valley Paiutes likely had another sobering thought in the 1930s: If the water disappears, what will become of the People? What will become of "water ditch Coyote children"? The drying of Frog Spring and Snake Spat Out and the disappearance of nā'hāvīta threatened the very identity of the People. Paiutes used their traditional stories to offer an alternative history of Paiute-Settler encounters and interpret the impact of those encounters on the water, and therefore the People, of the Owens Valley.[41]

Some Paiutes blamed Settlers and not the city of Los Angeles for their current predicament. Cashbaugh actually had kind words for Los Angeles: "The city of Los Angeles is a different proposition all together. They would meet the Indians part way, they realize they have made the Indians homeless and took their work from them, the means of bread and butter they had, just a living but today they are fair enough to compromise with the Federal Government so as to give better land to the Indians to at least make a living."[42] Los Angeles, according to Cashbaugh, pledged to work with the Paiutes, something that Owens Valley Settlers had never offered. Unlike the Settlers, who also "made the Indians homeless," Los Angeles promised to create a land base for the Paiutes and provided jobs in 1930 and 1931 on city-owned ranches, roads, and waterways.[43] Settlers, on the other hand, had marginalized Paiutes to the lowest rung of the region's economic ladder and usurped the valley's best land.[44] Yet Paiutes and their knowledge systems persisted despite violence and ethnic cleansing.

Paiute oral histories allude to the history of water in the Owens Valley. The stories of the giant and the Frog sisters refer to a predator entering the Owens Valley, moving across the Paiute landscape and harming the People. Both the giant and Rattlesnake mimic Los Angeles's actions. When the giant walks from Alabama Hills to Tupueseenata, he comes from the direction of Los Angeles (south) and parallels the pattern in which Los Angeles purchased land in the Owens Valley, moving from south to north. The Frog sisters story likewise resembles the history of Paiutes, Anglo Settlers, and Los Angeles. Someone—Paiute leaders, the Office of Indian Affairs, Owens Valley Settlers—slept when Rattlesnake crawled into the valley and stole the water. At this point it certainly looked bleak for Paiutes and water, with murderous giants and thieving rattlesnakes.[45]

The stories' conclusions, however, offer an empowering narrative for the future. The giant story suggests that the Paiutes were prepared for Los Angeles. They already knew that violent and threatening beings could invade from the south. Paiutes also knew that they and their water had the *puha* to defeat these large monsters. The story of Rattlesnake pointed out the folly of greed. Rattlesnake took too much water, for he could not swallow all of it. He eventually lost all the water and the Frog sisters returned the water to its rightful place. At the end of both stories, diminutive, ostensibly powerless characters reclaim the water, defeat powerful enemies, and heal the land. The small water baby throws the giant into the lake and devours him; the Frog sisters reclaim their water from poisonous Rattlesnake. Although things may have looked bleak in the oral histories and in 1935, when the women shared these stories, the future need not be. Paiutes had faced large foes like this before and won; Paiute cultural heroes returned the water to its proper place.

In 1935, when Paiute women told these stories, their leaders were negotiating with the United States and Los Angeles about the future of the Paiute People. In the early 1930s the federal government and Los Angeles had recommended removing the Paiutes from their homeland, from the site of the "water ditch" to a new reservation, near modern-day Merced, or to Nevada's Walker River Reservation. Many of the Paiutes interviewed in 1935, such as Cashbaugh and Bulpitt, were children when the federal government removed the Paiutes to Tejon at the end of the 1860s, and they told stories of that difficult experience. Los Angeles's suggestion for removal resurrected those memories of the forced march to Tejon and the awful living conditions there and at Tule River.[46]

Between 1935 and 1937 federal officials held outdoor meetings in the Owens Valley to explain the situation to the People. Paiute women appeared at these meetings in equal numbers with Paiute men. Perhaps the stories they told their leaders energized them in their effort to reclaim land, water, and power. At any rate the Paiute leaders, supported by their elders, insisted they were *not* leaving. Historian Steven Crum suggests that the Paiutes' "deep attachment" to the Owens Valley galvanized their resistance to removal.[47] Paiute history and oral tradition likewise bolstered their fight to remain near the water ditch.

Paiutes empowered themselves through their belief systems, which defined their worldview and shaped their reality.

In part Paiutes emerged victorious in their struggle with Los Angeles and Settlers. In the 1937 Land Exchange Act, Paiutes and the United States traded 2,914 acres of previously allotted lands to Los Angeles for 1,392 acres, which became the Bishop, Big Pine, and Lone Pine reservations.[48] Thus Paiutes ensured that they remained next to the water ditch forever. But this was a limited victory. The Land Exchange Act provided for Paiute water rights, but the federal government failed to secure them from Los Angeles. As part of the exchange, Los Angeles had promised to provide 6,064 acre-feet of water to the Paiutes, but at the same time, the city insisted it could not transfer water rights to the Paiutes without a two-thirds vote by city residents. Moreover the amount of water promised failed to meet the demands of a growing Paiute People and tribal economic development.[49] In 1994 the U.S. Department of the Interior investigated the water rights issue, which is still open to debate. The Owens Valley Indian Water Commission—a consortium made up of the Bishop, Big Pine, and Lone Pine reservations—fights for water rights and, like their traditional narratives, hopes for a positive future.[50]

By the Great Depression, Pomos and Paiutes, if not all California Indians, faced threats to their health. Pomos understood that the People were ill, suffering from trachoma and tuberculosis. Although newspapers and the Office of Indian Affairs denounced traditional healing methods as antimodern, Pomos argued that they possessed a history of healing and that their ways of knowing persisted. Paiutes noted that the land itself was imperiled by Settler colonialism. The siphoning of the Owens River and Owens Lake threatened their plants, history, and identity. Yet Paiutes told stories in which seemingly powerless people could persist and defeat apparently powerful entities. These narratives of persistence and power would serve the People as they entered a new historical phase after the Great Depression.

Conclusion

IN 1935 CALIFORNIA INDIANS IN MENDOCINO COUNTY AND THE OWENS Valley worked on a state public works project. Hired to provide information on precontact ways of life, California Indians used their oral traditions to tell and interpret California's history. This history began at creation, when Myth People made Indigenous land, People, and culture. The narrative then shifted to the naming of California's landscape. California Indians invested meanings in the landscape by telling traditional stories about specifically named places. Then California Indians told a history of the mid-nineteenth century. Prophecy narratives predicted the chaos that attended the encounter with Settler society. California Indian storytellers remembered and interpreted the Indian Wars, understanding those conflicts as part of a long history of Indigenous warfare, not as proof of their racial inferiority and disappearance. The storytellers said the same about Indian removal: Concows and Paiutes understood removal as a story of ethnogenesis and sovereignty, not their destruction or disappearance. Finally, California Indians confronted two issues that affected them during the Great Depression: health and water. They argued that they possessed the power to heal the People and the land. How was this indigenizing California history significant to American Indian history in the 1930s?

New Deal programs, such as the Federal Writers' Project (FWP), included folk and multicultural understanding of the U.S. past. Anticipating the development of social history in the 1960s, the FWP wanted to tell the history of the United States and define Americans' identity from the bottom up and with long-ignored voices. This effort on the part of the FWP produced the famous WPA slave narratives and brought anthropologists to California to record ethnographic information from Indigenous People. This book has demonstrated how California Indians told a version of history that reflected their ways of knowing and understanding the past.

Place, not time, mattered in the telling of this history. California Indians grounded their historical arguments in specific and known places on their landscapes, such as the Pomos' Mot ti coy, the Concows' West Mountain, and the Paiutes' Grant Lake. California Indians established human and nonhuman historical actors, such as Earth Maker, Coyote, and Lizard, as creative forces in California history. Finally, California Indians authored a version of California history that provided insight into their worlds. Unlike the WPA slave narratives, which the Jim Crow South's power relations influenced, California Indians controlled how they produced knowledge. Older California Indians shared oral traditions with younger community members. California Indians' version of the state's history emphasized the violence of Settler colonialism and the ongoing processes of colonialism that affected their daily lives.

California Indians' contribution to the folk and multicultural moment of the 1930s reminds us that the Pomo, Concow, and Paiute storytellers were part of a long line of California Indian and American Indian intellectuals. Historian Lisbeth Haas argues that California Indians translated Spanish and Mexican colonialism to other California Indians. Painters inscribed Indigenous meanings on mission walls and in paintings of saints. In the 1820s Luiseño Pablo Tac traveled to Rome and produced a dictionary of the Luiseno language and a history of his People's contact with the Spanish. Native leaders claimed citizenship and land rights according to the tenets of the liberal revolution of early nineteenth-century Mexico.[1] In the mid-nineteenth century, Cherokee, Anishinabeg, Pequot, and Haudenosaunee intellectuals articulated Indigenous sovereignty and nationhood against the backdrop of ethnic cleansing.[2] Acting in a similar vein during the 1930s, California Indian storytellers established their sources and intellectual traditions as viable ways of understanding California's past, present, and future. And they fought for their sovereignty.

California Indian oral traditions and historical arguments were important sources of political activism and self-determination in an anticolonial moment. African Americans used the WPA slave narratives to critique slavery, Reconstruction, and their current situation in Depression-era Jim Crow America. California Indians told their version of the state's history in a way that defied Settler understandings of the past. The so-called California story portrayed California Indians as racially degraded, docile, and disappearing. Histories of Indian removal justified ethnic cleansing in the name of economic development and humanitarianism. California Indian oral narratives subverted these understandings of the past. Pomos and Paiutes argued that they possessed their own rationale for warfare and were effective, if not superior, combatants. Concows and Paiutes interpreted Indian removal as a lived experience, one full of pain, trauma, and violence.

Traditional stories expressed everyday Peoples' politics. Scholars have done an excellent job of narrating the creation and rejection of Indian Reorganization Act (IRA) tribal governments. The focus on institutions and federal policy, however, has obscured the political activism of local Native People. California Indians expressed their sovereignty as much as those Native men and women who created and opposed tribal governments. Ojibwe scholar Scott Richard Lyon defines sovereignty as an effort to reclaim what has been lost during the processes of colonialism.[3] Concows used oral narratives and histories of their homeland to reclaim the land from which they had been ethnically cleansed. Paiutes established themselves as significant players in the Owens Valley Water Wars, with their identity and ways of knowing hanging in the balance. These stories charted a path forward for Indigenous People and established Indigenous power over historical events. Prophets knew how to deal with Settler newcomers. The Myth People, important to Concow oral traditions, had already traveled the path that Concows walked when they were removed in the 1860s. Paiutes instructed listeners that diminutive people possessed the power to shape and change the world. The subaltern voices from 1930s California challenged colonial understandings of the world and asserted alternative forms of power.

Yet California Indians' efforts to indigenize the state's history, like the New Deal itself, were limited. New Deal programs failed to challenge Jim Crow segregation at the same time that they helped realign party politics. The secretary of the interior, the commissioner of Indian affairs, and Congress retained control over Indigenous land and politics and even who had access to the positive aspects of the Indian Reorganization Act. Few people incorporated or understood California Indian oral narratives as history or criticism. *The Indians of California v. the United States* (1928) ignored the arguments that California Indians made in their traditional narratives. Rather than recognize California Indian understandings of identity and land as expressed in their creation stories, *Indians of California* rejected the notion that California Indians possessed legal rights to California's land and depicted them as wandering savages. Although California Indians won the case, the compensation was paltry: in 1950 they received a check for $150 for the lands lost because the U.S. Senate failed to ratify treaties. Although Susie Wathen and Lucy Young challenged the ideas that undergirded California and western history, scholars continued to use traditional stories as ethnographic information, not alterative historical narratives. It was not until the 1950s, when non-Indian historians challenged and problematized terms like *frontier* and *pioneer*, that ethnohistorians and then the New Western historians assaulted the frontier narrative. If anthropologists, lawyers, and historians did not listen to California Indians in the 1930s, then why should we?

Oral narratives contribute to a history of political activism in Indian Country. American Indians did not immediately become conquered peoples when moved to reservations. Instead they modified and maintained their traditional stories and deployed them as weapons against attempted oppression. During the Great Depression Native People empowered themselves. Rather than turn to federal Indian policy, California Indians looked inward, relying on their own oral traditions and ways of knowing to chart a path toward the future. Across Indian Country in the twentieth century, from Lakotas seeking the return of the Black Hills to Clyde Warrior's speech when he ran for president of the National Indian Youth Council to Indian gaming and "red capitalism," Native Peoples have made similar decisions. Rather than consider Indian history a narrative of defeat, perhaps we should look at these political forms. This book reminds us that Indigenous ways of knowing survived and found expression in the ongoing processes of colonialism.

NOTES

PREFACE

1 In this book I define *ethnic cleansing* as a war crime in which Settlers, or the United States, forcibly removed an ethnic group, in this case the Concow, from their homeland. For two books that utilize ethnic cleansing, see Anderson's *Ethnic Cleansing and the Indian* and *The Conquest of Texas*. By "utilizing ethnic cleansing," I do not mean to suggest that genocide did not occur in North America, as Anderson argues. Rather I see ethnic cleansing and genocide as two distinct crimes that require historical investigation.
2 For Charles Wright's life, see Bauer, *We Were All Like Migrant Workers Here*, 204-16.
3 Charles Wright (Concow), reel 204-3, notebook no. 204.26.

INTRODUCTION

1 Throughout the book I capitalize *People* and *Settler*. Borrowing from Vine Deloria Jr. and Robert K. Thomas, American Indian studies scholar Tom Holm argues that "peoplehood" "transcend[s] the notions of statehood, nationalism, gender, ethnicity and sectarian membership." Holm identifies four "interwoven and dependent" factors of peoplehood: language, sacred history, religion, and land. Holm et al., "Peoplehood," 11, 12. Scholar Adam Barker defines *Settlers* as "peoples who occupy lands previously stolen or in the process of being taken from their Indigenous inhabitants or who are otherwise members of the 'Settler society,' which is founded on co-opted lands and resources" ("The Contemporary Reality of Canadian Imperialism," 328).
2 Lucy Young (Lassik), reel 204-2, notebook no. 204.23: 1757. For Young's history, see Smith, "Lucy Young, or T'tcetsa"; Smith, *Freedom's Frontier*, 144–46. Other Native People who were interviewed in the early twentieth century also noted that non-Indian academics ignored Native histories. See, for instance, Jacoby, *Shadows at Dawn*, 143–44. I utilize "Wailacki" rather than "Walaki" because it is the preferred spelling on the Round Valley Reservation.
3 Baker and Baker, *The WPA Oklahoma Slave Narratives*; Shaw, "Using the WPA Ex-Slave Narratives to Study the Impact of the Great Depression"; Mangione, *The Dream and the Deal*, 257. The WPA also conducted fieldwork with Mexican and Mexican American women in New Mexico (Rebolledo and Marquez, *Women's Tales from the New Mexico WPA*).
4 The work yielded 160 notebooks, recording interviews with about one hundred California Indians.
5 Alfred Kroeber to Frank McLaughlin, State Director of SERA, April 9, 1935, and Alfred Kroeber to Roy Nash, April 9, 1935, both in Records of the Department of Anthropology, CU-23, box 134, folder SERA.
6 Jeff Joaquin (Hopland Pomo), reel 204-2, notebook no. 204.18: 1539. Similarly, in Inyo County anthropologist Frank Essene complained, "The material I'm getting is not so startling. Its quite similar to that [Frederick] Hulse got, I'm afraid the Paiute seem to have a remarkably uniform culture. Everyone knows the story of Hinanoo (the whistling dove)

and insists on telling it." Frank Essene to Alfred Kroeber, January 19, 1936, CU-23, box 54, folder Essene, Frank. It is clear that Paiutes considered the story important and insisted that each person record a version of it.

7. On authority in oral narratives, see Nabokov, *A Forest of Time*, 52–57.
8. Anthropologist Peter Nabokov describes "Indigenous ways of history" in *A Forest of Time*.
9. Waziyatawin, *Remember This!*, 27. Jan Vansina defines oral histories as those stories that have "passed from mouth to mouth, for a period beyond the lifetime of the [storyteller]" (*Oral Tradition as History*, 12–13).
10. Noenoe Silva writes, "One of the basic virtues of a genealogical world view is that it places people in a great chain of being: it links them not only to the past but to the future through children and grandchildren" (*Aloha Betrayed*, 110).
11. Anthropologist Keith Basso defines a "place world" as "a particular universe of objects and events ... wherein portions of the past are brought into being" (*Wisdom Sits in Places*, 6). On place and Indigenous ways of knowing, see Nabokov, *A Forest of Time*, 126–49; Cruikshank, *The Social Life of Stories*, 16–21; Fixico, *The American Indian Mind in a Linear World*; Lowman and Barker, "Indigenizing Approaches to Research."
12. On oral tradition as history, see Hill, *Rethinking History and Myth*; Waziyatawin, *Remember This!*; Vansina, *Oral Tradition as History*; Fixico, *American Indian Mind in a Linear World*; Nabokov, *A Forest of Time*; Deloria, *Red Earth, White Lies*. Anthropologist Marshall Sahlins has argued for a culturally relativistic approach to understanding history and historical production in *Islands of History*.
13. Cruikshank, *The Social Life of Stories*, xiii. Creek scholar Craig Womack writes, "Oral tradition has always contained within it this level of political critique" (*Red on Red*, 57). In a similar way Maori scholar Linda Tuhiwai Smith suggests that Indigenous Peoples have "two major strands" with which to criticize colonialism, and one of them "draws upon a notion of authenticity, of a time before colonization in which we were intact as indigenous peoples. We had absolute authority over our lives; we were born into and lived in a universe which was entirely of our making." The other strand is "an analysis of how we were colonized, of what that has meant in terms of our immediate past and what it means for our present and future" (*Decolonizing Methodologies*, 24). See also Alfred and Corntassel, "Being Indigenous," 597.
14. Platt, *Grave Matters*, 61.
15. Historians have found similar historical projects in New England, Arizona, and the Great Lakes. See O'Brien, *Firsting and Lasting*; Jacoby, *Shadows at Dawn*, 228–44; Buss, *Winning the West with Words*. Scholars interested in settler colonialism and frontier historiography owe a debt to the iconoclastic Jennings, *The Invasion of America*, esp. 3–14.
16. California Indian oral storytellers join with those Indigenous Peoples in North, Central, and South America who adopted literacy and reframed their history and reinterpreted the causes of historical change. See Silva, *Aloha Betrayed*; Konkle, *Writing Indian Nations*; O'Brien, *Firsting and Lasting*, 145–99; Haas, *Pablo Tac, Indigenous Scholar*; Rappaport, *The Politics of Memory*; Denetdale, *Reclaiming Diné History*; Waziyatawin, *Remember This!*
17. On the intersection of past and present in oral tradition, see also Nabokov, *A Forest of Time*, 85–104; Vansina, *Oral Tradition as History*; Wickwire, "Stories from the Margins," 456. On the significance of place, as opposed to land, see Schneider, "'There's Something in the Water,'" esp. 161n1.
18. Johnson, *K-344*.
19. For work on the theft of the Owens Valley water, see Libecap, *Owens Valley Revisited*; Hoffman, *Vision or Villainy*; Walton, *Western Times and Water Wars*; Reisner, *Cadillac*

Desert; Walter, "The Land Exchange Act of 1937"; Kahrl, *Water and Power*; Franklin, "Desiccating a Valley and a People.".

20 Anthropologist Peter Nabokov describes American Indian ways of history as a "thick rope, a long ladder, or a wide corridor, which also allows for two-way traffic" (*A Forest of Time*, 71).

21 Six years later the Indian Reorganization Act promised to revitalize tribal economies and reorganize tribal governments. For the Indian New Deal and the revitalization of Indian economies and reorganization of tribal governments, see Taylor, *The New Deal and American Indian Tribalism*; Kelly, *The Assault on Assimilation*; Philp, *John Collier's Crusade for Indian Reform*. For local histories of the Indian New Deal, see Frank and Goldberg, *Defying the Odds*; Rosier, *Rebirth of the Blackfeet Nation*; Iverson, *When Indians Became Cowboys*, 116–50; McPherson, *Navajo Land, Navajo Culture*; Weisiger, *Dreaming of Sheep in Navajo Country*; Parman, *Navahos and the New Deal*. For critical assessments of the Indian New Deal, see Lowery, *Lumbee Indians in the Jim Crow South*; Biolsi, *Organizing the Lakota*.

22 I have found the following work helpful in framing the New Deal and Great Depression: Fraser and Gerstle, *The Rise and Fall of the New Deal Order*. For concise overviews of the global impacts of the Depression, see Rothermund, *The Global Impact of the Great Depression*, 136–48; Rothermund, *The Routledge Companion to Decolonization*, 41–42. Helpful works on the Federal Writers' Project and the New Deal's folk focus are Hirsch, *Portrait of America*; Mangione, *The Dream and the Deal*; Stott, *Documentary Expression and Thirties America*. Helpful works on African Americans in the Great Depression and New Deal include Sklaroff, *Black Culture and the New Deal*; Sitkoff, *A New Deal for Blacks*; Weiss, *Farewell to the Party of Lincoln*.

23 Schrader, *The Indian Arts and Crafts Board*; Meyn, *More Than Curiosities*; McLerran, *A New Deal for Native Art*.

24 Morgan, "Constructions and Contestations of the Authoritative Voice."

25 Chantal Norrgard, "Beyond Folklore: Historical Writing and Treaty Rights Activism in the Bad River WPA," in Hosmer and Nesper, *Tribal Worlds*, 185–218; Adriana Greci Green, "Anishinaabe Gathering Rights and Market Arts: The WPA Indian Handicraft Project in Michigan," in Hosmer and Nesper, *Tribal Worlds*, 219–52.

26 Fixico writes, "The *longue durée* history of Indians existed long before relations with the United States and well before the arrival of Christopher Columbus" (*Call for Change*, 21).

27 Unlike in the contemporaneous court case involving Hualapai land, though, few listened to California Indian histories in the 1920s and 1930s.

CHAPTER 1. CREATING

1 Austin McLaine (Concow), reel 204-3, notebook no. 204.37: 1965. McLaine did not call this figure Earth Maker, only "a man." In other Concow and Maidu versions, scholars identify this figure as Earth Maker. See Loeb, "The Creator Concept among the Indians of North Central California," 472.

2 Hank Hunter (Independence Paiute), reel 153-155, notebook no. 48: 129.

3 Lizzie Tillotson (Yuki), reel 204-4, notebook no. 204.40: 3129. As with McLaine, Tillotson did not name Taikomol' in the story. She only described him as "a man." The Yuki creation story was part of the instruction young men underwent, perhaps explaining Tillotson's reluctance to provide the creator's name because it might have transgressed Yuki gender norms. For Taikomol' and the male religious school, see Kroeber, "Yuki Myths," 906; Loeb, "The Creator Concept among the Indians of North Central California," 472.

4   Tuan, *Topophilia*, 23.
5   Indigenous ways of knowing are, in part, experiential, "based in the experiences of each individual on and with the rest of the world." Lowman and Barker, "Indigenizing Approaches to Research."
6   Lizzie Tillotson (Yuki), reel 204-4, notebook no. 204.40: 3129–30. Throughout the book I utilize the spelling of Indigenous words, such as *me căus cō*, that I found in the original notebooks.
7   Austin McLaine (Concow), reel 204-3, notebook no. 204.27: 1964–66.
8   Hank Hunter (Independence Paiute), reel 153-155, notebook no. 48: 129–30.
9   Indigenous ways of knowing "stress a sociocultural kinship of relationships" (Fixico, *The American Indian Mind in a Linear World*, 22; see also Lowman and Barker, "Indigenizing Approaches to Research"). At its core labor is a "social phenomenon, carried on by human beings bonded to one another in society" (Wolf, *Europe and the People without History*, 74).
10 For work and labor in northern California, see Bauer, *"We Were All Like Migrant Workers Here."*
11 Sven Liljeblad, "Oral Tradition: Content and Style of Verbal Arts," 645–47, and Sven Liljeblad and Catherine Fowler, "Owens Valley Paiute," 428, both in d'Azevedo, *Handbook of North American Indians*. See Steward, "Ethnography of the Owens Valley Paiutes," 278–85, 320–21 for the Round or Circle Dance. Other singers specialized in antelope songs, which attracted antelope to kill sites.
12 "Indigenous ontology," Lowman and Barker explain, "is premised on the understanding that all life possess its own intelligence which can be learned from and interacted with" ("Indigenizing Approaches to Research").
13 Hank Hunter (Independence Paiute), reel 153-155, notebook no. 48: 130–31. Anthropologist Peter Nabokov points out that Coyote is sometimes the cocreator of the universe, as he appears in this Owens Valley Paiute story, which seems to contradicts his more famous guise as "glutton, thief, clown and mischief maker." Nabokov concludes that Coyote is the ultimate shape-shifter: "Sorting out Coyote's mutually contradictory range of personalities often exposes outsiders' deepest fantasies of escape from convention or institutionalization—simply proving, once again, his persistent power to outfox our psyches" (*A Forest of Time*, 108–16, quotes 110, 115).
14 Little Toby (Yuki) and George Moore (Yuki), reel 204-4, notebook no. 204.38: 2986–87.
15 Mary Saulque (Paiute) and Emma Washington (Paiute), reel 205, notebook no. 205.3: 99.
16 Polly Anderson (Concow), reel 204.3, notebook no. 204.34: 2705.
17 For the comparison between creation and baskets, see an earlier Yuki creation story in Kroeber, "Yuki Myths," 908.
18 There were three similar descriptions of Coyote's house. George Robinson, from Independence, said, "In the eastern part of the Round Valley [in Inyo County], a large rock stands alone by the side of the road, which was, as the legend say, the hut of the coyote" (reel 153-155, notebook no. 46: 39). Paiute Jim Tom Jones from Inyo County's Round Valley identified a different place but in the same region as Robinson: "This cave is near the Indian picture rock in Round Valley, close to the rock quarry" (reel 149-152, notebook no. 29: 129). Paiute Mattie Bulpitt described Coyote/first man's house as being a rock near a quarry in Round Valley (reel 153-155, notebook no. 33: 306).
19 Miller, "Basin Religion and Theology," 77, 78.
20 Jim Tom Jones (Paiute), reel 149-152, notebook no. 29: 129–32.
21 George Robinson (Paiute), reel 153-155, Notebook no. 46: 40.
22 In her introduction to *The WPA Guide to California* Gwendolyn Wright writes, "For an unknown age before the white man stumbled upon them in the sixteenth century, the

NOTES TO CHAPTER I 129

Indians of California had dwelt in their scattered bands, walled off from the rest of the aboriginal world, by mountains and deserts. . . . The scattered bands dwelt in isolation from one another. Each fishing in its own creek, catching game in its own preserves, gathering nuts, seeds and berries in its own forests" (33–34).

23 Anthropologist Keith Basso defined "place-world."
24 I owe a debt to the late Pacific Island scholar Epeli Hau'ofa for his idea of "world enlargement." Hau'ofa argues that throughout the history of Polynesia and Oceania Indigenous people have pushed the boundaries of their world ("Our Sea of Islands," 10–11). Wakuénis, a People living in the Isana-Guinía River drainage on the border of Colombia and Venezuela, possess a similar understanding of space and time: "The spatial movements of [first man] Kuwái and [first woman] Amáru in the primordial past are not described as mere journeys between places that already exist, but as a dynamic process of creating spatial distances between places" (Jonathan Hill and R. Wright, "Time, Narrative and Ritual: Historical Interpretations from an Amazonian Society," in Hill, *Rethinking History and Myth*, 87).
25 Nancy Dobey (Wailacki), reel 204-2, notebook no. 204.20: 1630. For humans' perceptions of dark and light, see Tuan, *Topophilia*, 25. The classic statement on Euro-American views of white and black is Jordan, *White over Black*. Historian Alden T. Vaughan describes how Euro-Americans began to identify American Indians as "red" in the mid-eighteenth century and established the color as a racial category in the nineteenth century ("From White Man to Redskin").
26 Susie Butcher (Paiute), reel 205-206, notebook no. 205.1: 16.
27 Austin McLaine (Concow), reel 204-3, notebook no. 204.27: 2084.
28 Jim Jones (Paiute), reel 149-152, notebook no. 29: 132.
29 Haas, *Pablo Tac, Indigenous Scholar*, 169. On the importance of language and "peoplehood," see Holm et al., "Peoplehood," 13.
30 Mary Saulque (Paiute) and Emma Washington (Paiute), reel 205-206, notebook no. 205.3: 99.
31 Jim Jones (Paiute), reel 149-152, notebook no. 29: 132.
32 George Robinson (Paiute), reel 153-155, notebook no. 46: 41.
33 Tuan writes that people construct ethnocentric understandings of place and people: "They saw their habitat not only as the world's geographic center, but also its cultural and population center" (*Topophilia*, 34).
34 Mose Weyland (Paiute), reel 153-155, notebook no. 35: 339; Austin McLaine (Concow), reel 204-3, notebook no. 204.27: 1966–67.
35 Nancy Dobey (Wailacki), reel 204-2, notebook no. 204.20: 1636–38.
36 Mose Weyland (Paiute), reel 153-155, notebook no. 35: 342. For a description of Paiute flutes, see Steward, "Ethnography of the Owens Valley Paiutes," 277.
37 Mose Weyland (Paiute), reel 153-155, notebook no. 35: 342–43.
38 Owens Valley Paiutes married within and outside their polity's boundaries. Within Owens Valley, Paiutes from the Bishop area often married those from Lone Pine. Owens Valley Paiutes and Mono Lake Paiutes also married Western Monos, Panamint Shoshones, and Awani Miwoks (Steward, "Ethnography of the Owens Valley Paiutes," 294). Theodore Binnema explains that exogamous marriage practices formed interethnic relations on the northern Plains (*Common and Contested Ground*, 13–14). For northern California, see Chase-Dunn and Mann, *The Wintu and Their Neighbors*, 108.
39 Steward, "Ethnography of the Owens Valley Paiutes," 295.
40 Mose Weyland (Paiute), reel 153-155, notebook no. 35: 339.
41 Steward, "Ethnography of the Owens Valley Paiutes," 289–90.

42 Austin McLaine (Concow), reel 204-3, notebook no. 204.27: 1967. Concows believe that upon a person's death his or her soul or "heart" left the body through the mouth and "retrace[d] every step taken in life." After taking this journey, the "heart" followed the Milky Way toward "Heaven Valley" or "a paradise of food and pleasure" (Francis A. Riddell, "Maidu and Konkow," in Heizer, *Handbook of North American Indians*, 382.

43 Mose Weyland (Paiute), reel 153-155, notebook no. 35: 339.

44 Austin McLaine (Concow), reel 204-3, notebook no. 204.27: 1973–76.

45 Roberts, *Concow-Maidu Indians of Round Valley*, 18–19. For Paiutes, see Steward, "Ethnography of the Owens Valley Paiutes," 285–86.

46 Austin McLaine (Concow), reel 204-3, notebook no. 204.37: 1969. In another Maidu oral tradition, Earth Maker planted the first acorn tree near Durham, California (Gifford and Harris Block, *California Indian Nights*, 85–91).

47 Lizzie Tillotson (Yuki), reel 204-4, notebook no. 204.40: 3131.

48 Austin McLaine (Concow), reel 204-3, notebook no. 204.37: 1969–70.

49 Jim Jones (Paiute), reel 149-152, notebook no. 29: 132; Mary Saulque and Emma Washington (Paiute), reel 205-206, notebook no. 205.3: 99. For a description of baskets, see Steward, "Ethnography of the Owens Valley Paiutes," 270–74.

50 During the nineteenth and twentieth centuries "big times" remained relevant social, cultural, and political events in California Indian communities. In the 1850s treaty negotiations afforded an opportunity for a big time as Maidus and Concows feasted on cattle provided by the federal government. In the late nineteenth and early twentieth century Concows left the Round Valley Reservation to pick hops on ranches in Mendocino County. When the workday concluded, Concows and other Round Valley Indians participated in grass game events until the wee hours of the night (Bauer, *"We Were All Like Migrant Workers Here,"* 28, 29, 74, 75, 81, 93, 119, 137, 143, 168, 172). In the twentieth century Miwoks hosted big times at their *rancherías* and traveled to Yosemite National Park for an annual July big time (Spence, "Dispossessing the Wilderness," 50–51; Maniery and Dutschke, "Northern Miwok at Big Bar," 488–90; Maniery, "A Chronicle of Murphey's Rancheria (Mol-Pee-So)," 191, 193; Currie, "Bidwell Rancheria," 315; Garth, "Emphasis on Industriousness among the Atsugewi," 556n9, 565).

51 Julian Steward reported that a Paiute *musa* still stood at Big Pine creek in the 1930s ("Ethnography of Owens Valley Paiutes," 265).

52 Gendzel, "Pioneers and Padres," 62–70; Weber, *The Spanish Frontier in North America*, 341–46; Platt, *Grave Matters*, 60–61.

53 Gendzel, "Pioneers and Padres," 59–61. For a brief history of the Native Sons, see Conmy, *The Origin and Purposes of the Native Sons and Native Daughters of the Golden West*.

54 McCulley, *The Mark of Zorro*.

55 Bancroft, *History of the Pacific States of North America*, 474.

56 Platt, *Grave Matters*, 58–59; Gendzel, "Pioneers and Padres," 74.

57 Bancroft, *History of the Pacific States of North America*, 474.

58 Platt, *Grave Matters*, 58, 60. By "genocide," I mean acts committed with the "intent to destroy" an ethnic group. For a definition and discussion of genocide, see Madley, "Reexamining the American Genocide Debate," esp. 103; Lindsay, *Murder State*; Madley, "California's Yuki Indians."

59 For a concise overview of treaty making in California, see Robert Heizer, "Treaties," in *Handbook of North American Indians*, 701–4.

60 Johnson, *K-344*, 58–59, 61–65; Heizer, "Treaties," 701–4; Omer Stewart, "Litigation and Its Effects," in Heizer, *Handbook of North American Indians*, 706; Edward Castillo, "Twentieth Century Secular Movements," in Heizer, *Handbook of North American Indians*, 715.

NOTES TO CHAPTER 1   131

While working for the Club, Frederick G. Collett, a controversial advocate for California Indians, canvassed the state raising money and support for California Indians to bring a claim against the U.S. government. Collett collected dues from California Indians, but an investigation into his activities revealed that he used $30,000 of the dues for personal expenses. For an insightful look at Frederick Collett, see Wright, "'We Cast Our Lot with the Indians from That Day On.'"

In 1920 Lakotas in South Dakota successfully lobbied to bring a claim against the United States for the theft of the Black Hills (Lazarus, *Black Hills, White Justice*, 119–49). For Hualapais, see McMillen, *Making Indian Law*. For Tlingits, see Baumgarte, "Alaska Natives and the Power of Perseverance."

61   Quoted in U.S. House of Representatives, "To Amend an Act Entitled 'An Act Authorizing the Attorney General of the State of California to Bring Suit in the Court of Claims on Behalf of the Indians of California,'" 1. See also Johnson, *K-344*, 64, 67; Goldberg and Champagne, "Ramona Redeemed?," 43.

62   Costo and Costo, *Natives of the Golden State*, 301; Burnett quote from Johnson, *K-344*, 54; Harold Driver, "Excerpts from the Writings of A. L. Kroeber on Land Use and Political Organization of California Indians, with Comments by Harold E. Driver," in *California Indians IV*, 107 (pagination refers to the book, not the report, which in this case is 32). For *tribelet*, see also Alfred Kroeber, "Basic Report on California Indian Land Holdings," in Driver, *California Indians IV*, 19, 25–26; and Kroeber, "The Patwin and Their Neighbors," 258–59. Despite opposition from California Indians since the 1980s, *tribelet* has persisted as a way of describing California Indian tribal nations. California Indians argue that the tribelet may have been a post-Spanish and postgenocide "social grouping" rather than one that existed in precontact California. The term also connotes an "impression of pre-contact California as a region of extremely small-scale, provincial cultures that lacked forms of large-scale integration." In a sense the term freezes California Indians in stasis and leads scholars away from considering how Indigenous peoples interacted with their neighbors and Indigenous peoples in more distant locales, such as modern-day Vancouver Island and the Great Basin (Leventhal et al., "The Ohlone Back from Extinction," 300). See also Costo and Costo, *Natives of the Golden State*, 44–45.

63   Nancy Dobey (Wailacki), reel 204-2, notebook no. 204.20: 1638–39.

64   Ibid.

65   Little Toby and George Moore (Yuki), reel 204-4, notebook no. 204.38: 2987–88.

66   The Doctrine of Discovery dates to the Crusades, when Pope Innocent IV declared that Christian nations could invade the lands of non-Christians. The legal implications of this papal decree were applied to North America in the fifteenth and sixteenth centuries. For an overview of the Doctrine of Discovery, see Miller, *Native America, Discovered and Conquered*.

67   For an overview of these land policies, see Banner, *Dispossessing the Pacific*, 163–94.

68   Adams and Schneider, "'Washington Is a Long Way Off.'"

69   For an overview of the Western Shoshone case, see Crum, *The Road on Which We Came*; Rusco, "Historic Change in Western Shoshone Country." For the Lakota case, see Lazarus, *Black Hills, White Justice*.

70   Johnson, *K-344*, 81–82; Stewart, "Litigation and Its Effects," 706.

CHAPTER 2. NAMING

1. The Paiute suffixes *-witü* and *-patü* translate into "place" (Steward, "Ethnography of the Owens Valley Paiute," 236–37). Similarly the Yuki suffix *-nom* means "people of" (Elmendorf and Shepherd, "Another Look at Wappo-Yuki Loans," 223, 225).
2. Jake Gilbert (Mono Paiute), reel 149-152, notebook no. 26: 21.
3. Billy Rice (Pomo), reel 204-1, notebook no. 204.5: 290.
4. Austin McLaine and Annie Feliz (Concow), reel 204-3, notebook no. 204.30: 2309–10.
5. As Maori scholar Linda Tuhiwai Smith argues, the presence of Indigenous People confronts colonial hegemony. The existence of Indigenous place-names challenges the historical narratives on which colonial hegemony is established (*Decolonizing Methodologies*, 24).
6. The mapping and (re)naming of the American West, historian Jared Farmer notes, was as much a part of colonialism and colonization as the military or the railroad (*On Zion's Mount*, 18). For discovery ritual, see Miller, *Native America, Discovered and Conquered*, 110–13, 126–56.
7. O'Brien, *Firsting and Lasting*.
8. "Naming," geographer Yi-Fu Tuan reminds us, "is power . . . the creative power to call something into being, to render the invisible visible, to impart a certain character of things" ("Language and the Making of Place," 688).
9. Anthropologist Rodney Frey called these actors Myth People ("Oral Traditions," in Biolsi, *A Companion to the Anthropology of American Indian*, 155). Apaches understand their history and place-naming in a similar fashion. Charles Henry told anthropologist Keith Basso a narrative of Apache migration that culminated with Apache leaders naming a place so that "we must be able to speak about this place and remember it clearly and well" (Basso, *Wisdom Sits in Places*, 11–12).
10. Susie Wathen (Pomo), reel 204.1, notebook no. 204.1: 104–18. Other names for these lakes include *xa-siliū* or *xala-xatū*, which translates into Clam Lake; *dilē-xa* (middle water); and *xa-cīnal* (water head). See Barrett, "The Ethno-Geography of the Pomo and Neighboring Indians," 130, n114.
11. John McWhinney (Ukiah Pomo), reel 204-1, notebook no. 204.3: 182–92. On the commonality of the story, see Dangel, "Bear and Fawns."
12. Sally McLendon, "Cultural Presuppositions and Discourse Analysis: Patterns of Presupposition and Assertion of Information in Eastern Pomo and Russian Narrative," in Saville-Troike, *Linguistics and Anthropology*, 162.
13. See, for instance, Lowie, "Oral Tradition and History."
14. Susie Wathen (Pomo), reel 204.1, notebook no. 204.1: 104–18. For Bagi'l and another oral tradition about this place, see Barrett, "The Ethno-Geography of the Pomo and Neighboring Indians," 130–31, n114.
15. M. Kat Anderson writes, "The roots of *Angelica* sp. were most prized for medicine and as a talisman when collected from plants growing in cold places" (*Tending the Wild*, 53).
16. John McWhinney (Ukiah Pomo), reel 204-1, notebook no. 204.3: 188.
17. Susie Wathen (Pomo), reel 204.1, notebook no. 204.1: 116.
18. Gudde, *California Placenames*, 39.
19. Parkman, "The Supernatural Frontier in Pomo Cosmology."
20. Susie Wathen (Pomo), reel 204.1, notebook no. 204.1: 110, 118.
21. Ibid., 112.
22. Ibid., 105–6.

NOTES TO CHAPTER 2   133

23 For an overview of Pomo trade trails and others in California, see Davis, "Trail Routes and Economic Exchange."
24 Susie Wathen (Pomo), reel 204.1, notebook no. 204.1: 116–17.
25 Ibid., 117.
26 In his famous critique of the Indian Wars, Dee Brown writes, "Americans who have always looked westward when reading about this period should read this book facing eastward" (*Bury My Heart at Wounded Knee*, xii). Historian Daniel Richter uses the phrase *facing east* to "outline stories of North America during the period of European colonization rather than of the European colonial of North America" (*Facing East from Indian Country*, 1, 7–9, quote 9).
27 Historian Brian DeLay, for instance, argues that the U.S. victory in the Mexican-American War was made possible by nearly a decade of Comanche and Kiowa raids into northern Mexico. See his *A War of a Thousand Deserts*.
28 On pioneers, see Buss, *Winning the West with Words*.
29 Gilbert appeared in the 1905–6 census of off-reservation Indians in California with an unnamed wife and three children (Kelsey, *Census of Non-Reservation California Indians*, 80).
30 Jake Gilbert (Paiute), reel 149-152, notebook no. 26: 4–5.
31 On place in Numic-speaking People's oral tradition, see Gelo, "Recalling the Past in Creating the Present."
32 Paiutes called their doctors *pühá'ga, pü'hükü, puhagü,* or *pü'nagi* (Steward, "Ethnography of the Owens Valley Paiutes," 311).
33 Ibid., 308. For a concise overview of *puha*, see Miller, "Basin Religion and Theology."
34 Jake Gilbert (Mono Paiute), reel 149-152, notebook no. 26: 21–22.
35 Bridgeport Tom (Paiute), reel 149-152, notebook no. 27: 56–57.
36 For wolves, see Coleman, *Vicious*.
37 Steward, "Ethnography of the Owens Valley Paiutes," 250, 256.
38 Laylander, "California's Prehistory as a Remembered Past," 170.
39 Steward, "Ethnography of the Owens Valley Paiutes," 236, 329. Owens Valley Paiutes informed Steward that few Owens Valley and Mono Paiutes could understand the Northern Paiute language.
40 Makley and Makley, *Cave Rock*, 10–11. Anthropologist Julian Steward refers to the Washoe as the Paiutes' "traditional enemies," but there are no direct references to conflict in this story ("Ethnography of the Owens Valley Paiutes," 235).
41 Zappia, *Traders and Raiders*.
42 For the naming of Owens Valley, see Chalfant, *The Story of Inyo*, 47. For Owens Valley's history, see Dean et al., *Weaving a Legacy*, 16–20; Bahr, *Viola Martinez, California Paiute*, 13, 18, 20–22, 28; Michael, "At the Plow and in the Harvest Field," 16–19; Wilson, "Owens Valley Paiutes," 12, 23–24.
43 Blackhawk, *Violence over the Land*, 133–44.
44 Chalfant, *The Story of Inyo*, 42–44.
45 Miller, *Native America, Discovered and Conquered*; Miller et al., *Discovering Indigenous Lands*, 72–73.
46 Chalfant, *The Story of Inyo*, frontispiece. Jean O'Brien writes about New England in *Firsting and Lasting*.
47 Chalfant, *The Story of Inyo*, chaps. 3 and 4, p. 9. In the twentieth century archaeologists and anthropologists dismissed Chalfant's ideas. They argue that people occupied the Owens Valley as early as 3500 bce and that Owens Valley Paiute ethnogenesis occurred

sometime between 600 and 1000 CE (Sven Liljeblad and Catherine Fowler, "Owens Valley Paiute," in d'Azevedo, *Handbook of North American Indians*, 412).

48 For place-names, see Gudde, *California Place Names*, 187, 156, 363, 415.
49 For Paiute removal, see Crum, "Deeply Attached to the Land."
50 See Kahrl, *Water and Power*; Reisner, *Cadillac Desert*; Libecap, *Owens Valley Revisited*; Hoffman, *Vision or Villainy*.
51 There are correctives. See Walter, "The Land Exchange Act of 1937"; Walton, *Western Times and Water Wars*; Franklin, "Desiccating a Valley and a People."
52 Austin McLaine (Concow), 204-3, notebook no. 204.28: 2131–46. For the Maidu term, see Luthin, *Surviving through the Days*, 250; Shipley, *The Maidu Indian Myths and Stories of Hanc'ibyjim*, 6; Shipley, "Maidu Texts and Dictionary," 174.
53 Annie Feliz (Concow), reel 204-3, notebook no. 204.31: 2438–39.
54 My discussion of landmarks benefits from historian Jared Farmer's definition: "a legible feature of the landscape where meaning is concentrated" (*On Zion's Mount*, 13–15).
55 For the history of fire, see Pyne, *Fire*. For a discussion of fire stories in California, Oregon, and Nevada oral histories, see Shinn, "Man and the Land," 24–28.
56 Anthropologist Don Laylander argues that California Indian oral traditions cannot accurately date volcanic eruptions, though "the basic phenomenon of eruptions would have been familiar to the region's inhabitants." He adds, "It would not have been surprising for [northeastern California Indians] to have inferred the volcanic origins of [geological features] without any orally transmitted testimony from contemporary witnesses" ("California's Prehistory as a Remembered Past," 167–69). Countering Laylander's pessimistic view of California oral tradition is, of course, the work of the late Vine Deloria Jr., who argued that oral traditions about volcanoes and other geological events provide evidence for a long Indigenous occupation of North America (*Red Earth, White Lies*, 161–209).
57 Others viewed West Mountain from very different vantages. In 1883, for instance, the U.S. Geological Survey conducted a reconnaissance of Lassen Peak. After acquiring supplies at Red Bluff, the survey team approached Lassen from the west and then proceeded north (Diller, *Geology of the Lassen Peak District*, 401).
58 For West Mountain as a Concow border, see Shipley, "Maidu and Nisenan," 46; Kroeber, *Handbook of the Indians of California*, 391.
59 Aron and Adelman, "From Borderlands to Borders," 816. For an important corrective to some of Adelman and Aron's arguments, see Wunder and Hämäläinen, "Of Lethal Places and Lethal Essays," esp. 1229, 1231; Barr, "Geographies of Power."
60 Sapir and Swadesh, *Yana Dictionary*, 172; Sapir, "Yana Texts," 161. Atsugewis named the mountain Wicuhirdiki (Schulz, *Indians of Lassen Volcanic Park and Vicinity*, 145). Achumawis called the mountain Yēttĭjena (Olmstead, *Achumawi Dictionary*, 59).
61 On Esto Jamáni serving as a border between the Maidu and Wintu, see Dixon, "The Northern Maidu," 25n1.
62 Charles Wathen (Nomlacki), reel 204-4, notebook no. 204.47: 3678. For sharing, see Kroeber, *Handbook of the Indians of California*, 381. For borderlands as zones of intercultural exchange, see White, *The Middle Ground*; Anderson, *Kinsmen of Another Kind*.
63 Austin McLaine (Concow), reel 204-3, notebook no. 204.27: 1974–79.
64 The name of the figure in the story is said to be Wappen-doc-co. The name for Old Man Coyote, according to William Shipley, is Wépam Májdy or Wépam Wájsi ("Maidu Texts and Dictionary," 186).
65 Annie Feliz (Concow), reel 204-3, notebook no. 204.32: 2522–23.
66 Nabokov, *Where the Lightning Strikes*, 270; Starn, *Ishi's Brain*, 259.

NOTES TO CHAPTER 3   135

67 For agents of colonialism, which include fur traders, see Whaley, *Oregon and the Collapse of Illahee*.
68 On discovery rituals, see Miller, *Native America, Discovered and Conquered*, 20.
69 For an overview of the park's history, see Krahe and Catton, *Little Gem of the Cascades*. For naming, see Gudde, *California Place Names*, 173. For the connection between Indian removal and the National Parks, see Spence, *Dispossessing the Wilderness*; Burnham, *Indian Country, God's Country*.
70 Dixon, "The Northern Maidu," 181.
71 Annie Feliz (Concow), reel 204-3, notebook no. 204.32: 2519–24.
72 *Calque* "is a linguistic term that designates an instance in which the meaning of a word in one language has been translated into another language" (Chase-Dunn and Mann, *The Wintu and Their Neighbors*, 125). See 125–32 for a discussion of calques in Wintu territory and how the lack of calques suggests hostile relationships between two groups.

CHAPTER 3. DISCOVERING

1   On prophecies and history, see Nabokov, *A Forest of Time*, 218–32.
2   Atherton, *California*, 24. A similar rendition of contact between Miwoks and the pirate Sir Francis Drake appears in Wright, introduction, 33.
3   Mary Louise Pratt defines an anticonquest as a "[strategy] of representation" that "secure[d Settlers'] innocence in the same moment they assert . . . hegemony" (*Imperial Eyes*, 9).
4   Smoak, *Ghost Dances and Identity*; Dowd, *A Spirited Resistance*; Edmunds, *The Shawnee Prophet*; Martin, *Sacred Revolt*; Wallace, *The Death and Rebirth of the Seneca*; DuBois, *The 1870 Ghost Dance*. For female prophets, see Fur, *A Nation of Women*, 147–56.
5   Little Toby and George Moore (Yuki), reel 204-4, notebook no. 204.38: 3063–69.
6   Annie Feliz (Concow), reel 204-3, notebook no. 204.33: 2638–39.
7   Smith, "Lucy Young, or T'tcetsa."
8   Lucy Young (Lassik), reel 204-2, notebook no. 204.23: 1750–52.
9   Little Toby and George Moore (Yuki), reel 204-4, notebook no. 204.38: 3063.
10 For the role of the elderly in American Indian communities, see Basso, *Wisdom Sits in Places*, 105–50; Simmons, *The Role of the Aged in Primitive Society*, chap. 6; Pamela Amoss, "Coast Salish Elders," in Amoss and Harrell, *Other Ways of Growing Old*, 227–47; Gerry C. Williams, "Warriors No More: A Study of the American Indian Elderly," in Fry, *Aging in Culture and Society*, 101–11.
11 Kroeber, "The Patwin and Their Neighbors"; Loeb, "The Western Kuksu Cult" and "The Eastern Kuksu Cult."
12 In the late 1860s, probably 1869, a Paiute man named Wodziwob (or Fish Lake Joe), who lived at Nevada's Walker River Reservation, had a vision about the return of the dead and the restoration of a Paiute ecology. The Ghost Dance featured a Paiute Round Dance, in which dancers locked hands and danced in a left-to-right direction. After a while some dancers fell into a trance and dreamed of the dead. The dreamers informed the People of their visions and proclaimed that the dead would return if the People continued to dance. A group of prophets emerged from among the Paiutes who took the Ghost Dance message to other Native People. Prophets used modern forms of transportation, such as horseback riding and railroads, to visit reservations, remote Indigenous communities, and agricultural worksites where Native People congregated and preached the Ghost Dance. Shoshone and Paiute preachers Weneyuga (Frank Spencer) and Tavivo, or Numataivo, spread the religion to Indigenous People in Nevada and California (Hittman, "The 1870

Ghost Dance at the Walker River Reservation," 260). Hittman suggests that Wodziwob was a Fish Lake Valley Paiute. See also Thornton, *We Shall Live Again*, 1–6, 16; Kroeber, "A Ghost-Dance in California," 32, 33; Kroeber, *Handbook of the Indians of California*, 870.

13. Thornton, *We Shall Live Again*, 5, 6; Kroeber, *Handbook of the Indians of California*, 269, 376, 870; Gifford, "Southern Maidu Religious Ceremonies," 217; Lowell John Bean and Sylvia Brakke Vane, "Cults and Their Transformations," in Heizer, *Handbook of North American Indians*, 665, 670–71; Sarris, *Mabel McKay*.
14. Lucy Young, reel 2, notebook no. 204.23: 1749–50.
15. Foster, "Summary."
16. Little Toby and George Moore (Yuki), reel 204-4, notebook no. 204.38: 3064.
17. From a Yuki perspective, strangers did not speak the Yuki language and lacked kin in Yuki communities (Foster, "The Yuki," 161).
18. Shipley, "Maidu Texts and Dictionary," 149.
19. In the Pacific Northwest, for instance, Indigenous People called Englishmen (including Hawaiians, Iroquois, and French Canadians) "King George Men" and Americans (including Europeans and Asian and Latin American immigrants) "Bostons." As historian Alexandra Harmon points out, these categories were as fluid and historically contingent as conceptions of race (*Indians in the Making*, 10, 13–42).
20. In addition to oral traditions, California Indian languages adapted to include racialized understandings of People's differences. In Maidu, *wólem májdy* translates into "white person," while *pibútim májdy* translates into "charred person" or a black person. The phrase *ťadákym májdy* means "braided person" and stood for the Chinese (Shipley, "Maidu Texts and Dictionary," 149, 150).
21. Horsman, *Race and Manifest Destiny*.
22. Bancroft, *The Native Races of the Pacific States of North America*, 325.
23. Almaguer, *Racial Fault Lines*.
24. Atherton, *California*, 15.
25. Across North America, Native Peoples used prophecies and traditional stories to contemplate and create strategies to deal with the invasion of plants and animals. On the southern Plains, for instance, Kiowas tell of their cultural hero Saynday encountering Smallpox near the Washita River. Saynday first observed cattle grazing within a fenced open range on the Washita, an ominous portent of the reservation system. Then Saynday met Smallpox, who rode a black horse, powdered red by dust that plows had kicked up. Smallpox dressed like a missionary: black suit and a high hat. After exchanging pleasantries, Smallpox informed Saynday that he would be a blight on any People, killing children, scarring beautiful women, and striking down strong warriors. The quick-thinking Saynday informed Smallpox that his People, the Kiowa, were poor, but his neighbors, the Pawnees, were not. Saynday urged Smallpox to find another People to bother. After Smallpox began to travel north and visit the Pawnee, Saynday took out a flint and steel and started a prairie fire in order to make a ring of safety around Kiowa camps Calloway, *Our Hearts Fell to the Ground*, 51–53).
26. Little Toby and George Moore (Yuki), ED reel 204-4, notebook no. 204.38: 3064.
27. In *The Red Atlantic* Jace Weaver defines the "Red Atlantic" as the movement of Indigenous People and exchange of material goods across the Atlantic Ocean.
28. Nunn and Qian, "The Columbian Exchange," 171–72.
29. Weeks, *Farewell, My Nation*, 12. On gardens and farming at Round Valley, see Bauer, "We Were All Like Migrant Workers Here," 61–63; Newman. "'There Will Come a Day When White Men Will Not Rule Us,'" 192–203.
30. Little Toby and George Moore (Yuki), reel 204-4, notebook no. 204.38: 3065–66.

NOTES TO CHAPTER 3

31 Anderson, "King Philip's Herds." For the role of livestock in Indian assimilation, see Iverson, *When Indians Became Cowboys*.
32 Lucy Young (Wailacki-Lassik), reel 204-2, notebook no. 204.23: 1751.
33 For sheep and other livestock in northern California, see Carranco and Beard, *Genocide and Vendetta*, 196–97; Isenberg, *Mining California*, 128–29. Kiowas on the Southern Plains also observed the impact of ungulates' feet. When Saynday reached the Washita River before meeting Smallpox, he observed that cattle had replaced bison on the Plains: "The Washita River, which once ran bankful with clear water, was soggy with red mud" (Calloway, *Our Hearts Fell to the Ground*, 51).
34 Anderson, "King Philip's Herds," 601–24.
35 See, for instance, Adams and Schneider, "'Washington Is a Long Way Off.'"
36 Breen, "Horses and Gentlemen," 248–50.
37 Little Toby and George Moore (Yuki), reel 204-4, notebook no. 204.38: 3063–69.
38 Lucy Young (Wailacki-Lassik), reel 204-2, notebook no. 204.23: 1751.
39 In recent years the debate concerning genocide in California has been revived. Historians Benjamin Madley and Brendan C. Lindsay have persuasively applied genocide studies to California history, especially in Mendocino County and the Owens Valley. See Madley, "Reexamining the American Genocide Debate"; Madley, "California's Yuki Indians"; Lindsay, *Murder State*. Older works in California also employed the term; see Carranco and Beard, *Genocide and Vendetta*; Costo and Costo, *The Missions of California*; Norton, *Genocide in Northwestern California*.

   Historian Gary Clayton Anderson argues that what occurred in California was ethnic cleansing, not genocide (*Ethnic Cleansing and the Indian*, 3–22 generally, 192–218 specifically).
40 Keyes, "'Like a Roaring Lion,'" 20–21, 36.
41 Little Toby and George Moore (Yuki), reel 204-4, notebook no. 204.38: 3066.
42 Historian Andrew Isenberg examines the transition from an Indigenous landscape to an extractive resource landscape in California (*Mining California*, esp. 131–62 for impact on Modocs).
43 Little Toby and George Moore (Yuki), reel 204-4, notebook no. 204.38: 3067.
44 For intermarriage and the strategies that Native women employed during the fur trade, see Sleeper-Smith, *Indian Women and French Men*. Historian Elliott West describes how Cheyennes and traders used marriage to forge social and economic ties. However, with the arrival of American Settlers and prospectors, the trader husbands, Cheyenne women, and Métis offspring were pushed to the social margins (*The Contested Plains*, 78–82, 266).
45 Little Toby and George Moore (Yuki), reel 204-4, notebook no. 204.38: 3067.
46 Margaret Jacobs in *White Mother to a Dark Race* applies settler colonialism to the process of removing Indigenous children from their homes. The go-to book on Indian education remains Adams, *Education for Extinction*.
47 In *History's Shadow* historian Steven Conn argues that the development of professional history turned American Indians into "history's shadow," or people who possessed a past but not a history.
48 Bauer, *"We Were All Like Migrant Workers Here,"* 61, 66; Newman, "'There Will Come a Day,'" 203–8.
49 Little Toby and George Moore (Yuki), reel 204-4, notebook no. 204.38: 3063–64, 3069.
50 Annie Feliz (Concow), reel 204-3, notebook no. 204.33: 2638.
51 Hämäläinen, "The Rise and Fall of Plains Indian Horse Cultures," 846. For Columbia River, see Fisher, *Shadow Tribe*, 27.

52 Buechel and Manhart, *Lakota Dictionary*, 290.
53 Annie Feliz (Concow), reel 204-3, notebook no. 204.33: 2638–39.

CHAPTER 4. FIGHTING

1 By the 1930s many Americans agreed with historian Frederick Jackson Turner, who argued that the fear of Indians was a "consolidating agent" on the frontier. Historian Elliott West notes that many Americans viewed the 1877 surrender of Chief Joseph and the Nez Perce as the "last Indian War." The pursuit of Joseph signified "a sense of [white racial] superiority, the pleasure of painless reconciliation, and the catharsis of cost-free guilt" (*The Last Indian War*, 288–92, 306). See too Jacoby, *Shadows at Dawn*, 220–44; Blackhawk, *Violence over the Land*. For American innocence, see Cothran, *Remembering the Modoc War*. A classic revision of the Indian Wars is Brown, *Bury My Heart at Wounded Knee*.
2 Atherton, *California*, 15. These ideas persisted well into the twentieth century. As lawyer Kenneth Johnson wrote in the 1960s, "The California Indian, though somewhat quarrelsome, was not warlike" (*K-344*, 10).
3 Gray, *History of California from 1542*, 337. Robert Glass Cleland added the Pit River and Klamaths to the bellicose Modocs, who "wantonly attacked and massacred small parties of whites" (*From Wilderness to Empire*, 286).
4 Indian-white violence has been a popular theme and topic in California Indian studies. See Madley, "Reexamining the American Genocide Debate" and "California's Yuki Indians"; Lindsay, *Murder State*; Baumgardher, *Killing for Land in Early California*; Secrest, *When the Great Spirit Died*; Carranco and Beard, *Genocide and Vendetta*; Norton, *Genocide in Northwestern California*.
5 Kroeber, *Handbook of the Indians of California*, 152–53.
6 Tony Francisco (Lake County), reel 204-1, notebook no. 204.9: 694. For Kabe'lal and Kabedile, see McLendon and Oswalt, "Pomo: Introduction," in Heizer, ed., *Handbook*, 284. For Kulukau, see Stewart, "Notes on Pomo Ethnogeography," 34. For Balo Kay, see McLendon and Oswalt, "Pomo: Introduction," 284. Pomos use thirty different seeds for pinole making (Anderson, *Tending the Wild*, 261).
7 For Kabekel, see Stewart, "Notes on Pomo Ethnogeography," 48. For Kodalau, see Kroeber, *Handbook of the Indians of California*, 232.
8 Steve Parrish (Coast Pomo), reel 204-2, notebook no. 204.12: 1046.
9 Billy Rice and Frank Miller (Ukiah Pomo), reel 204-1, notebook no. 204.5: 428–57. In 1905 and 1906 Rice lived with his wife in Potter Valley before relocating to Ukiah by the Great Depression (Kelsey, *Census of Non-Reservation California Indians*, 65). Lassik Lucy Young's war story begins in a similar fashion: "There was a big war." A group of Indians from the north invaded and "killed all the Indians off." Lucy Young (Lassik), reel 204-2, notebook no. 204.23: 1768.
10 Steve Parrish (Coast Pomo), reel 204-2, notebook no. 204.12: 1046–50.
11 Jeff Joaquin (Hopland Pomo), reel 204-2, notebook no. 204.16: 1418–27. For alternative place-names, see Stewart, "Notes on Pomo Ethnogeography," 45; Kroeber, *Handbook of the Indians of California*, 233.
12 Steve Parrish (Coast Pomo), reel 204-2, notebook no. 204.12: 1046–50.
13 For the location of Buldam, see Stewart, "Notes on Pomo Ethnogeography," 33. For Cabus, see 48. Stewart explains, "Buldam, situated near the mouth of Big River, was considered by Barrett and Kroeber to constitute a separate political group. However, two Mato informants, two Mitom informants, one Katca informant and one Canel informant said that Buldam belonged to the Mitom poma and was not occupied until historic times when

NOTES TO CHAPTER 4

the whites made life in the [Willits] valley unsafe. Indians from Nabo and other Mitom towns under chief Kaianika (Captain George) settled permanently at Buldam shortly before 1851, the date being remembered by the people because of its coincidence with the wrecking of a steamer off Point Cabrillo. Before the settlement of Buldam there were no Pomo villages on the coast north of the area occupied by the Point Arena group of the Central Dialect and it is probably that the latter felt they owned all the coast. However, it is certain that the coast territory was not usually held by one group to the exclusion of all others, as is evidenced by the fact that the tribes from the upper Russian River went regularly to the mouth of Big River in the Mitom Poma area for sea food. Several accounts of a war between the Point Arena Indians and the Buldam Indians reveal that, later, the ridge north of the Navarro was recognized as the division line between these two groups. One account of the war was told by [Willie Williams] as he learned it from his aunt. It seems that the Point Arena Indians objected to the permanent settlement of Buldam and attacked the Mitom people there, carrying off a young woman. This woman married into her captors' group and remained with them until her children died. Then she returned to her Mitom relatives, dying about 1912 in [Williams's] house, a very old woman" ("Notes on Pomo Ethnogeography," 37).

14 Harvey James and Andrew White (Coast Pomo), reel 204-2, notebook no. 204.15: 1393–417.
15 Gudde, *California Placenames*, 191.
16 Hurtado, *Indian Survival on the California Frontier*, 104–6.
17 Billy Rice and Frank Miller (Ukiah Pomo), reel 204-1, notebook no. 204.5: 428–57. For sneak attack, see Baumgardner, *Killing for Land*, 81, 86.
18 Billy Rice and Frank Miller (Ukiah Pomo), reel 204-1, notebook no. 204.5: 428–57. Indeed devastating attacks occurred in another narrative. At K'e Bay Cho-k'lal the attackers from P'hŏ,ŏl, K'öy killed the People at K'e Bay, except for M,ti-ge-nam, the hell diver, his wife, daughter, and two sons, and some girls. Tony Francisco (Lake County), reel 204-1, notebook no. 204.9: 694.
19 Cook, *The Conflict between the California Indians and White Civilization*, 255.
20 Billy Rice and Frank Miller (Ukiah Pomo), reel 204-1, notebook no. 204.5: 428–57.
21 Emily Siegel (Pomo), reel 204-1, notebook no. 204.10: 981–83.
22 The Dinés defended themselves against an invading U.S. Army until Kit Carson's winter campaign forced them to surrender, after which they endured the Long Walk to Bosque Redondo. See, for example, Iverson, *Diné*, 48–65. In Colorado the Colorado Cavalry conducted a surprise attack against Cheyennes and Arapahos at Sand Creek. For Sand Creek and its contested memory, see Kelman, *A Misplaced Massacre*. Dakotas revolted against the U.S. failure to uphold treaty obligations in Minnesota. See Anderson, *Kinsmen of Another Kind*. These conflicts have been seared into Indigenous Peoples' memories and oral histories. Although Native People have recalled the trauma of violence and ethnic cleansing that followed these conflicts, they also understand the Indian Wars as instrumental to their persistence in the twentieth century. Historian Benjamin Madley has begun to revise understandings of the Owens Valley War. He argues that the war constitutes an act of genocide committed against Owens Valley Paiutes. See Madley, "American Genocide," 456–60, and "The Forgotten Genocide in Eastern California's Owens Valley."
23 Madley, "American Genocide," 456–60; Bahr, *Viola Martinez*, 21–22; Dean et al., *Weaving a Legacy*, 19–21; Wilson, "Owens Valley Paiutes," 14–15; Michael, "'At the Plow and in the Harvest Field,'" 50–58; Chalfant, *The Story of Inyo*, 96–97. For a concise overview of the 1861–62 winter, see Isenberg, *Mining California*, 68–74, 124. For the Klamath Indian Reservation, see *Annual Report of the Commissioner of Indian Affairs for 1862*, 457–58, 460–62.

24 Madley, "American Genocide," 456–60; Dean et al., *Weaving a Legacy*, 21–22; Michael, "'At the Plow and in the Harvest Field,'" 51–67; Wilson, "Owens Valley Paiutes," 15; Chalfant, *The Story of Inyo*, 148.
25 Chalfant, *The Story of Inyo*, 110, 111.
26 In 1906 he was a bachelor, living with his two children. Kelsey, *Census of Non-Reservation California Indians*, 37.
27 Hank Hunter (Paiute), reel 153-155, notebook no. 48: 119.
28 Jeffrey Shepherd explains, "European notions of land and topography privileged private tenure and bureaucratic definitions of space, while the science of geography, techniques of mapping, and the power of surveying worked as tools of conquest. Physical conquest and colonial settlement redefined Indigenous lands in terms that made sense to non-natives: latitude and longitude, township and block" (*We Are an Indian Nation*, 10).
29 Hank Hunter (Paiute), reel 153-155, notebook no. 48: 119.
30 Jennie Cashbaugh (Paiute), reel 153-155, notebook no. 31: 199, 200.
31 Jim Jones (Paiute), reel 149-152, notebook no. 28: 90.
32 Ibid., 88–92. Chalfant suggested that the dance, apparently held in the fall of 1861, made the stockmen "anxious." Ostensibly Paiute doctors were "mixing war medicine . . . [and] claimed that their magic would make the white men's guns so they could not be fired" (*The Story of Inyo*, 99).
33 Jim Jones (Paiute), reel 149-152, notebook no. 28: 90.
34 Jennie Cashbaugh (Paiute), reel 153-155, notebook no. 31: 200.
35 Ibid., 201.
36 Historian Juliana Barr explains, "Native visiting parties included women and children to emphasize the diplomatic nature of the mission" (*Peace Came in the Form of a Woman*, 33). In colonial Pennsylvania the Lenapes positioned themselves as a "nation of women" to act as peacekeepers (Fur, *A Nation of Women*, esp. 169–75).
37 Hank Hunter (Paiute), reel 153-155, notebook no. 48: 122. In January 1862 Chief George and other Paiute leaders met with Settlers at the San Francis Ranch. Settlers agreed not to harm Paiutes while they hunted or harvested, and Paiutes agreed not to destroy Settlers' property or kill livestock (Chalfant, *The Story of Inyo*, 99–100).
38 Hank Hunter (Paiute), reel 153-155, notebook no. 48: 122. Chalfant notes, "The treaty proved to be merely a passing incident. Within two months war was on in earnest" (*The Story of Inyo*, 100).
39 Maggie Earl (Paiute), reel 153-155, notebook no. 46: 86.
40 Some accounts suggest that Van Fleet instigated the violence by leveling his rifle at the Paiutes, and Chalfant indicates that there was some debate among the cowboys as to the responsibility for the skirmish. Nevertheless he suggests that those accounts do "not well accord with the narration of the fight as above printed on the statements of McGee and Van Fleet" (*The Story of Inyo*, 102–3).
41 Maggie Earl (Paiute), reel 153-155, notebook no. 46: 86.
42 Jim Jones (Paiute), reel 149-152, notebook no. 28: 91.
43 Maggie Earl (Paiute), reel 153-155, notebook no. 46: 87, 85–93.
44 Ibid., 87.
45 Hank Hunter (Paiute), reel 153-155, notebook no. 48: 123, 124.
46 Ibid., 124.
47 Ibid., 125, 126.
48 Maggie Earl (Paiute), reel 153-155, notebook no. 46: 87.

CHAPTER 5. CLEANSING

1. Hank Hunter (Paiute), reel 153-155, notebook no. 46: 118.
2. For the original letter, see Abraham Lincoln to Jesse W. Fell, December 20, 1859, in Basler, *The Collected Works of Abraham Lincoln*, 3: 511–12.
3. For a concise discussion of Jefferson's removal policy, see Miller, *Native America, Discovered and Conquered*, 90–91. Miller notes that Jefferson supported removing Cherokees and Shawnees during the American Revolution.
4. The literature on Indian removal is extensive. For a concise overview of removal policy, see Prucha, *The Great Father*, 64–77.
5. Sellers, *The Market Economy*, 308–12; Usner, "American Indians on the Cotton Frontier."
6. Prucha, "Andrew Jackson's Indian Policy"; Remini, *Andrew Jackson and His Indian Wars*. Recent scholars have been more critical. Historian Alfred Cave, for instance, argues in "Abuse of Power" that Jackson shirked his duty as the leader of the executive branch, overstepped his powers, and bowed to political pressure from western politicians. Historian Gary Clayton Anderson has used the concept of ethnic cleansing to discuss events in Texas and other parts of North America in *The Conquest of Texas* and *Ethnic Cleansing and the Indian*.
7. Phillips, *"Bringing Them under Subjection,"* 33, 227, 232, 235–36. See also Banner, *Dispossessing the Pacific*, 186. For the reservation policy, see Trennert, *Alternative to Extinction*; Rockwell, *Indian Affairs and the Administrative State in the Nineteenth Century*; Genetin-Pilawa, *Crooked Paths to Allotment*.
8. Conners, "The Chico to Round Valley Trail of Tears."
9. Phillips, *"Bringing Them under Subjection,"* 245, 248.
10. Cruikshank, *The Social Life of Stories*, 16–21.
11. Jennie Cashbaugh (Paiute), reel 153-155, notebook no. 31: 188.
12. Baumgardner, *Killing for Land in Early California*, 78, 79. Historian Angela Pulley Hudson argues that Creeks killed livestock that trespassed on their territory (*Creek Paths and Federal Roads*, 50).
13. Potter, "Reminiscences of the Early History of Northern California and of the Indian Troubles." For the Kibbe campaign, see Shover, "The Politics of the 1859 Kibbe Campaign." In *Murder State* historian Brendan C. Lindsay argues that democratic processes enabled Settlers to commit acts of genocide against California Indians. I suggest a similar process worked in ethnic cleansing.
14. Conners, "The Chico to Round Valley Trail of Tears," 7; Wilson, "Remove Them beyond the West," 134–56.
15. Conners, "The Chico to Round Valley Trail of Tears," 14, 18–40.
16. Shover, "The Politics of the 1859 Kibbe Campaign," 32.
17. Quoted in Baumgardner, *Killing for Land in Early California*, 83.
18. John Heenan (Pit River), reel 204-4, notebook no. 204.45: 3556.
19. Bob Green (Concow), reel 204-3, notebook no. 204.35: 2797.
20. John Heenan (Pit River), reel 204-4, notebook no. 204.45: 3556.
21. Bob Green (Concow), reel 204-3, notebook no. 204.35: 2797.
22. Polly Anderson (Concow), reel 204-3, notebook no. 204.34: 2705.
23. Ibid.
24. Bob Green (Concow), reel 204-3, notebook no. 204.35: 2797.
25. Austin McLaine and Annie Feliz (Concow), reel 204-3, notebook no. 204.32: 2551.
26. Historian Kathleen DuVal defines "native ground" as a space where Native Peoples maintained sovereignty and "set the terms of engagement" (*The Native Ground*, 5).

27 Bob Green (Concow), reel 204-3, notebook no. 204.35: 2797.
28 Polly Anderson (Concow), reel 204-3, notebook no. 204.35: 2706.
29 John Heenan (Pit River), reel 204-4, notebook no. 204.45: 3557–58.
30 Bob Green (Concow), reel 204-3, notebook no. 204.35: 2799.
31 Polly Anderson (Concow), reel 204-3, notebook no. 204.35: 2707.
32 Shover, "The Indian Removal to Round Valley in 1863."
33 For Cherokee removal, see Perdue and Green, *The Cherokee Nation and the Trail of Tears*, 116–32.
34 Bob Green (Concow), reel 204-3, notebook no. 204.35: 2803–4.
35 Polly Anderson (Concow), reel 204-3, notebook no. 204.35: 2707.
36 Bob Green (Concow), reel 204-3, notebook no. 204.35: 2804.
37 John Heenan (Pit River), reel 204-4, notebook no. 204.45: 3559.
38 Theodoratus and Evans, "Native American Interview."
39 N. Scott Momaday featured in *We Shall Remain: The Trail of Tears*, Chris Eyre, producer (PBS, 2009). See also "The Becoming of the Native: Man in America before Columbus," in Josephy, *America in 1492*, 16.
40 Austin McLaine (Concow), reel 204-3, notebook no. 204.27: 2084.
41 Polly Anderson (Concow), reel 204-3, notebook no. 204.34: 2708.
42 Austin McLaine and Annie Feliz (Concow), reel 204-3, notebook no. 204.32: 2552–54.
43 Ibid., 2555.
44 Ibid., 2565–68.
45 Dean et al., *Weaving a Legacy*, 21–22; Michael, "'At the Plow and in the Harvest Field,'" 51–58, 64–67; Wilson, "Owens Valley Paiutes," 15.
46 Phillips, *"Bringing Them under Subjection,"* 245–48, 250.
47 Frank and Goldberg, *Defying the Odds*, 24–25.
48 Mary Harry identified one man as Joe Bowers, and Hank Hunter named a man Jose Chico. Mary Looker (Paiute), reel 153-155, notebook no. 47: 99–102; Hank Hunter (Paiute), reel 153-155, notebook no. 48: 125–29. Scholars are divided about the status of these individuals. Anthropologist Richard Wilson argues, "Joe Bowers, a Paiute who helped a settler after he was attacked, was resented by other Paiutes for years" ("Owens Valley Paiutes," 30). Mary Harry, however, recalled that Bowers did not tell all Paiutes about the removal and soldiers punished him for his alleged transgression. Jose Chico, meanwhile, had a long history of involvement in the Owens Valley. In 1859 he led Captain J. W. Davidson into the Owens Valley in search of horse thieves. By the 1860s he lived near the two forks of the Kern River and raised livestock. He later joined the California Volunteers as an interpreter (Michael, "'At the Plow and in the Harvest Field,'" 19, 121–24; Phillips, *"Bringing Them under Subjection,"* 244). For go-betweens, see Merrell, *Into the American Woods*, 19, 27, 38–34.
49 Hank Hunter (Paiute), reel 153-155, notebook no. 48: 125–26.
50 Mary Looker (Paiute), reel 153-155, notebook no. 47: 102.
51 Jennie Cashbaugh (Paiute), reel 153-155, notebook no. 31: 187, 188.
52 Hank Hunter (Paiute), reel 153-155, notebook no. 48: 126.
53 Maggie Earl (Independence Paiute), reel 153-55, notebook no. 46: 88, 89.
54 Jennie Cashbaugh (Paiute), reel 153-155, notebook no. 31: 187. Cashbaugh's history of removal aligns with that of nineteenth-century Choctaws. On the eve of their removal, historian Donna Akers writes, "[Choctaw] women covered their heads with their skirts, keening the death songs all night long." Upon leaving their homeland, Choctaws made sure to touch the leaves and branches of every tree they passed, a final tangible connection with the land they were leaving ("Removing the Heart of the People," 70). Elsie Cavender

(Dakota) also remarked that the Dakota removal from Minnesota "must have been heartbreaking for them, as this valley had always been their home" (Angela Cavender Wilson, "Grandmother to Granddaughter: Generations of Oral History in a Dakota Family," in Mihesuah, *Natives and Academics*, 31).
55 Maggie Earl (Paiute), reel 153-155, notebook no. 46: 88.
56 Hank Hunter (Paiute), reel 153-155, notebook no. 48: 127.
57 Maggie Earl (Paiute), reel 153-155, notebook no. 46: 88; Hank Hunter (Paiute), reel 153-155, notebook no. 48: 127.
58 Gelo, "Recalling the Past in Creating the Present."
59 Hank Hunter (Paiute), reel 153-155, notebook no. 46: 127.
60 Jennie Cashbaugh (Paiute), reel 153-155, notebook no. 31: 188, 189.
61 Dakota women, historian Waziyatawin argues, understood removal as an act of violence, wherein soldiers killed the elderly (Wilson, "Grandmother to Granddaughter," 7–13). Diné Gus Bighorse's history of the Long Walk included incidents of soldiers killing pregnant women (Bighorse, *Bighorse the Warrior*, 34).
62 Mary Harry (Paiute), reel 205-206, notebook no. 1: 40.
63 Jennie Cashbaugh (Paiute), reel 153-155, notebook no. 31: 190.
64 Mary Harry (Paiute), reel 205-206, notebook no. 1: 40.
65 Maggie Earl (Paiute), reel 153-155, notebook no. 46: 85–86. Government officials at San Sebastian ignored the Paiutes while they lived at the reservation. Dean et al., *Weaving a Legacy*, 23; Wilson, "Owens Valley Paiutes," 15–16.
66 Hank Hunter (Paiute), reel 153-155, notebook no. 46: 128, 129. In January 1864 the 380 Paiutes at Tejon were starving. Captain John Schmidt transferred them to the Tule River Farm, later named Tule River Reservation (Dean et al., *Weaving a Legacy*, 23; Wilson, "Owens Valley Paiutes," 15–16).
67 Jennie Cashbaugh (Paiute), reel 153-155, notebook no. 31: 190.
68 D'Azevedo, *Handbook of North American Indians*, 431; Dean et al., *Weaving a Legacy*, 31.
69 Crum, "Deeply Attached to the Land."
70 Jennie Cashbaugh (Paiute), reel 153-155, notebook no. 31: 187.

CHAPTER 6. PERSISTING

1 Hoxie, *Talking Back to Civilization*; Hertzberg, *The Search for an American Indian Identity*. For John Collier, see Philp, *John Collier's Crusade for Indian Reform*; Kelly, *The Assault on Assimilation*.
2 I am indebted to Annette Reed for my thinking about how California Indians persisted and thrived, as opposed to simply surviving, in the nineteenth and twentieth century.
3 Hosmer, *American Indians in the Marketplace*, 37, 217. See also Arnold, *The Fishermen's Frontier*, 132–33; White, *The Roots of Dependency*, 321.
4 Subaltern studies scholar Dipesh Chakrabarty notes that "the biography [and] the autobiography" are two of the "basic genres that help express the modern self." Although other biographies and autobiographies of American Indians might deny Native Peoples a role in "modern America," California Indian oral biographies and autobiographies accomplished quite the opposite ("Postcoloniality and the Artifice of History," 8). "Modernity," historian Pablo Mitchell writes, "is a collapsing of time and space into new sets of measurable relationships." Mitchell demonstrates that in New Mexico the human body and "bodily comportment" were central to the processes of modernization, imperialism, and colonialism. Intent on asserting power over people of color in the American West, Anglo-Americans attempted to create a proper and racialized order and cultivate a belief

in Indian and Chicano/a assimilation in order to prove that the American West was ready for statehood and citizenship. To assimilate and modernize American Indians, the Office of Indian Affairs and other state officials introduced Indians to professional doctors and attempted to eradicate unscientifically trained folk healers (Mitchell, *Coyote Nation*). Other helpful works on modernity include Wiebe, *The Search for Order*; Hayes, *The Response to Industrialism*; Deloria, *Indians in Unexpected Places*.

5   George Brierly (Paiute), reel 205-206, notebook no. 206.6: 358.
6   For a concise overview of these policies and their effort to weaken and control Native populations on reservations, see Rockwell, *Indian Affairs and the Administrative State in the Nineteenth Century*, 266–69. For case studies, see Trennert, *White Man's Medicine*; Trafzer, *Death Stalks the Yakama*.
7   For the extensive newspaper coverage of this incident, see the *Detroit Free Press*, November 5, 1929; *Miami News*, November 12, 1929. For the Pomo opposition to Keenan, see Wilson, "Ukiah Valley Pomo Religious Life, Supernatural Doctoring and Beliefs," 55–56.
8   In New Mexico, Mitchell writes, "the evaluation and characterization of human bodies and body practices . . . helped define citizenship, structure opportunity, and provide the scaffolding around which new sets of social hierarchies were to be constructed" (*Coyote Nation*, 25).
9   For a concise discussion of the matron program, see Cahill, *Federal Fathers and Mothers*, 46–47. See more extended discussions in Trennert, *White Man's Medicine*, chap. 5; Lisa Emmerich, "'Save the Babies!' American Indian Women, Assimilation Policy and Scientific Motherhood, 1912–1918," in Jameson and Armitage, *Writing the Range*, 393–411.
10 Trennert, *White Man's Medicine*, 136–54.
11 Young men usually learned healing skills from their fathers. Among Pomos, shamans learned healing skills from older shamans. In some instances healing was a hereditary craft, whereby fathers passed the skills and spirits to their sons. At other times a shaman might identify a novice who possessed the potential to heal and would trained the young man to follow in his footsteps. Kroeber, *Handbook of the Indians of California*, 258–59; Heizer, *Handbook of North American Indians*, 297.
12 Billy Rice (Pomo), reel 204-1, notebook no. 204.4: 281–89.
13 For a concise discussion of the "memory culture" method, see Lightfoot, *Indians, Missionaries and Merchants*, 46–47.
14 Chakrabarty, "Postcoloniality and the Artifice of History," 8.
15 Billy Rice, reel 204-1, notebook no. 204.4: 281–89.
16 John McWhinney (Pomo), reel 204-1, notebook no. 204.4: 265–71.
17 Compare Calvin Martin's treatment of disease in the Great Lakes in *Keepers of the Game*, 40–65, with Paul Kelton's analysis of the Southeast in "Avoiding the Smallpox Spirits."
18 See Craig Womack's definition of *traditionalism*: "anything that is useful to Indian people in retaining their values and world views, no matter how much it deviates from what people did one or two hundred years ago" (*Red on Red*, 42).
19 Susie Baker, reel 149-152, notebook no. 152.4: 296–98.
20 Ibid., 298.
21 There are correctives that include Paiutes in Owens Valley water history. See Walter, "The Land Exchange Act of 1937"; Walton, *Western Times and Water Wars*; Franklin, "Desiccating a Valley and a People."
22 Steward, "Ethnography of the Owens Valley Paiute," 235.
23 Ibid., 247.
24 Mary Saulque and Emma Washington, reel 205-206, notebook no. 205.3: 159.
25 Susie Baker, reel 149-152, notebook no. 152.4: 288–92.

NOTES TO CHAPTER 6

26 Richard Stoffle, Richard Arnold, Kathleen Van Vlack, Larry Eddy, and Betty Cornelius, "Nuvagantu, 'Where the Snow Sits': Origin Mountains of the Southern Paiutes," in Christie, *Landscapes of Origin in the Americas*, 36, 38.
27 Cruikshank, *The Social Life of Stories*, 17, 18.
28 Yi-Fu Tuan defines space as "that which allows movement." *Space and Place: The Perspective of Experience* (Minneapolis: University of Minnesota Press, 2001), 6. Here, too, I am influenced by Daniel Gelo's work on Comanche understandings of topography. "Recalling the Past in Creating the Present: Topographic References in Comanche Narrative," *Western Folklore* 53 (October 1994): 295–312.
29 For a similar narrative structure, see Gelo, "Recalling the Past in Creating the Present."
30 Susie Baker, reel 149-152, notebook no. 152: 321–22.
31 Ibid.
32 Mattie Bulpitt (Paiute), reel 149-52, notebook no. 43: 336–38.
33 Basso, *Wisdom Sits in Places*, 15, 16. Basso notes that Western Apaches recognized that water too had left their homeland. Many Western Apache place-names referenced water existing in places that are now dry.
34 Erwin Gudde, *California Place Names: The Origin and Etymology of Current Geographic Names*, Fourth edition (Berkeley: University of California Press, 1998, 1949), 6. Anglo Americans named Tinemaha after a Paiute chief. Ibid., 394.
35 Jennie Cashbaugh, reel 153-155, item 154, notebook no. 31: 198–206.
36 For a concise overview of removal see George Harwood Phillips, *"Bringing Them Under Subjection": California's Tejón Indian Reservation and Beyond, 1852–1864* (Lincoln: University of Nebraska Press, 2004), 248–49. See also Walton, *Western Times and Water Wars*, 24–52; Sharon Dean, et al, *Weaving A Legacy: Indian Baskets & the People of Owens Valley, California* (Salt Lake City: University of Utah Press, 2004), 23–26.
37 Susie Baker, reel 149-152, notebook no. 152.4: 296–98, 321–22.
38 Jennie Cashbaugh, reel 153-155, item 154, notebook no. 31: 196–97.
39 Jim Jones, reel 149-152, notebook no. 29: 129–33.
40 Walton, *Western Times and Water Wars*, 25–27.
41 Cruikshank, *The Social Life of Stories*, xiii.
42 Jennie Cashbaugh, reel 153-155, item 154, notebook no. 31: 198–206.
43 Kahrl, *Water and Power*, 356.
44 Jennie Cashbaugh, reel 153-155, item 154, notebook no. 31: 198–206. For the Paiutes, events during the next couple of years ensured that they would remain in their homeland. In 1937 the Land Exchange Act created reservations at Bishop, Big Pine, and Lone Pine. On behalf of the Paiutes, the federal government exchanged nearly 3,000 acres of land with the City of Los Angeles for nearly 1,400 acres of land. Questions remain about Paiute water rights, and modern-day Paiutes and scholars argue that the United States failed to protect Paiute water rights and fulfill its trust responsibility to the Paiute Nation (Walter, "The Land Exchange Act of 1937").
45 Anthropologist Julie Cruikshank notes that for Indigenous People of the Yukon Territory, "if one has optimistic stories about the past . . . one can draw on internal resources to survive and make sense of arbitrary forces that might otherwise seem overwhelming" (*The Social Life of Stories*, xii).
46 For Owens Valley Paiute removal, see Crum, "Deeply Attached to the Land." Crum also notes that in 1873 the federal government proposed returning the Paiutes from Owens Valley to Tule River. However, Owens Valley Settlers, who needed Paiute labor, blocked these efforts.
47 Ibid.

48 Dean et al., *Weaving a Legacy*, 31–33.
49 Walter, "The Land Exchange Act of 1937," 213, 379.
50 Owens Valley Indian Water Commission, "Protecting Preserving Our Water Rights," 2011, http://www.oviwc.org/index.html (accessed August 1, 2012).

CONCLUSION

1 Haas, *Saints and Citizens*; Haas, *Pablo Tac, Indigenous Scholar*.
2 Konkle, *Writing Indian Nations*.
3 Lyons, "Rhetorical Sovereignty."

BIBLIOGRAPHY

ARCHIVAL COLLECTIONS

Bancroft Library, University of California, Berkley

Elijah Renshaw Potter, "Reminiscences of the Early History of Northern California and of the Indian Troubles"
Ethnological Documents of the Department and Museum of Anthropology, BANC FILM 2216
Susie Baker, reel 149–152, Notebook no. 4
Jake Gilbert, reel 149–152, Notebook no. 26
Bridgeport Tom, reel 149–152, Notebook no. 27
Jim Tom Jones, reel 149–152, Notebook no. 29
Jennie Cashbaugh, reel 153–155, Notebook no. 31
Mattie Bulpitt, reel 153–155, Notebook no. 33
Mose Weyland, reel 153–155, Notebook no. 35
Mattie Bulpitt, reel 153–155, Notebook no. 43
George Robinson, reel 153–155, Notebook no. 46
Mary Looker, reel 153–155, Notebook no. 47
Maggie Earl, reel 153–155, Notebook no. 46
Hank Hunter, reel 153–155, Notebook no. 48
Susie Wathen, reel 204-1, Notebook no. 204.1
John McWhinney, reel 204-1, Notebook no. 204.3
John McWhinney, reel 204-1, Notebook no. 204.4
Billy Rice, reel 204-1, Notebook no. 204.4
Billy Rice, reel 204-1, Notebook no. 204.5
Tony Francisco, reel 204-1, Notebook no. 204.9
Emily Siegel, reel 204-1, Notebook no. 204.10
Steve Parrish, reel 204-2, Notebook no. 204.12
Harvey James and Andrew White, reel 204-2, Notebook no. 204.15
Jeff Joaquin, reel 204-2, Notebook no. 204.18
Nancy Dobey, reel 204-2, Notebook no. 204.20
Lucy Young, reel 204-2, Notebook no. 204.23
Charles Wright, reel 204-3, Notebook no. 204.26
Austin McLaine, reel 204-3, Notebook no. 204.27
Annie Feliz, reel 204-3, Notebook no. 204.31
Annie Feliz, reel 204-3, Notebook no. 204.32
Polly Anderson, reel 204-3, Notebook no. 204.34
Austin McLaine, reel 204-3, Notebook no. 204.37
Little Toby and George Moore, reel 204-4, Notebook no. 204.38
Lizzie Tillotson, reel 204-4, Notebook no. 204.40
John Heenan reel 204-4, Notebook no. 204.45
Susie Butcher, reel 205–206, Notebook no. 205.1
Mary Saulque and Emma Washington reel 205–206, Notebook no. 205.3

George Bierly, reel 205–206, Notebook no. 206.6
Records of the Department of Anthropology, University Archives, BANC MSS CU-23

PRIMARY AND SECONDARY SOURCES

Adams, David Wallace. *Education for Extinction: American Indians and the Boarding School Experience*. Lawrence: University of Kansas Press, 1995.

Adams, Kevin, and Khal Schneider. "'Washington Is a Long Way Off': The 'Round Valley War' and the Limits of Federal Power on a California Indian Reservation." *Pacific Historical Review* 80 (November 2011): 557–96.

Akers, Donna. "Removing the Heart of the People: Indian Removal from a Native Perspective." *American Indian Culture and Research Journal* 23.3 (1999): 63–76.

Alfred, Taiaike, and Jeff Corntassel. "Being Indigenous: Resurgences against Contemporary Colonialism." *Government and Opposition* 40.4 (2005): 597–614.

Almaguer, Tomas. *Racial Fault Lines: The Historical Origins of White Supremacy in California*. Berkeley: University of California Press, 2008.

Amoss, Pamela, and Stevan Harrell, eds. *Other Ways of Growing Old: Anthropological Perspectives*. Stanford: Stanford University Press, 1981.

Anderson, Gary Clayton. *The Conquest of Texas: Ethnic Cleansing in the Promised Land, 1820–1875*. Norman: University of Oklahoma Press, 2005.

———. *Ethnic Cleansing and the Indian: The Crime That Should Haunt America*. Norman: University of Oklahoma Press, 2014.

———. *Kinsmen of Another Kind: Dakota-White Relations in the Upper Mississippi Valley, 1650–1862*. 1997; Minneapolis: Minnesota Historical Society Press, 1984.

Anderson, M. Kat. *Tending the Wild: Native American Knowledge and the Management of California's Natural Resources*. Berkeley: University of California Press, 2005.

Anderson, Virginia DeJohn. "King Philip's Herds: Indians, Colonists, and the Problem of Livestock in Early New England." *William and Mary Quarterly* 51 (October 1994): 601–24.

Annual Report of the Commissioner of Indian Affairs for 1862. Washington, D.C.: Government Printing Office, 1863.

Arnold, David. *The Fishermen's Frontier: People and Salmon in Southeast Alaska*. Seattle: University of Washington Press, 2009.

Aron, Stephen, and Jeremy Adelman. "From Borderlands to Borders: Empires, Nation-States and the Peoples in between in North American History." *American Historical Review* 104 (June 1999): 814–41.

Atherton, Gertrude. *California: An Intimate History*. New York: Boni & Liveright, 1927.

Bahr, Diana. *Viola Martinez, California Paiute: Living in Two Worlds*. Norman: University of Oklahoma Press, 2003.

Baker, T. Lindsay, and Julie Baker, eds. *The WPA Oklahoma Slave Narratives*. Norman: University of Oklahoma Press, 1996.

Bancroft, Hubert Howe. *History of the Pacific States of North America*. 19 vols. Vol. 7: *California, 1860–1890*. San Francisco: History Company, 1890.

———. *The Native Races of the Pacific States of North America*. Vol. 1: *Wild Tribes*. New York: D. Appleton, 1874.

Banner, Stuart. *Dispossessing the Pacific: Land, Settlers and Indigenous People from Australia to Alaska*. Cambridge, MA: Harvard University Press, 2007.

Barker, Adam. "The Contemporary Reality of Canadian Imperialism: Settler Colonialism and the Hybrid Colonial State." *American Indian Quarterly* 33 (Summer 2009): 325–51.

Barr, Juliana. "Geographies of Power: Mapping Indian Borders in the 'Borderlands' of the Early Southwest." *William and Mary Quarterly* 68 (January 2011): 5–46.

———. *Peace Came in the Form of a Woman: Indians and Spaniards in the Texas Borderlands*. Chapel Hill: University of North Carolina Press, 2007.

Barrett, S. A. "The Ethno-Geography of the Pomo and Neighboring Indians." *University of California Publications in American Archaeology and Ethnology* 6.1 (1908): 1–322.

Basler, Roy, ed. *The Collected Works of Abraham Lincoln*. New Brunswick, NJ: Rutgers University Press, 1953.

Basso, Keith. *Wisdom Sits in Places: Landscape and Language among the Western Apache*. Albuquerque: University of New Mexico Press, 1996.

Bauer, William J., Jr. *"We Were All Like Migrant Workers Here": Work, Community and Memory on Northern California's Round Valley Reservation, 1850–1941*. Chapel Hill: University of North Carolina Press, 2009.

Baumgardner, Frank, II. *Killing for Land in Early California: Indian Blood at Round Valley, 1856–1863*. New York: Algora, 2005.

Baumgarte, Bridget. "Alaska Natives and the Power of Perseverance: The Fight for Sovereignty and Land Claims in Southeast Alaska, 1912–1947." MA thesis, University of Nevada–Las Vegas, 2015.

Bighorse, Tiana. *Bighorse the Warrior*. Tucson: University of Arizona Press, 1990.

Binnema, Theodore. *Common and Contested Ground: A Human and Environmental History of the Northwestern Plains*. Norman: University of Oklahoma Press, 2001.

Biolsi, Thomas, ed. *A Companion to the Anthropology of American Indians*. Malden, MA: Blackwell, 2004.

———. *Organizing the Lakota: The Political Economy of the New Deal on the Pine Ridge and Rosebud Reservations*. Tucson: University of Arizona Press, 1992.

Blackhawk, Ned. *Violence over the Land: Indians and Empires in the Early American West*. Cambridge, MA: Harvard University Press, 2006.

Breen, T. H. "Horses and Gentlemen: The Cultural Significance of Gambling among the Gentry of Virginia." *William and Mary Quarterly* 34 (April 1977): 239–57.

Brown, Dee. *Bury My Heart at Wounded Knee: An Indian History of the American West*. New York: Bantam Books, 1972.

Buechel, Eugene, and Paul Manhart, comps. and eds. *Lakota Dictionary: Lakota-English/English-Lakota*. New comprehensive edition. Lincoln: University of Nebraska Press, 2002.

Burnham, Philip. *Indian Country, God's Country: Native Americans and the National Parks*. Covelo, CA: Island Press, 2000.

Buss, James Joseph. *Winning the West with Words: Language and Conquest in the Lower Great Lakes*. Norman: University of Oklahoma Press, 2011.

Cahill, Cathleen. *Federal Fathers and Mothers: A Social History of the United States Indian Service, 1869–1933*. Chapel Hill: University of North Carolina Press, 2011.

Calloway, Colin, ed. *Our Hearts Fell to the Ground: Plains Indian Views on How the West Was Lost*. Boston: Bedford Books, 1996.

Carranco, Lynwood, and Estle Beard. *Genocide and Vendetta: The Round Valley Wars of Northern California*. Norman: University of Oklahoma Press, 1981.

Cave, Alfred. "Abuse of Power: Andrew Jackson and the Indian Removal Act of 1830." *Historian* 65 (Winter 2003): 1330–53.

Chakrabarty, Dipesh. "Postcoloniality and the Artifice of History: Who Speaks for 'Indian' Pasts." *Representations* 37 (Winter 1992): 1–26.

Chalfant, William. *The Story of Inyo*. Chicago: Hammond Press, 1922.

Chase-Dunn, Christopher, and Kelly M. Mann. *The Wintu and Their Neighbors: A Very Small World-System in Northern California*. Tucson: University of Arizona Press, 1998.

Cleland, Robert Glass. *From Wilderness to Empire: A History of California, 1542–1900*. New York: Knopf, 1954.

Christie, Jessica Joyce, ed. *Landscapes of Origin in the Americas: Creation Narratives Linking Ancient Places to Present Communities*. Tuscaloosa: University of Alabama Press, 2009.

Coleman, Jon. *Vicious: Wolves and Men in America*. New Haven, CT: Yale University Press, 2006.

Conmy, Peter Thomas. *The Origin and Purposes of the Native Sons and Native Daughters of the Golden West*. San Francisco: Dolores Press, 1956.

Conn, Steven. *History's Shadow: Native Americans and Historical Consciousness in the Nineteenth Century*. Chicago: University of Chicago Press, 2004.

Conners, Pamela. "The Chico to Round Valley Trail of Tears." Willows, CA: Mendocino National Forest, 1993.

Cook, Sherburne. *The Conflict between the California Indians and White Civilization*. Berkeley: University of California Press, 1976.

Costo, Rupert, and Jeanette Costo. *The Missions of California: A Legacy of Genocide*. San Francisco: Indian Historian Press, 1987.

Costo, Rupert, and Jeanette Costo. *Natives of the Golden State: The California Indians*. San Francisco: Indian Historian Press, 1995.

Cothran, Boyd. *Remembering the Modoc War: Redemptive Violence and the Making of American Innocence*. Chapel Hill: University of North Carolina Press, 2014.

Cruikshank, Julie. *The Social Life of Stories: Narrative and Knowledge in the Yukon Territory*. Lincoln: University of Nebraska Press, 1998.

Crum, Steven J. "Deeply Attached to the Land: The Owens Valley Paiutes and Their Rejection of Indian Removal, 1863–1937," *News from Native California* 14 (Summer 2001): 18–20.

———. *The Road on Which We Came: A History of the Western Shoshones*. Salt Lake City: University of Utah Press, 1994.

Currie, Anne. "Bidwell Rancheria." *California Historical Society Quarterly* 36 (December 1957): 313–25.

Dangel, R. "Bear and Fawns." *Journal of American Folklore* 42 (July–September 1929): 307–8.

Davis, James T. "Trade Routes and Economic Exchange among the Indians of California." *University of California Archaeological Survey* 54 (1961): 1–71.

d'Azevedo, Warren, ed. *Handbook of North American Indians*. Vol. 11: *Great Basin*. Washington, DC: Smithsonian Institution, 1986.

Dean, Sharon, Peggy Ratcheson, Judith Finger, Ellen Daus, and Craig Bates. *Weaving a Legacy: Indian Baskets and the People of Owens Valley, California*. Salt Lake City: University of Utah Press, 2004.

Deloria, Philip. *Indians in Unexpected Places*. Lawrence: University of Kansas Press, 2004.

Deloria, Vine, Jr. *Red Earth, White Lies: Native Americans and the Myth of Scientific Fact*. 1977; Boulder, CO: Fulcrum, 1997.

Denetdale, Jennifer Nez. *Reclaiming Diné History: The Legacies of Navajo Chief Manuelito and Juanita*. Tucson: University of Arizona Press, 2007.

Diller, Joseph Siller. *Geology of the Lassen Peak District*. Washington, DC: Government Printing Office, 1889.

Dixon, Roland. "The Northern Maidu." *Bulletin of the American Museum of Natural History* 17 (May 1905): 119–346.

Dowd, Gregory Evans. *A Spirited Resistance: The Struggle for North American Indian Unity, 1745–1815*. Baltimore: Johns Hopkins University Press, 1992.

Driver, Harold, comp. *California Indians IV*. American Indian Ethnohistory: California and Basin-Plateau Indians. New York: Garland, 1974.
DuBois, Cora. *The 1870 Ghost Dance*. Introduction by Thomas Buckley. Lincoln: University of Nebraska Press, 2007.
DuVal, Kathleen. *The Native Ground: Indians and Colonists in the Heart of the Continent*. Philadelphia: University of Pennsylvania Press, 2006.
Edmunds, R. David. *The Shawnee Prophet*. Lincoln: University of Nebraska Press, 1982.
Elmendorf, William, and Alice Shepherd. "Another Look at Wappo-Yuki Loans." *Anthropological Linguistics* 41 (Summer 1999): 209–29.
Farmer, Jared. *On Zion's Mount: Mormons, Indians and the American Landscape*. Cambridge, MA: Harvard University Press, 2008.
Fisher, Andrew H. *Shadow Tribe: The Making of Columbia River Indian Identity*. Seattle: University of Washington Press, 2010.
Fixico, Donald. *The American Indian Mind in a Linear World: American Indian Studies and Traditional Knowledge*. New York: Routledge, 2003.
———. *Call for Change: The Medicine Way of American Indian History, Ethos and Reality*. Lincoln: University of Nebraska Press, 2013.
Foster, George. "A Summary of Yuki Culture." *Anthropological Records* 5.3 (1944): 155–244.
Frank, Geyla, and Carole Goldberg. *Defying the Odds: The Tule River Tribe's Struggle for Sovereignty in Three Centuries*. New Haven, CT: Yale University Press, 2011.
Franklin, Andrew. "Desiccating a Valley and a People: The Effects of the Los Angeles Department of Water and Power on Owens Valley and Its Inhabitants, 1924–1931." MA thesis, California State University–Sacramento, 2000.
Fraser, Steve, and Gary Gerstle, eds. *The Rise and Fall of the New Deal Order, 1930–1980*. Princeton, NJ: Princeton University Press, 1989.
Fry, Christine L., ed. *Aging in Culture and Society: Comparative Viewpoints and Strategies*. New York: Praeger, 1980.
Fur, Gunlög. *A Nation of Women: Gender and Colonial Encounters among the Delaware Indians*. Philadelphia: University of Pennsylvania Press, 2009.
Garth, Thomas R., Jr. "Emphasis on Industriousness among the Atsugewi." *American Anthropologist* 47 (October–December 1945): 554–66.
Gelo, Daniel. "Recalling the Past in Creating the Present: Topographic References in Comanche Narratives." *Western Folklore* 53 (October 1994): 295–312.
Gendzel, Glen. "Pioneers and Padres: Competing Mythologies in Northern and Southern California, 1850–1930." *Western Historical Quarterly* 32 (Spring 2001): 55–81.
Genetin-Pilawa, Joseph. *Crooked Paths to Allotment: The Fight over Federal Indian Policy after the Civil War*. Chapel Hill: University of North Carolina Press, 2014.
Gifford, Edward. "Southern Maidu Religious Ceremonies." *American Anthropologist* 29 (July 1927): 214–57.
Gifford, Edward, and Gwendoline Harris Block. *California Indian Nights*. Glendale, CA: Arthur H. Clark, 1930.
Goldberg, Carole, and Duane Champagne. "Ramona Redeemed? The Rise of Tribal Political Power in California." *Wicazo Sa Review* 17.1 (2002): 43–63.
Gray, A. A. *History of California from 1542*. Boston: D. C. Heath, 1934.
Gudde, Erwin G. *California Placenames: The Origins and Etymology of Current Geographical Names*. 4th edition. 1949; Berkeley: University of California Press, 2004.
Haas, Lisbeth. *Pablo Tac, Indigenous Scholar: Writing on Luiseno Language and Colonial History, c. 1840*. Berkeley: University of California Press, 2011.

———. *Saints and Citizens: Indigenous Histories of Colonial Missions and Mexican California.* Berkeley: University of California Press, 2013.

Hämäläinen, Pekka. "The Rise and Fall of Plains Indian Horse Cultures." *Journal of American History* 90 (December 2003): 833–62.

Harmon, Alexandra. *Indians in the Making: Ethnic Relations and Indian Identities around Puget Sound.* Berkeley: University of California Press, 1998.

Hau'ofa, Epeli. "Our Sea of Islands." In Vijay Naidu, Eric Waddell, and Epeli Hau'ofa, eds., *A New Oceania: Rediscovering Our Sea of Islands.* Suva, Fiji: School of Social and Economic Development, University of the South Pacific, 1993.

Hayes, Samuel. *The Response to Industrialism, 1885–1914.* Chicago: University of Chicago Press, 1995.

Heizer, Robert, ed. *Handbook of North American Indians: California.* Vol. 8. Washington, DC: Smithsonian Institution Press, 1978.

Hertzberg, Hazel. *The Search for an American Indian Identity: Modern Pan-Indian Movements.* Syracuse, NY: Syracuse University Press, 1971.

Hill, Jonathan D., ed. *Rethinking History and Myth: Indigenous South American Perspectives on the Past.* Urbana: University of Illinois Press, 1988.

Hirsch, Jerrold. *Portrait of America: A Cultural History of the Federal Writers' Project.* Chapel Hill: University of North Carolina Press, 2003.

Hittman, Michael. "The 1870 Ghost Dance at the Walker River Reservation: A Reconstruction." *Ethnohistory* 20 (Summer 1973): 247–78.

Hoffman, Abraham. *Vision or Villainy: Origins of the Owens Valley–Los Angeles Water Controversy.* College Station: Texas A&M University Press, 2001.

Holm, Tom, J. Diane Pearson, and Ben Chavis. "Peoplehood: A Model for the Extension of Sovereignty in American Indian Studies." *Wicazo Sa Review* 18 (Spring 2003): 7–24.

Horsman, Reginald. *Race and Manifest Destiny: Origins of American Racial Anglo-Saxonism.* Cambridge, MA: Harvard University Press, 1986.

Hosmer, Brian. *American Indians in the Marketplace: Persistence and Innovation among the Menominees and Metlakatlans, 1870–1920.* Lawrence: University of Kansas Press, 1999.

Hosmer, Brian C., and Larry Nesper, eds. *Tribal Worlds: Critical Studies in American Indian Nation Building.* Albany: SUNY Press, 2012.

Hoxie, Frederick E. *Talking Back to Civilization: Indian Voices from the Progressive Era.* Boston: Bedford Books, 2001.

Hudson, Angela Pulley. *Creek Paths and Federal Roads: Indians, Settlers, and Slaves and the Making of the American South.* Chapel Hill: University of North Carolina Press, 2010.

Hurtado, Albert. *Indian Survival on the California Frontier.* New Haven, CT: Yale University Press, 1988.

Isenberg, Andrew. *Mining California: An Ecological History.* New York: Hill and Wang, 2005.

Iverson, Peter. *Diné: A History of the Navajos.* Albuquerque: University of New Mexico Press, 2002.

———. *When Indians Became Cowboys: Native Peoples and Cattle Ranching in the American West.* Norman: University of Oklahoma Press, 1994.

Jacobs, Margaret. *White Mother to a Dark Race: Settler Colonialism, Maternalism and the Removal of Indigenous Children in the American West and Australia, 1880–1940.* Lincoln: University of Nebraska Press, 2009.

Jacoby, Karl. *Shadows at Dawn: The Apache Massacre and the Violence of History.* New York: Penguin, 2009.

Jameson, Elizabeth, and Susan Armitage, eds. *Writing the Range: Race, Class and Culture in the Women's West.* Norman: University of Oklahoma Press, 1997.

Jennings, Francis. *The Invasion of America: Indians, Colonialism and the Cant of Conquest.* New York: Norton, 1977.
Johnson, Kenneth. *K-344; Or the Indians of California vs. the United States.* Los Angeles: Dawson's Books, 1966.
Jordan, Winthrop. *White over Black: American Attitudes toward the Negro, 1550–1812.* Chapel Hill: University of North Carolina Press, 1968.
Josephy, Alvin M., Jr., ed. *America in 1492: The World of the Indian Peoples before the Arrival of Columbus.* New York: Vintage Books, 1993.
Kahrl, William. *Water and Power: The Conflict over Los Angeles Water Supply in the Owens Valley.* Berkeley: University of California Press, 1983.
Kelly, Lawrence *The Assault on Assimilation: John Collier and the Origins of Indian Policy Reform.* Albuquerque: University of New Mexico Press, 1983.
Kelman, Ari. *A Misplaced Massacre: Struggling over the Memory of Sand Creek.* Cambridge, MA: Harvard University Press, 2013.
Kelsey, C. E. *Census of Non-Reservation California Indians, 1905–1906.* Edited by Robert Heizer. Berkeley: Archaeological Research Facility, 1971.
Kelton, Paul. "Avoiding the Smallpox Spirits: Colonial Epidemics and Southeastern Indian Survival." *Ethnohistory* 51 (Winter 2004): 45–72.
Keyes, Sarah "'Like a Roaring Lion': The Overland Trail as a Sonic Conquest." *Journal of American History* 96 (June 2009): 19–43.
Krahe, Diane, and Theodore Catton. *Little Gem of the Cascades: An Administrative History of Lassen Volcanic National Park.* http://www.nps.gov/lavo/learn/historyculture/upload/Lassen-Volcanic-National-Park-Administrative-History.pdf. Accessed August 18, 2015.
Kroeber, Alfred. "A Ghost-Dance in California." *Journal of American Folklore* 17 (January–March 1904): 32–35.
———. *Handbook of the Indians of California.* New York: Dover, 1976.
———. "The Patwin and Their Neighbors." *University of California Publications in American Archaeology and Ethnology* 29 (1930–32): 312–40.
———. "Yuki Myths." *Anthropos* 37 (September–December 1932): 905–39.
Konkle, Maureen. *Writing Indian Nations: Native Intellectuals and the Politics of Historiography, 1827–1863.* Chapel Hill: University of North Carolina Press, 2004.
Laylander, Don. "California's Prehistory as a Remembered Past." *Journal of California and Great Basin Anthropology* 26.2 (2006): 153–77.
Lazarus, Edward. *Black Hills, White Justice: The Sioux Nation versus the United States, 1775 to the Present.* Lincoln: University of Nebraska Press, 1999.
Leventhal, Alan, Les Field, Hank Alvarez, and Rosemary Cambr. "The Ohlone Back from Extinction." In Lowell Jean Bean, ed., *The Ohlone Past and Present: Native Americans of the San Francisco Bay Region.* Menlo Park, CA: Ballena Press, 1994.
Libecap, Gary. *Owens Valley Revisited: A Reassessment of the West's First Great Water Transfer.* Palo Alto, CA: Stanford Economics, 2007.
Lightfoot, Kent. *Indians, Missionaries and Merchants: The Legacy of Colonial Encounters on the California Frontiers.* Berkeley: University of California Press, 2005.
Lindsay, Brendan C. *Murder State: California's Native American Genocide, 1846–1873.* Lincoln: University of Nebraska Press, 2012.
Loeb, Edwin. "The Creator Concept among the Indians of North Central California." *American Anthropologist* 28 (July–September 1926): 467–93.
———. "The Eastern Kuksu Cult." *University of California Publications in American Archaeology and Ethnology* 33 (1932–34): 139–232.

———. "The Western Kuksu Cult." *University of California Publications in American Archaeology and Ethnology* 33 (1932–34): 1–138.

Lowery, Malinda Maynor. *Lumbee Indians in the Jim Crow South: Race, Identity, and the Making of a Nation*. Chapel Hill: University of North Carolina Press, 2010.

Lowie, Robert. "Oral Tradition and History." *American Anthropologist* 17 (July–September, 1915): 597–99.

Lowman, Emma, and Adam Barker. "Indigenizing Approaches to Research." The Sociological Imagination, 2004. http://sociologicalimagination.org/archives/2004/comment-page-1. Accessed December 5, 2012.

Luthin, Herbert W., ed. *Surviving through the Days: Translations of Native California Stories and Songs*. Berkeley: University of California Press, 2002.

Lyons, Scott Richard. "Rhetorical Sovereignty: What Do American Indians Want from Writing?" *College Composition and Communication* 51 (February 2000): 447–68.

Madley, Benjamin. "American Genocide: The California Indian Catastrophe, 1846–1873." PhD dissertation, Yale University, 2009.

———. "California's Yuki Indians: Defining Genocide in Native American History." *Western Historical Quarterly* 39 (Autumn 2008): 303–32.

———. "The Forgotten Genocide in Eastern California's Owens Valley, 1862–1868." Paper Presented at the American Society for Ethnohistory Annual Conference, Las Vegas, November 5–7, 2015.

———. "Reexamining the American Genocide Debate: Meaning, Historiography, and New Methods." *American Historical Review* 120 (February 2015): 98–140.

Makley, Michael J., and Matthew Makley. *Cave Rock: Climbers, Courts, and a Washoe Indian Sacred Place*. Reno: University of Nevada Press, 2010.

Mangione, Jerre. *The Dream and the Deal: The Federal Writers' Project, 1935–1943*. Syracuse, NY: Syracuse University Press, 1996.

Maniery, James Gary. "A Chronicle of Murphey's Rancheria (Mol-Pee-So): An Historical Central Sierra Miwok Village." *Journal of California and Great Basin Anthropology* 5 (Summer–Winter 1983): 176–98.

Maniery, James Gary, and Dwight Dutschke. "Northern Miwok at Big Bar: A Glimpse into the Lives of Pedro and Lily O'Connor." *American Indian Quarterly* 13 (Autumn 1989): 481–95.

Martin, Calvin. *Keepers of the Game: Indian-Animal Relationships and the Fur Trade*. Berkeley: University of California Press, 1978.

Martin, Joel. *Sacred Revolt: The Muskogees' Struggle for a New World*. Boston: Beacon Press, 1991.

McCulley, Johnston. *The Mark of Zorro: The Curse of Capistrano*. Kindle eBook.

McLerran, Jennifer. *A New Deal for Native Art: Indian Arts and Federal Policy, 1933–1943*. Tucson: University of Arizona Press, 2009.

McMillen, Christian. *Making Indian Law: The Hualapai Land Case and the Birth of Ethnohistory*. New Haven, CT: Yale University Press, 2007.

McPherson, Robert. *Navajo Land, Navajo Culture: The Utah Experience in the Twentieth Century*. Norman: University of Oklahoma Press, 2001.

Merrell, James. *Into the American Woods: Negotiators on the Pennsylvania Frontier*. New York: Norton, 1999.

Meyn, Susan Labry. *More Than Curiosities: A Grassroots History of the Indian Arts and Crafts Board and Its Precursors, 1920–1942*. New York: Lexington Books, 2001.

Michael, William. "At the Plow and in the Harvest Field: Indian Conflict and Accommodation in the Owens Valley, 1860–1889." MA thesis, University of Oklahoma, 1993.

Mihesuah, Devon, ed. *Natives and Academics: Researching and Writing about American Indians*. Lincoln: University of Nebraska Press, 1998.

Miller, Jay. "Basin Religion and Theology: A Comparative Study of Power (*Puha*)." *Journal of California and Great Basin Anthropology* 5.1–2 (1983): 66–86.

Miller, Robert J. *Native America, Discovered and Conquered: Thomas Jefferson, Lewis and Clark and Manifest Destiny*. Lincoln: University of Nebraska Press, 2008.

Miller, Robert J., Jacinta Ruru, Larissa Behrendt, and Tracy Lindberg. *Discovering Indigenous Lands: The Doctrine of Discovery in the English Colonies*. New York: Oxford University Press, 2010.

Mitchell, Pablo. *Coyote Nation: Sexuality, Race, and Conquest in Modernizing New Mexico, 1880–1920*. Chicago: University of Chicago Press, 2005.

Morgan, Mindy J. "Constructions and Contestations of the Authoritative Voice: Native American Communities and the Federal Writers' Project, 1935–1941." *American Indian Quarterly* 29 (Winter–Spring 2005): 56–83.

Nabokov, Peter. *A Forest of Time: American Indian Ways of History*. New York: Cambridge University Press, 2002.

———. *Where the Lightning Strikes: The Lives of American Indian Storied Places*. New York: Viking Books, 2006.

Newman, Jason C. "'There Will Come a Day When White Men Will Not Rule Us': The Round Valley Indian Tribe and Federal Indian Policy, 1856–1934." PhD dissertation, University of California–Davis, 2004.

Norton, Jack. *Genocide in Northwestern California: When Our Worlds Cried*. San Francisco: Indian Historian Press, 1979.

Nunn, Nathan, and Nancy Qian. "The Columbian Exchange: A History of Disease, Food and Ideas." *Journal of Economic Perspectives* 24 (Spring 2010): 163–88.

O'Brien, Jean. *Firsting and Lasting: Writing Indians Out of Existence in New England*. Minneapolis: University of Minnesota Press, 2010.

Olmstead, D. L. *Achumawi Dictionary*. University of California Publications in Linguistics, vol. 45. Berkeley: University of California Press, 1966.

Parkman, E. Breck. "The Supernatural Frontier in Pomo Cosmology." California Department of Parks and Recreation. http://www.parks.ca.gov/?page_id=23014. Accessed July 12, 2015.

Parman, Donald. *Navahos and the New Deal*. New Haven, CT: Yale University Press, 1976.

Perdue, Theda, and Michael Green. *The Cherokee Nation and the Trail of Tears*. New York: Penguin, 2008.

Phillips, George Harwood. *"Bringing Them under Subjection": California's Tejón Indian Reservation and Beyond, 1852–1864*. Lincoln: University of Nebraska Press, 2004.

Philp, Kenneth. *John Collier's Crusade for Indian Reform*. Tucson: University of Arizona Press, 1981.

Platt, Tony. *Grave Matters: California's Buried Past*. Berkeley: Heyday Books, 2011.

Pratt, Mary Louise. *Imperial Eyes: Travel Writing and Transculturation*. 2nd edition. New York: Routledge, 2008.

Prucha, Francis Paul. "Andrew Jackson's Indian Policy: A Reassessment." *Journal of American History* 56 (December 1969): 527–39.

———. *The Great Father: The United States Government and the American Indians*. Abridged edition. Lincoln: University of Nebraska Press, 1986.

Pyne, Stephen. *Fire: A Brief History*. Seattle: University of Washington Press, 2001.

Rappaport, Joanne. *The Politics of Memory: Native Historical Interpretation in the Colombian Andes*. New York: Cambridge University Press, 1990.

Rebolledo, Tey Diana, and Maria Teresa Marquez, eds. *Women's Tales from the New Mexico WPA: La Diabla a Pie*. Houston: Arte Público Press, 2000.

Reisner, Marc. *Cadillac Desert: The American West and Its Disappearing Water*. Revised edition. New York: Penguin Books, 1993.

Remini, Robert. *Andrew Jackson and His Indian Wars*. New York: Penguin Books, 2002.
Richter, Daniel. *Facing East from Indian Country: A Native History of Early America*. Cambridge, MA: Harvard University Press, 2001.
Roberts, Helen Heffron. *Concow-Maidu Indians of Round Valley—1926*. Edited by Dorothy J. Hill. Chico: Association for Northern California Records and Research, 1980.
Rockwell, Stephen. *Indian Affairs and the Administrative State in the Nineteenth Century*. New York: Cambridge University Press, 2010.
Rosier, Paul. *Rebirth of the Blackfeet Nation, 1912–1954*. Lincoln: University of Nebraska Press, 2004.
Rothermund, Dietmar. *The Global Impact of the Great Depression, 1929–1939*. New York: Routledge, 1996.
———. *The Routledge Companion to Decolonization*. New York: Routledge, 2006.
Rusco, Elmer R. "Historic Change in Western Shoshone Country: The Establishment of the Western Shoshone National Council and Traditionalist Land Claims." *American Indian Quarterly* 16 (Summer 1992): 337–60.
Sahlins, Marshall. *Islands of History*. Chicago: University of Chicago Press, 1987.
Sapir, Edward. "Yana Texts." *University of California Publications in American Archaeology and Ethnology* 9 (February 1910): 1–235.
Sapir, Edward, and Morris Swadesh. *Yana Dictionary*. University of California Publications in Linguistics, vol. 22. Berkeley: University of California Press, 1960.
Sarris, Greg. *Mabel McKay: Weaving the Dream*. Berkeley: University of California Press, 1998.
Saville-Troike, Muriel, ed. *Linguistics and Anthropology*. Washington, DC: Georgetown University Press, 1977.
Schneider, Lindsay. "'There's Something in the Water': Salmon Runs and Settler Colonialism on the Columbia River." *American Indian Culture and Research Journal* 37.2 (2013): 149–63.
Schrader, Robert Fay. *The Indian Arts and Crafts Board: An Aspect of New Deal Indian Policy*. Albuquerque: University of New Mexico Press, 1983.
Schulz, Paul. *Indians of Lassen Volcanic Park and Vicinity*. 1954; Mineral, CA: Loomis Museum Association, 1988.
Secrest, William B. *When the Great Spirit Died: The Destruction of the California Indians, 1850–1860*. Sanger, CA: Word Dancer Press, 2003.
Sellers, Charles. *The Market Economy: Jacksonian America, 1815–1846*. New York: Oxford University Press, 1991.
Shaw, Stephanie J. "Using the WPA Ex-Slave Narratives to Study the Impact of the Great Depression." *Journal of Southern History* 69 (August 2003): 623–58.
Shepherd, Jeffrey. *We Are an Indian Nation: A History of the Hualapai People*. Tucson: University of Arizona Press, 2010.
Shinn, Dean. "Man and the Land: An Ecological History of Fire and Grazing on Eastern Oregon Rangelands." MA thesis, Oregon State University, 1977.
Shipley, William. "Maidu and Nisenan: A Binary Survey." *International Journal of American Linguistics* 27 (January 1961): 46–51.
———. *The Maidu Indian Myths and Stories of Hanc'ibyjim*. Berkeley: Heyday Books, 1991.
———. *Maidu Texts and Dictionary*. University of California Publications in Linguistics, vol. 33. Berkeley: University of California Press, 1963.
Shover, Michele. "The Indian Removal to Round Valley in 1863, A Reconsideration: Part Two, The Indians' Account: Soldier Savagery." *Dogtown Territorial Quarterly* 57.4 (2004): 4–16.
———. "The Politics of the 1859 Kibbe Campaign: Northern California Indian-Settler Conflicts of the 1850s." *Dogtown Territorial Quarterly* 38 (1999): 4–39.
Silva, Noenoe. *Aloha Betrayed: Native Hawaiian Resistance to American Colonialism*. Durham, NC: Duke University Press, 2004.

Simmons, Leo. *The Role of the Aged in Primitive Society*. 1945; New York: Archon Books, 1970.
Sitkoff, Harvard. *A New Deal for Blacks: The Emergence of Civil Rights as a National Issue*. New York: Oxford University Press, 2008.
Sklaroff, Lauren. *Black Culture and the New Deal: The Quest for Civil Rights in the Roosevelt Era*. Chapel Hill: University of North Carolina Press, 2009.
Sleeper-Smith, Susan. *Indian Women and French Men: Rethinking Cultural Encounter in the Western Great Lake*. Amherst: University of Massachusetts Press, 2001.
Smith, Eric Krabbe. "Lucy Young, or T'tcetsa: Indian/White Relations in Northwest California, 1846–1944." MA thesis, University of California–Santa Cruz, 1990.
Smith, Linda Tuhiwai. *Decolonizing Methodologies: Research and Indigenous Peoples*. New York: Zed Books, 1999.
Smith, Stacey L. *Freedom's Frontier: California and the Struggle over Unfree Labor, Emancipation, and Reconstruction*. Chapel Hill: University of North Carolina Press, 2013.
Smoak, Gregory. *Ghost Dances and Identity: Prophetic Religion and American Indian Ethnogenesis in the Nineteenth Century*. Berkeley: University of California Press, 2006.
Spence, Mark. *Dispossessing the Wilderness: Indian Removal and the Making of the National Parks*. New York: Oxford University Press, 2000.
———. "Dispossessing the Wilderness: Yosemite Indians and the National Park Ideal, 1864–1930." *Pacific Historical Review* 65 (February 1996): 27–59.
Starn, Orin. *Ishi's Brain: In Search of America's Last "Wild" Indian*. New York: Norton, 2004.
Steward, Julian. "Ethnography of the Owens Valley Paiutes." *University of California Publications on American Archaeology and Ethnology* 33.3 (1933): 233–338.
Stewart, Omer. "Notes on Pomo Ethnogeography." *University of California Publications in American Archaeology and Ethnology* 40 (1956): 29–61.
Stott, William. *Documentary Expression and Thirties America*. New York: Oxford University Press, 1973.
Taylor, Graham D. *The New Deal and American Indian Tribalism: The Administration of the Indian Reorganization Act, 1934–1945*. Lincoln: University of Nebraska Press, 1980.
Theodoratus, Dorothea, and Nancy H. Evans. "Native American Interview." College of the Siskyous. http://www.siskiyous.edu/shasta/fol/nat/theo.htm. Accessed August 19, 2015.
Thornton, Russell. *We Shall Live Again: The 1870 and 1890 Ghost Dance Movements as Demographic Revitalization*. New York: Cambridge University Press, 2006.
Trafzer, Clifford. *Death Stalks the Yakama: Epidemiological Transitions and Mortality on the Yakama Indian Reservation, 1888–1964*. East Lansing: Michigan State University Press, 1997.
Trennert, Robert A., Jr. *Alternative to Extinction: Federal Indian Policy and the Beginnings of the Reservation System, 1846–51*. Philadelphia: Temple University Press, 1975.
———. *White Man's Medicine: Government Doctors and the Navajo, 1863–1955*. Albuquerque: University of New Mexico Press, 1998.
Tuan, Yi-Fu. "Language and the Making of Place: A Narrative-Descriptive Approach." *Annals of the Association of American Geographers* 81 (December 1991): 684–96.
———. *Space and Place: The Perspective of Experience*. Minneapolis: University of Minnesota Press, 2001.
———. *Topophilia: A Study of Environmental Perception, Attitudes and Values*. Englewood Cliffs, NJ: Prentice Hall, 1974.
U.S. House of Representatives. "To Amend an Act Entitled 'An Act Authorizing the Attorney General of the State of California to Bring Suit in the Court of Claims on Behalf of the Indians of California,' Approved May 18, 1928, (45 Stat. L. 602), by Amending Certain Portions of Sections 3 and 6 Thereof." 74th Congress, 1st Session, Report no. 1520.
Usner, Daniel. "American Indians on the Cotton Frontier: Changing Economic Relations with

Citizens and Slaves in the Mississippi Territory." *Journal of American History* 72 (September 1985): 297–317.
Vansina, Jan. *Oral Tradition as History*. Madison: University of Wisconsin Press, 1985.
Vaughan, Alden T. "From White Man to Redskin: Changing Anglo-American Perceptions of the American Indian." *American Historical Review* 87 (October 1982): 917–53.
Wallace, Anthony F. C. *The Death and Rebirth of the Seneca*. New York: Vintage Books, 1972.
Walter, Nancy. "The Land Exchange Act of 1937: Creation of the Indian Reservations at Bishop, Big Pine, and Lone Pine, California, through a Land Trade between the United States of America and the City of Los Angeles." PhD dissertation, Union Graduate School, 1986.
Walton, John. *Western Times and Water Wars: State, Culture and Rebellion in California*. Berkeley: University of California Press, 1993.
Waziyatawin Angela Wilson. *Remember This! Dakota Decolonization and the Eli Taylor Narratives*. Lincoln: University of Nebraska Press, 2005.
Weaver, Jace. *The Red Atlantic: American Indigenes and the Making of the Modern World, 1000–1927*. Chapel Hill: University of North Carolina Press, 2014.
Weber, David. *The Spanish Frontier in North America*. New Haven, CT: Yale University Press, 1992.
Weeks, Philip. *Farewell, My Nation: The American Indian and the United States, 1820–1890*. Wheeling, WV: Harlan Davidson, 1990.
Weisiger, Marsha. *Dreaming of Sheep in Navajo Country*. Seattle: University of Washington Press, 2011.
Weiss, Nancy. *Farewell to the Party of Lincoln: Black Politics in the Age of FDR*. Princeton, NJ: Princeton University Press, 1983.
West, Elliott. *The Contested Plains: Indians, Goldseekers and the Rush to Colorado*. Lawrence: University of Kansas Press, 1998.
———. *The Last Indian War: The Nez Perce Story*. New York: Oxford University Press, 2009.
Whaley, Gray. *Oregon and the Collapse of Illahee: U.S. Empire and the Transformation of an Indigenous World, 1792–1859*. Chapel Hill: University of North Carolina Press, 2010.
White, Richard. *The Middle Ground: Indians, Empires and Republics in the Great Lakes Region, 1650–1815*. New York: Cambridge University Press, 1991.
———. *The Roots of Dependency: Subsistence, Environment and Social Change among the Choctaws, Pawnees and Navajos*. Lincoln: University of Nebraska Press, 1983.
Wickwire, Wendy. "Stories from the Margins: Toward a More Inclusive British Columbia Historiography." *Journal of American Folklore* 118.470 (2005): 453–74.
Wiebe, Robert. *The Search for Order, 1877–1920*. New York: Hill and Wang, 1966.
Wilson, Angela Cavender. "From Grandmother to Granddaughter: Generations of Oral History in a Dakota Family." *American Indian Quarterly* 20 (Winter 1996): 7–13.
Wilson, Birbeck. "Ukiah Valley Pomo Religious Life, Supernatural Doctoring and Beliefs: Observations of 1939–1941." Edited by Caroline Hills. In *Reports of the University of California Archaeological Survey* 72. Berkeley: University of California Archaeological Research Facility, 1968.
Wilson, Darryl Babe. "Remove Them beyond the West: California, Gold." PhD dissertation, University of Arizona, 1997.
Wilson, Richard Allen. "Owens Valley Paiutes: Dependency or Interdependency." MA thesis, University of Nevada–Las Vegas, 1979.
Wright, Gwendolyn. Introduction to *The WPA Guide to California: The Federal Writers' Project Guide to 1930s California*. 1939; New York: Pantheon Books, 1984.
Wright, Tim. "'We Cast Our Lot with the Indians from That Day On': The California Indian Welfare Work of Frederick G. Collett and Beryl Bishop-Collett, 1910 to 1914." MA thesis, California State University–Sacramento, 2004.

Wolf, Eric. *Europe and the People without History*. 1982; Berkeley: University of California Press, 1997.
Womack, Craig. *Red on Red: Native American Literary Separatism*. Minneapolis: University of Minnesota Press, 1999.
Wunder, John R., and Pekka Hämäläinen. "Of Lethal Places and Lethal Essays." *American Historical Review* 104 (October 1999): 1229–34.
Zappia, Natale. *Traders and Raiders: The Indigenous World of the Colorado Basin, 1450–1859*. Chapel Hill: University of North Carolina Press, 2014.

INDEX

Aberdeen, California, 85
Acorns, 57
Alabama Hills, 112, 114, 117, fig14
Allen, Lawrence, 29
Anchorite Hills, California, 36
Anderson, Polly, 14, 92–95, 101
Atherton, Gertrude, 49, 53, 56, 59, 62, 73
Autobiography, 106, 110

Bagi'l, 30, 32
Baker, Susie, 112, 113, 115, 116
Ball Mountain, California, 93, 94
Bancroft, Hubert Howe, 5, 7, 22, 23, 38, 55
Bear, 30, 57, 79, 92
Bear Doctor, 79
Bear Lady, 76, 79
Benton, California, 14, 28, 34, 106
Big Pine, California, 16, 81, 85, 86, 112
Big Pine Reservation, 119
Big River, California, 77
Big Time, 21, 22, 130n50
Biography, 106, 108
Birch Mountains, California, 34
Bishop Creek, California, 80, 113
Bishop Reservation, 119
Bishop, California, 14, 34, 35, 81, 84, 85, 86, 90, 99, 113, 116
Bloody Island Massacre, 78, 79
Bole Maru, 54
Borderland, 44, 47
Bowers, Joe, 142n48
Bridgeport Tom, 35, 36, fig4
Brierly, George, 106
Britton, Frank, 52
Brush Creek, California, 77
Buldam (Pomo town), 77, 78
Bulpitt, Mattie, 14, 115, 116, 118
Butcher, Evelyn, 16
Butcher, Susie, 16
Butte County, California, 28, 89, 90, 97

Cabbacal (Kabekel), 75, 76, 77
California Indian Brotherhood, 24, 107, 108, fig13
California Indian Jurisdiction Act, 25, 27
California Story, 10, 38
California Volunteers, 86, 87, 91, 116
Camp Independence, 80, 85, 86, 98, 99, 100, 104, fig10
Campbell, Clarence, 29
Captain George (Paiute), 80, 89
Captain George (Pomo), 139n13
Carbayo (Kabeyo), 77
Cardalaow (Kodalau), 75, 76, 77
Cashbaugh, Jennie, 81, 82, 90, 99, 101, 102, 103, 104, 116, 117, 118
Cattle, 56, 57, 59, 80
Cha-boos, 77, 78
Chalfant, Pleasant, 38
Chalfant, William, 38, 39, 80, 83, 84
Chaum chä pö we (Coyote Valley), 32
Chico, California, viii, ix, 5, 24, 89
Chico, Jose, 98, 99, 104, 142n48
Civil War, 8, 37, 47, 57, 80
Clear Lake, California, 29, 32
Cloverdale, California, 77
Collett, Frederick, 107, 131n60
Collier, John, 105
Colonialism, 107, 116
Commonwealth Club, 24
Concow, 5, 8, 120, 121, 125n1; Big Times, 21; Creation, 10, 11, 14; Creation of, 17; Ethnic Cleansing, 90–97; Place Names, 41–47; Prophecy, 52, 55, 61
Concow Valley, California, 93, fig11
Cowan Station, California, 100
Coyote, viii, ix, 13, 14, 15, 16, 17, 18, 19, 21, 27, 35, 41, 43, 44, 45, 57, 82, 86, 88, 96, 97, 100, 121
Coyote's Knee Rancheria, 75, 76, 78, 79
Creation Story—California, 22

161

Cŭză'vi (cŭt'za), 22, 34, 36

Daowaya (Lake Tahoe, California), 36
Dawson Creek, California, 85
Dĕ-yas, 31, 32
Deer, 35, 57, 59, 110
Deer Creek, California, 45, 90
Devil, 62, 92
Disease, 3, 102
Division Creek, California, 86
Dobey, Nancy, 15, 18, 22, 25
Doctrine of Discovery, 7, 26, 27, 37, 38, 40, 131n66
Dog, 61
Domesticated Livestock, 56. *See also* Cattle; Horses; Pigs; Sheep
Dorrington, L.A., 107
Dos Rios, California, 95
Dragonfly Brothers, 13. *See also* Esha; Oonoop
Dreamer, 50, 53
Drum, Colonel R.C., 98
Durham, California, 28, 46
Dyer, Nevada, 113, 114

Eagle, ix, 41, 43
Earl, Maggie, 83, 84, 85, 87, 100, 101, 102
Earth Maker, 7, 10, 11, 12, 17, 20, 21, 43, 44, 96, 121, 127n1
Ecological Imperialism, 56
Eden Valley, California, 93
Education, 60
Eel River, 5, 18, 94
Encounters, Native-Newcomer, vii, 3
Esha, 10, 12, 13, 14, 15, 35
Essene, Frank, 4
Ethnic Cleansing, vii, ix, 6, 8, 56, 58, 89, 92, 117, 122, 125n1, 137n39; Lived Experience, 90; Violence of, 100
Ethnogenesis, 90, 113
Evans, Lieutenant George, 80

Fall River Mills, California, 92
Father (Paiute), 117
Fawns, 30
Feather River, California, 14
Federal Indian Policy, vii, 56
Federal Writer's Project, 120

Feliz, Annie, 24, 42, 45, 47, 50, 52, 53, 54, 92, 96, 97
First Man (Paiute), 21
First Man (Wailacki), 18, 25
First Woman (Paiute), 82, 86, 100
Fish, 34, 35, 36, 39, 113
Fort Bragg, California, 88, 91, 94
Fort Crook, California, 91
Fort Seward, California, 3
Fort Tejon, California, 80, 86, 90, 116
Franciscans, 22, 23, 50
Francisco, Tony, 75, 76, 78
Fremont, John C., 37, 38
French Ranch, California, 93
Frog Sisters, 114, 115, 116, 117, 118
Frog Spring, 115, 116, 117
Frontier, 32, 33, 123

Garberville, California, 3
Genocide, 23, 56, 58, 74, 89, 125n1, 130n58, 137n39
George Creek, California, 100
Ghost Dance, 35, 135n12
Gilbert, Jake, 28, 33, 36, 38, 39
God, vii, viii
Gold Rush, 22, 23, 94
Government Flat, California, 93
Grandfather (Wailacki), 18
Grant Lake, California, 28, 34, 121
Green, Bob, 92, 94, 95, 101
Gull Lake, California, 34, 39
Guns, 58, 111

Habematolel, 75
Harry, Mary, 101
Heenan, John, 92, 93, 94, 95
History, 60; Place-Centered, ix; Relationships, x; Veracity, 30
Honey Lake, California, 44
Hopland, California, 77
Horses, 57, 58, 59, 61
"How the Coyote Tried to Hold Fire", 41
Hu se lell (Mud Lake), 29, 31, 32
Huchnom, 28
Hulse, Frederick, 3
Hummingbird, 35
Hunter, Hank, 10, 15, 81, 88, 90, 98, 99, 100, 101, 102

INDEX

Independence, California, 10, 15, 83, 85, 88, 100
Indian Board of Cooperation, 107
Indian Citizenship Act, 105
Indian Health Service, 105, 106
Indian Removal Act, 89
Indian Reorganization Act, 75, 97, 122, 127n1
Indian Wars, 7, 8, 73, 74, 78, 88, 120; Lived Experience, 74, 84
Indian Wells, California, 100
Inyo County, California, 38, 116
Inyo Register, 38

Jackson, Edgar, 28, 75, 108, 109
James, Albert, 24
Jesus, viii, 14
Joaquin Jim, 80
Joaquin, Jeff, 4, 77, 78
Jones, Jim Tom, 14, 15, 16, 82, 84
June Lake, California, 34, 39

K'e Bāy Cho k'lal (Kabe'lal or Kabedile), 75
"K'e Bāy Cho k'lal Rancheria," 75
K'ŏ,ŭl K'ŏy (Kulakau), 75
Kama (Rabbit), 14
Katomal (Canel), 77
Kauca, 77, 78
Keenan, Lucy, 107, 108
Keeper Ranch, California, 93
Kĕläbehché, 110
Kelseyville, California, 78
Keough Hot Springs, California, 84, 85
Kibbe, William, 91
Kibbe's Guards, 91
Kinship, 17, 55, 74, 90
Kit Carson Pass, California, 44
Knight, Stephen, 24, 107, 108, fig13
Komshō, 110, 111
Koyoom K'awi, vii, ix
Kroeber, Alfred, vii, 25, 74
Kuksu, 44, 50, 53, 54

Lake County, California, 32, 75
Lake Crowley, California, 84
Lake Tahoe, California, 34, 36, 39, 44
Land, 26, 59
Land Exchange Act of 1937, 119
Landmark, 31, 43, 95, 134n54

Language, 7, 16, 31, 55, 92
Lassen County, California, 46
Lassen National Forest, 46
Lassen National Park, 43, 46
Lassen, Peter, 46
Lassik, 52, 55, 57, 61, 73
Lee Vining, California, 28, 33
Lincoln, Abraham, 88, 89
Little Toby, 13, 50, 52, 53, 54, 56
Little Valley, California, 93
Lizard, 41, 42, 43, 47, 121
Log Springs, California, 93
Lone Pine Reservation, 119
Lone Pine, California, 100
Long Valley, California (Inyo County), 82, 84
Long Valley, California (Mendocino County), 95
Looker, Mary, 98
Los Angeles Department of Water and Power, 40
Los Angeles, California, 6, 8, 80, 87, 103, 104, 106, 112, 116, 117, 118
Lummis, Charles, 7, 22

Mä pō me nä, 30, 31, 32
Maidu, 46, 55, 90
Manchester Pomo Community Council, 75
McGee Creek, 84
McLaine, Austin, 10, 16, 20, 21, 24, 28, 41, 42, 44, 45, 47, 93, 96, 97
McLaughlin, Captain Moses, 80
McWhinney, John, 29, 30, 31, 32, 110
Measles, 102
Memory Culture, 109
Mendocino Bay, California, 78
Mendocino County, California, 4, 29, 57, 120
Mendocino Reservation, 88, 91, 93, 94, 95
Mendocino, California, 77
Merced, California, 118
Meriam Report, 105, 108
Metlock, Tony, 107, 108
Middle Mountain (Sutter's Buttes), ix, 44, 45, 46, 47, fig8
Mill Creek, California, 90
Mill Ranch, California, 93
Mochu toca bayo (Kcakaleyo), 77
Modernity, 107, 111

Molala (Sea Lion Rock, California), 75, 76, 77
Mole, 42
Mono Lake (Cū'tza üp), 34, 35, 36, 37, 39, 48, fig5
Moore, George, 53
Mot ti coy (Blue Lake, California), 29, 31, 32, 33, 48, 121, fig3
Mount Dana, California, 34
Mount Shasta, California, 44, 95
Mountain House, California, 93
Mouse, ix, 41, 42, 43, 47
Myth People, 132n9

Nahavita (taboose), 116
Nationhood, 85
Native Sons of the Golden West, 23
Nevada City, California, 45
Nome Cult Walk, 97, fig12
Nome Lackee Reservation, 98
Noyo River, 93, 95

Office of Indian Affairs, 40, 98, 103, 106, 107, 108, 118
Ogden, Peter Skene, 37
Olancha, California, 100
Oonoop, 10, 12, 13, 15
Oral Tradition, 53, 74, 114
Oregon Jack, 92
Oroville, California, vii, viii, 42, 93
Owens Lake, California, 34, 112, 114, fig15
Owens River, 88, 113, fig16
Owens Valley, California, 4, 15, 29, 36, 37, 38, 39, 40, 46, 80, 86, 89, 104, 112, 114, 116, 117, 118, 120
Owens Valley Indian Water Commission, 119
Owens Valley Paiutes, 6, 8, 119, 120, 121, fig2; Creation, 10, 12, 13, 16, 17, 19, 22; Ethnic Cleansing, 88 90, 98–104; Place Names, 28, 29, 33–40; War Stories, 73, 74, 79–87
Owens Valley War, 8, 73, 80, 81, 88, 98
Owens Valley Water Wars, 8, 40, 87, 106, 112, 113, 116

P'hŏ,ŏl, K'öy (Balo Kai), 75
Parrish, Steve, 75, 76, 77
Pasasa'a (Casa Diablo Hot Springs), 113, 114
Paskenta, California, 91, 93
Patwin, 32, 33, 45, 54

Pdahau, 75
Peoplehood, 125n1
Pettit, Topsy, 107, 108
Pigs, 57, 59
Pine Creek Canyon, California, 14, 15
Pine Lake, California, 14, 15
Pinoleville, California, 29
Pioneer, 32, 33, 38, 116, 123; Pioneer Societies, 22
Pit River, 90, 91, 92, 94
Place, 28, 47, 55, 74, 76, 85, 121
Place Names, 7, 28, 29, 34, 36, 39, 40, 42, 46, 47, 48, 115
Place World, 45, 84, 95, 126n11
Point Arena, California, 75
Pomo, 4, 8, 54, 121; Bokeya, 75; Bulldam, 78; Healing, 105, 106–111; Place Names, 28, 29–33; War Stories, 73, 74, 78–79
Porterville, California, 98, 116
Potter, Elijah, 91
Potter Valley, California, 28
Pudding Creek, California, 95
Puha, 8, 14, 34, 36, 114, 118
Putnam Ranch, California, 83

Race, 55, 56
Rainy Springs Canyon, California, 86
Rancho Chico Treaty, 24
Rattlesnake (Concow), 20, 44
Rattlesnake (Paiute), 114, 115, 116, 117, 118
Red Bluff, California, 91, 93
Relationships, 30; Human-Animal, 13
Removal, 8, 40, 94, 120. *See also* Ethnic Cleansing
Rice, Billy, 28, 75, 76, 78, 79, 108, 109, 110
Richards, Arthur, 17
Robinson, George, 14, 15, 17
Round Valley (Inyo County, California), 14, 24, 28, 82, 84, 86, 115, 128n18
Round Valley Reservation, vii, ix, 3, 10, 13, 15, 52, 57, 88, 89, 91, 93, 95, 96, 97
Roundhouse, 22, 26, 42, 54, 55, 96
Rush Creek, California, 34, 113

Sacramento River, 91, 93, 94
Sacramento Valley, 29, 32, 42, 43, 45, 46, 76, 90
Sacramento, California, 80, 94
Salque, Mary, 17

INDEX

San Diego, California, 80
San Francisco, California, 22, 91, 93, 94
San Sebastian Reservation, 80, 87
Settler Colonialism, 6, 46, 50, 59, 61, 81, 82, 83, 104, 116
Settlers, Definition, 125n1
Shä kä' bä, 30
Shä pä lä mel' (Willits Hill, California), 30, 32
Shapda (Shepda/Cepda), 77
Sheep, 57, 59
Sherwin Hill, California, 84
Sherwood, California, 93
Siegel, Emily, 79
Silver Lake, California, 34, 39
Singing, 12, 13
Smith, Jedediah, 38, 45
Snake Spat Out, 115, 116, 117
Society of American Indians, 105
Sovereignty, 25, 85
State Emergency Relief Act, 4, 6, 75

Table Mountain, California, viii, 42, 47, fig7
Taboose Ranch, California, 85, 98, 99
Taikomol', 10, 11, 12, 14, 21, 26, 127n3
Tehama County, California, 90
Tehama, California, 93
Tejon Reservation, 88, 89, 98, 100, 102
Ten Mile River, California, 95
Terra Nullis, 7, 29, 46
The Curse of Capistrano, 23
Thibaut Creek, 85
Thomas Creek, 93
Tieyamunne (Anthony Peak), 97
Tillotson, Lizzie, 10
Tinemaha, 112, 114, 117
Togoqua (Rattlesnake), 35, 36
Trachoma, 8, 106, 119
Travel Narrative, 90, 94
Tribelet, 25, 74, 131n62
Tuberculosis, 8, 105, 106, 110, 119
Tule River Reservation, 88, 98, 102, 103, 116
Tupuseenata (Hammil Valley, California), 112, 114, 117

Turner, Frederick Jackson, 32, 33
Turner, Luella, 35
Turtle, 11, 12, 13

Ukiah, California, 28, 29, 32, 75, 108
U.S. Army, 40, 58, 78, 85, 87, 88, 89, 91, 100

Van Fleet, Arlen, 83, 84
Violence, 7, 73, 94, 95, 101, 117

Wailacki, 107, Creation, 15, 16, 18, 22, 25; Warfare, 74
Walker, Joe, 37, 38
Walker Lake, Nevada, 36, 39
Walker River Reservation, 118
Washington, Emma, 17
Water, 113, 114
Water Baby, 35, 101, 112, 114, 116, 117
"Water Baby," 34
Wathen, Charles, 44
Wathen, Susie, 29, 31, 33, 39, 122
Weller, John, 90, 91
West Mountain (Lassen Peak), ix, 41, 42, 43, 44, 47, 48, 88, 121, fig6
Weyland, Mose, 17, 18, 19, 22
Whiskey Flat, California, 36
Wilderness, 33
Williams, Billy (Paiute), 16
Williams, Billy (Pomo), 106, 107, 111
Williams, Catherine, 107, 110
Williams, Geraldine, 106, 107
Wise Creek, California, 77
Wolf, 17, 18, 19
World Enlargement, 15, 32
Wright, Charles, vii, ix, x, 3, 9, 24
Wright, Eva, ix, 4

Yomuch, 77
Young, Lucy, 3, 4, 9, 32, 50, 52, 53, 54, 122, fig1
Young, Sam, 3, 52
Yuki, 28, 73; Creation, 10, 11, 13, 26; Prophecy, 50, 52, 55, 56, 58, 59, 60, 61

Indigenous Confluences

Charlotte Cotè, Matthew Sakiestewa Gilbert, and Coll Thrush, *Series Editors*

Indigenous Confluences publishes innovative works that use decolonizing perspectives and transnational approaches to explore the experiences of Indigenous peoples across North America, with special emphasis on the Pacific Coast.

A Chemehuevi Song: The Resilience of a Southern Paiute Tribe
by Clifford E. Trafzer

Education at the Edge of Empire: Negotiating Pueblo Identity in New Mexico's Indian Boarding Schools
by John R. Gram

Native Students at Work: American Indian Labor and Sherman Institute's Outing Program, 1900–1945
by Kevin Whalen

California through Native Eyes: Reclaiming History
by William J. Bauer, Jr.

Indian Blood: HIV and Colonial Trauma in San Francisco's Two-Spirit Community
by Andrew J. Jolivette

Unlikely Alliances: Native Nations and White Communities Join to Defend Rural Lands
by Zoltán Grossman

Dismembered: Native Disenrollment and the Battle for Human Rights
by David E. Wilkins and Shelly Hulse Wilkins

Network Sovereignty: Building the Internet across Indian Country
by Marisa Elena Duarte

Chinook Resilience: Heritage and Cultural Revitalization on the Lower Columbia River
by Jon Daehnke

Power in the Telling: Grand Ronde, Warm Springs, and Intertribal Relations in the Casino Era
by Brook Colley

We Are Dancing for You: Native Feminisms and the Revitalization of Women's Coming-of-Age Ceremonies
by Cutcha Risling Baldy

www.ingramcontent.com/pod-product-compliance
Lightning Source LLC
Chambersburg PA
CBHW030655230426
43665CB00011B/1107